Gill Thorn has held research posts at both Manchester and Nottingham universities and was a teacher for the National Childbirth Trust for ten years, during which time she also developed courses on pregnancy and birth. She is a birth counsellor and still runs a range of weekly antenatal and post-natal classes. Gill has written feature articles for a number of national magazines and journals, and is a regular contributor to *Practical Parenting* magazine. Her previous books include *Practical Parenting: Pregnancy and Birth* which was published in 1995. She is the mother of three grown-up children and lives in Sussex with her husband.

NOT TOO LATE

HAVING
A
BABY
AFTER 35

GILL THORN

BANTAM BOOKS

LONDON · NEW YORK · TORONTO · SYDNEY · AUCKLAND

NOT TOO LATE: HAVING A BABY AFTER 35
A BANTAM BOOK : 0 553 50538 6

First publication in Great Britain

PRINTING HISTORY
Bantam edition published 1998

5 7 9 10 8 6 4

Set in Century Old Style by
Phoenix Typesetting, Ilkley, West Yorkshire.

Bantam Books are published by Transworld Publishers,
61-63 Uxbridge Road, London W5 5SA,
a division of The Random House Group Ltd,
in Australia by Random House Australia (Pty) Ltd,
20 Alfred Street, Milsons Point, Sydney, NSW 2061, Australia,
in New Zealand by Random house New Zealand Ltd,
18 Poland Road, Glenfield, Auckland 10, New Zealand
and in South Africa by Random House (Pty) Ltd,
Endulini, 5a Jubilee Road, Parktown 2193, South Africa.

Reproduced, printed and bound in Great Britain by
Cox & Wyman Ltd, Reading, Berks.

Dedicated to my mother, Edith Teresa Partington
1911–1996
In Loving Memory

Acknowledgements

I AM GRATEFUL TO ALL THE WOMEN WHO SHARED THEIR FEELINGS and their hands-on experience of older motherhood with me, especially those who were coping with the stress of infertility or loss. I should also like to thank Jayne Marsden, Editor-in-Chief of *Practical Parenting* magazine and a first-time mother; and Margaret Orr, a GP with three small children. They were both on maternity leave when they read the manuscript and made helpful comments, fitting it in around new babies and showing how positive the experience of older motherhood can be.

My thanks to Rose Elliot, vegetarian cookery writer, who checked the section on diet; and finally to Joanna and Annabel Thorn, who are enjoying careers and are in no hurry to start a family, but who made constructive comments as only one's own offspring can.

Contents

Introduction

A TIDAL WAVE OF OLDER MOTHERS IS GATHERING STRENGTH; women who are expecting their first baby, having enjoyed a career; women who are adding a new baby to a family of toddlers or teenagers; women who are having a baby with a new partner. A century ago average life expectancy was around 50 and you were nearing the end of your life at 35. Today you are in your prime: you work, you have important relationships, you lead a full, satisfying life and you *choose* motherhood.

The pre-war generation of women stopped work when they married and, without reliable contraception, many of them raised large families. Almost one birth in five was to a woman over 35 in the 1940s: sympathy, not congratulations, was frequently offered when another pregnancy was announced. As soon as the contraceptive pill arrived the birth rate to older women took a serious nose-dive.

Social change takes time, however. The post-war generation, the first to have early access to the pill, worked for a year or two after marriage, but did not put off having a family to establish a career. Most of us had children and 'retired'. Sympathy was reserved for mothers who had to work; good jobs and childcare were about as available as contraception was to the previous generation.

Today, women delay having children or combine work and motherhood as they wish, and the over-35 birth rate is rising steadily again (currently to about one birth in eight). The difference is that the majority have chosen to have a baby and are pleased to be pregnant. Forget the sympathy, crack open the champagne!

Until quite recently, a woman over 30 expecting her first baby was called an *elderly primigravida*, or an *elderly primip* if she already had a child. Labels with geriatric associations now seem ludicrous and there is plenty of evidence that health is more important than age when you are having a baby. Thirty-five is still seen by many people as a significant milestone, however, beyond which conception is not always easy nor pregnancy straightforward.

Women over 35 are increasingly aware that the choice of having a child will not be there for ever, yet choice is not always easy. The more you have to lose the harder it can be to weigh up the pros and cons of whether to have a baby. Little demons of doubt that were absent when you were younger niggle away. You start to wonder if you really want the changes a baby would bring to your life, how you would cope physically with pregnancy and birth, and whether it is fair to have an only child or to turn up at the school gates in a smart suit and wrinkles.

If you decide to go ahead you feel pressure to conceive quickly (with mounting anxiety if nothing happens immediately). Once pregnant you become conscious of being outside the 'safest' age range for having babies, and face something that past generations never had to worry about: fetal tests, which change your perception of the risks of having a baby, focus attention on your age and compel some difficult decisions.

Notwithstanding these drawbacks, more than 80,000 women

over 35 (and some 500 over 45) give birth in Britain every year. When push comes to shove, the advantages of older motherhood far outweigh the disadvantages.

This has become increasingly obvious to me from looking at the recent research, and especially from listening to the women who have come to my antenatal classes over the past twenty-five years. Older women talk realistically about the challenges of parenthood. They never claim that everything in the garden grows without effort, but point out that a mature outlook teaches you to take the rough with the smooth and enjoy life; that having organisational and practical skills to draw on improves most experiences, and that it is easier to make decisions when you know yourself well and have the confidence to seek out information.

It is hard to explain something as intangible as joy, but older mothers are overwhelmingly positive and feel especially privileged. A baby seems to give more meaning to almost everything they do.

Gill Thorn
Emsworth, June 1997

Older Mothers' Experiences

I ASKED SOME OF THE OLDER MOTHERS IN MY ANTENATAL classes to complete an open-ended questionnaire describing their experiences. Friends of theirs and past clients heard about it and contacted me. Women phoned after a request was displayed on doctors' notice boards. Replies flooded in, many of them written in great detail. They pointed out anxieties and losses as well as gains (as there are with any venture), but on the whole they felt fulfilled and rejuvenated and found the experience of older motherhood extremely rewarding. A mother aged 42 wrote:

> *I thought I might regret not having a child, but I kept putting it off because my life was pretty good and I couldn't imagine it being better. A baby certainly changes your life but you learn things that you can't get from books or from other people. You see the world through a child's eyes again. I'm just glad that in my case it was not too late . . .*

The experiences of Elizabeth, Valerie, Lesley, Sue and Anne appear at the end of each chapter. Although fictional, they are drawn from and represent the responses to the questionnaires and issues raised in numerous discussions with older mothers. It remains to introduce the five women.

Elizabeth (42) makes documentary programmes and her partner, Michael (47) is a foreign news reporter for a TV company. Elizabeth and Michael have been together for 11 years. While she was building her career Elizabeth felt no urge to have a child, and it was not until she was approaching her forties that she became aware that time was running out. She is fit and active, often travels to join Michael after he has completed an assignment, and has a varied social life when he is home. They enjoy a good income and standard of living, and Elizabeth is used to running her life independently.

Valerie (44) is a nurse with two daughters, Emma (14) and Claire (9), from a previous relationship. She has lived with Barry (35), who manages a small factory, for a year. Barry is confident and optimistic; he gets on well with Emma and Claire and is looking forward to having his first child. Valerie worries and tends to act cautiously; her health is not as good as it could be and she suffers from backache and diabetes. With two older children and very different personalities, Valerie and Barry's family life is volatile at times, but their relationship is close.

Lesley (36) is a receptionist and her husband Phil is a plumber and part-time youth leader. They married when they were both 18 and live in the town where they grew up and where most of Lesley's large family live. After stressful and unsuccessful infertility investigations in their twenties they turned their minds to other activities, but the longing to have a child remained and

Lesley is having IVF treatment. Although she worries, she has a down to earth approach to life and feels her past experience has made her more philosophical.

Sue (39) is a marine biologist who lectures at a local university. She met Kenneth (58) five years ago when testing new technology for his firm, and they married three months later. They have a four-year-old son, Jack. Ken sold his highly successful business and retired early so that he could spend more time with his family, something he feels he missed out on when Robert, his son from his first marriage, was growing up. Robert has twin daughters, Sophie and Kate, and the two families are close.

Anne (46) brought her children up alone, having divorced twenty years ago when they were aged six and four. Her son lives abroad while her daughter works in the next town and Anne shares a house with her mother, who at 87 is beginning to need more care. Since her children grew up Anne has returned to her sculpture and has made a name for herself through exhibitions. For the past few years she has had an on-off relationship with a television producer. Through him she met Elizabeth, who became an admirer of her work and, more recently, a friend.

1 *Do You Want to Have a Baby?*

HAVING A BABY WHEN YOU ARE OVER 35 HOLDS THE PROMISE OF great joy along with some uncertainties. Do you really want a baby? Many older women, especially those who have an absorbing career, waver between certainty and ambivalence. You may have too much to lose to take a chance, so if you are unsure this chapter may help to clarify your feelings. If your mind is made up and the answer is 'yes', turn to the at-a-glance chart, pages 34–5, which will take you on to the next step.

Thinking about having a baby or discussing it with your partner may not lead you directly to deciding one way or the other but it will help to prepare the ground. The issues are not quite the same as considering the pros and cons of moving house or changing your job. Having a baby has far-reaching consequences and even after you have thought about it a great deal you may still be undecided. If so, you will lose nothing by putting the matter aside for a while.

Once the ground is prepared, a trivial incident when you are not even thinking about babies – a child watching a line of ducks waddling down the road, a little train going round and round in a toy shop window, a harassed mother coping with a whining toddler in a supermarket – will often result in an emotional leap forward. In that instant you may make your decision, one way or the other, knowing that it instinctively feels right.

Time spent in contemplation can be usefully used to improve your fitness and health as suggested in Chapter 4. This will benefit you generally and if you decide you want to have a baby you will have done your best to achieve your wish. It is worth considering pre-conceptual care as soon as you think you might want a child because it can become a dauntingly serious business when you are trying to get pregnant, especially if a few months pass without success.

Age in perspective: the historical view

Women in their late thirties and forties have always had babies. Before the advent of effective birth control they kept on having them until the menopause or death put a stop to it. Mothers who had numerous pregnancies and brought up large families, often without enough money or help, frequently endured ill-health along the way, so older mothers suffered more complications during pregnancy and birth. This was linked in general to their poor health and long childbearing history rather than to their age. When reliable contraception became available they could prevent further pregnancies and avoid the draining effects of continual childbearing by planning their family.

The contraceptive pill was widely introduced in the 1960s and as women chose to have smaller families the number of births to women over 35 fell. It rose again in the late 1970s and early 80s, because women born in the post-war baby boom reached their mid thirties, and there were more of them. However, these older mothers had grown up with contraception; for them marriage and motherhood was not the only possible career, and relatively few of them had large families. A poorly nourished older mother having her ninth child during the Depression of the 1930s was far more likely to experience problems during pregnancy or birth than a healthy older woman who chooses to have her first or even her fourth child today.

Why older women are having babies

The average age for having a baby continues to rise because more women in their late thirties or early forties are having babies. They tend to fall into three groups: those who have delayed motherhood for career or personal reasons, those who are adding to their existing family or having a family with a new partner, and those who have not had a baby earlier because they have had fertility problems.

Creating security for a family takes time and money and some women delay motherhood as part of a long-term plan to establish themselves in a career first. They wait until they feel confident about their economic situation for the present and foreseeable future, but after the freedom and satisfactions of their twenties and early thirties some become aware of an empty space in their life. Parenthood is a shared experience achieved rather easily by most adults, and although you do not need to have a child to be fulfilled it is not called 'the club' for nothing.

A huge slice of luck goes into finding the right partner at the right time, and choice affects men too. A man may not feel strongly drawn to the idea of having a child because of his own experience of childhood; or he may have doubts about the restrictions and responsibilities of parenthood and his ability to be a good parent. It takes time to change your partner, or his views on the subject.

Fertility problems affect only a minority of couples of any age, but there can be few things more upsetting when you want a child than to fail repeatedly at the first fence, especially when you think time is running out. Choosing not to have a child is one thing, but the instinct to procreate is strong. Memories of your own child-hood, the half-remembered happiness of an outing or treat, friends or relatives announcing a pregnancy, or a growing sense of the value of relationships spur you on. Once you decide that you want a child it is hard to put the idea aside. You start to notice pregnant women, families, advertisements featuring cute babies. They seem to be all over the place.

Some older mothers are adding to a family born in their early- or mid-thirties, or have older children or teenagers and are starting again after a long gap. Change often triggers a desire for a second family. Some women, for instance, have a child after losing their job or being made redundant; others form a new relationship and want to cement or publicly acknowledge it, and some simply want to have a baby before time runs out.

Does age make much difference?

There are two major concerns for older women contemplating having a baby: 'Will I get pregnant?' and 'If I do, how risky is it?'

Conceiving tends to get harder the older you are, but the rate at which fertility declines is very individual. Some women have great difficulty at 26 or 36 while a few have no trouble at 46. If you are healthy and ovulate regularly, however, your chances of conceiving are probably good. More older women suffer a miscar-riage as abnormalities in eggs and sperm increase with age; and there has been more time for hormone imbalances or chronic illness to have developed.

Pregnancy and birth are safer than ever before, so serious risks to your health are minimal. The chances of having a baby with a chromosomal abnormality increase with age, and the develop-ment of tests for certain fetal abnormalities has brought this fact of life into sharp focus for women over 35. Tests give the chance of terminating an affected pregnancy, but they can also cause a great deal of unnecessary anxiety. These issues are discussed in Chapter 3.

The care you receive during pregnancy and birth will depend on your circumstances. If you are healthy and have had no difficulty conceiving it may be the same as a younger woman's. Nobody is likely to bat an eyelid if you have had a child within the last two or three years, whatever your age. If this is your first baby or there has been a long gap you may be offered additional antenatal checks, and if you are over 40 (a significant birthday for doctors as well as everyone else) a special eye may be kept on you. Some women find this daunting, but there is often room for negotiation, especially if you feel that the advice you have been given is based on personal views rather than objective research.

Some women feel that loss of energy makes pregnancy, birth and bringing up a child harder work when you are older, but others feel that it gives them a new lease of life and more vitality. Exhaustion is part of motherhood at any age, but sensible planning and the sheer pleasure a child brings can be great compensations.

The changes a baby brings

Whether you are contemplating having your first baby or adding to your family the decision will change you physically and affect your lifestyle and your career as much as, if not more than, it would have done when you were younger.

Body and mind: You may worry about whether your body can carry a child successfully or even whether it might harm a baby. Physically, age makes no difference but things that are associated with being older, such as having a pre-existing illness, may be significant. How easily your body copes with pregnancy and birth depends to some extent on whether everything is straight-forward. No woman can ascertain this in advance but the best approach, for your own and a baby's sake, is to make sure that you are as fit and healthy as possible to start with.

A wanted pregnancy is generally easier to cope with physi-cally: pride and pleasure affect your whole approach, including how you view discomfort. The ambivalent feelings that often accompany an unplanned pregnancy can be a source of added stress, and only you know how you feel and whether the time is right to have a baby. Pregnancy following a miscarriage or fertility treatment is also more stressful, as you are likely to have doubts and anxieties about your ability to have a child. Extra emotional support will help in such circumstances.

An unexpected bonus of having a baby later in life is that the other parents you come into contact with will probably be a mix of ages and personalities. Parents with small children become one of your reference groups; their approach to life will moderate yours and even may have a rejuvenating effect on it.

Lifestyle: Lifestyle changes are likely to be fairly dramatic with your first baby. You cannot get out and about so easily with a small child, although this is not a life sentence but a temporary grounding. If you and your partner thrive on travel or change your child may inherit your adaptability.

Spontaneity and the freedom to do exactly what you want fly out of the window when you become a parent, perhaps more than anyone can imagine in advance. Other possibilities fly in, however, and slowing down can be a welcome opportunity to develop different interests.

Your daily routine will change less if you already have young children, as you will have adapted to their needs. Your children will be affected emotionally and materially, however, as your attention will inevitably be partially taken up with the new baby.

Looking after a baby, especially when you work or have other children, is hard work physically. Two people can share the load, but fatigue is likely to be a constant bedfellow for the first year or two, even if your baby sleeps well and you have plenty of help.

The cost of a baby varies with income and preferences but even without everything you are tempted to buy, children are expensive. On a tight budget what you spend in the first year might pay for a fortnight's package holiday for four. At the other end of the scale it might finance a new family car. The expense tends to grow with the child, reaching a peak if you have to move to larger accommodation.

It is almost impossible to explain to someone without children the extra dimension that they bring to life. They are a long-term source of fascination, and the restrictions are matched by welcome changes such as a shared interest with your partner, a curb on an overcrowded social life, and a chance to revisit childhood. Having a baby forces you to give unselfishly; and when you do, even if it is not your natural inclination, it is surprising how good it can make you feel about yourself and about life in general.

Before you have a child the responsibilities may seem all too certain while the joys of parenthood are unknown. Making any major change to your lifestyle when you are relatively contented means taking a risk, but one of the reasons older women give for wanting a child is that life has become just too comfortable and predictable. For many couples, children are a risk worth taking.

Career: Combining work and family responsibilities can be successful with good organisation and child care arrangements, but emotionally it is not easy. Becoming a mother changes your priorities; you no longer think of parenthood as another domestic duty that can be efficiently delegated to somebody else. Top jobs often require dedication of the sort that mothers are reluctant to give. However committed they are, they begin to feel ambivalent about having to work until a task is finished, staying late at the office for a meeting arranged by colleagues without family responsibilities, going on a course or jumping on a plane at the drop of a hat. Suddenly there is more satisfaction to be found at home.

If the demands of your job force you to put your mothering relationship on hold you will feel that your child is growing up without you, and you are missing a time that you can never get back because life moves on. Men, too, are discovering that work commitments affect the intimacy they have with their children.

With a few honourable exceptions, society does not make life easy for working mothers; they are expected to behave as though they did not have children. Work patterns are beginning to change but there is a long way to go before job culture becomes 'family friendly'. Many a previously dedicated career woman finds to her surprise that she prefers a job where she can leave on time every evening without taking work home, where she can take her child to the dentist or attend the school play, because such commitments are accepted.

For women who work and have children there is no perfect solution. You may decide to take a break or mark time as far as your career is concerned, and if you are in your thirties interesting jobs will still be around when your children are older. If the nature of your work makes this impossible, however, or you have reached the age or stage in your career where it would seriously affect your employability, the choice between what your career means to you and what bringing up your child would mean is harder; either way there will be sacrifices. Some possible compromises are discussed in Chapter 13.

Choice and responsibility

Effective birth control indirectly improves women's health by reducing the problems linked to frequent childbearing, and it allows choice. You can have an active sex life without an unwanted pregnancy, but you also have to choose whether or when to take the plunge.

The messages given by society are mixed. Every child should be a wanted child, so you should not have a baby until you feel ready. At the same time if you delay too long the hard facts are that your eggs may run out, fertility treatment does not always succeed and, if you conceive, your baby has more chance of disability.

The penalties for having a child are high and when children are seen as personal indulgences mothers are unrealistically expected to give their all. If you choose to have a baby, the argument goes, you should earn a good salary or depend on your partner. You have no right to depend on state benefits, complain that you are exhausted or leave your child with other people to follow your career.

Motherhood does not get any easier; every new step involves gains as well as losses. A new baby is a bundle of needs and demands. It is unrealistic to expect it to shore up a rocky marriage, unite step-children, heal the hurt of an infidelity or help you to forget a child you lost. Difficult feelings cannot be resolved by patching them up with nappies. If you worry about wanting a baby for the 'right' reasons, think about what you could offer a child rather than what a child might offer you.

The responsibility of choosing to have a child only extends as far as an honest attempt to do your best, which most parents do instinctively. You cannot see into the future; freedom of choice is always affected by individual circumstances.

When the effort of actually making a decision feels too heavy some couples simply take a risk or switch to a less effective method of contraception, giving fate the chance to play a part in the creation of a new life.

Some advantages of being older

Responsibilities that can be daunting for younger parents can seem like pleasures when you have had time to get your career and home established first. You may be financially secure, having achieved most of what you want from a career; content to stay at home and no longer hankering after a social whirl. If your lifestyle has been hectic, parenthood may bring a gentler pace to it.

The benefits of older motherhood depend on your perspective. You are likely to be better motivated to plan ahead for a healthy pregnancy, you know more about yourself and what you want out of life. You probably have the confidence to ask questions, make choices and get the most out of any experience. You may have suffered physical pain in the past and developed inner resources to cope with labour. You may be more tolerant and patient as a parent, and, especially if you have other children, less likely to be disappointed if your baby doesn't reach a milestone on time or frustrated by trying to do three things at once and failing.

Friends with older children may discourage you with tales of sleepless nights and toddler tantrums, or look back nostalgically at supposedly angelic toddlers while pointing out how much worse it will be when you are trying to cope with a teenager while creeping towards retirement. Mothers of all ages get exhausted, however, while most toddlers go through the tantrum phase and teenagers can be easy or difficult according to their – and your – nature.

Every parent faces problems as a child grows up, but no parent gets them all. Babies may not come with instruction manuals and guarantees, but problems can be easier to handle simply because you are older. You may accept the difficult times more readily, be less affected by what other people think, and more open to seeking help at an early stage.

When tackling the challenges of parenthood, maturity, experience and a more realistic attitude to life can be great advantages.

Making a decision

Ultimately the decision whether to have a baby will be affected by how you and your partner feel, but try this exercise to weigh up the practical considerations:

Score each statement 1, 2 or 3 according to how important it is to you. For example, if not being able to go out spontaneously would make little difference to you score 1, but if you would really miss the freedom to travel or socialise score 3.

For:

I like family life and children in general ☐

I feel I (or we) can afford to have a child ☐

My partner is keen to have a baby ☐

I would regret it later if I didn't have a child ☐

I want a reason to slow down and act responsibly ☐

Any other reasons . . . . (fill this one in yourself)

Against:

I would miss the freedom to go out spontaneously ☐

My career is very important to me ☐

My partner is not keen to have a baby ☐

I have other stresses in my life at present ☐

My health is not as good as it could be ☐

Any other reasons . . . . (fill this one in yourself

Add up your scores for and against. If you have decided that you want to have a child, turn to the at-a-glance chart on pages 34–5 to take the next step. If you are still uncertain put the exercise aside to give your mind time to work away quietly and make the decision clearer. Try it again in three or six months' time.

Another way to help you and your partner decide how you feel about having a baby is to make 'His and Hers' lists of your feelings individually. You could head them, 'for and against parenthood', or 'this is what I want and this is what I am afraid of', for example. Take your time to write down everything that is relevant, and then put your statements away for a few days. When you look at them again the main themes may become clear. You might realise, for instance, that your list in favour of parenthood expresses all your optimism in life while your list against it is about fear of failure. It will give you something concrete to discuss.

If you decide you want to have a child while your partner definitely does not, and you simply cannot reach a compromise or agreement, at least you will know where you stand. You may have to be realistic about shouldering the main burden of bringing up a child yourself; you may feel there is no alternative but to part company and look for someone who feels the same as you; or if your relationship is too valuable to risk losing, you may accept the decision and go on to have different adventures in life.

Unplanned pregnancy

Older women sometimes take a chance, or stop using contraception, in the belief that they are unlikely to conceive. A study in America found almost two-thirds of pregnancies in women over 40 were unplanned – similar to the rate among teenagers. On average fertility declines with age, but this tells you as much about your own chances of getting pregnant as average height says about whether you can reach something off a top shelf.

A planned pregnancy is wanted; an unplanned one can be a nasty shock. It can be as devastating for an older woman as for a teenager, although many women change their minds and welcome it later on. As you get older you gather commitments, obligations and an outlook on life that sometimes makes the unexpected initially harder to accept.

Your career may have reached a point where it requires extra time or effort and taking maternity leave might be out of the question or it could let people down. Family or other commitments may make having a baby at this time unthinkable. You may be thrilled to be pregnant initially, but discover with utter dismay that your family is not supportive or your partner abandons you. If you have painfully broken free from a long-standing relationship you may be unsure what the future holds.

Pregnancy and birth are no more hazardous for a healthy older woman than for a younger one, but with the normal passage of time older women are more likely to have developed an illness or disability that could make motherhood more difficult.

Five per cent of abortions in Britain are requested by women over 40. It is neither possible nor the right decision for everyone to continue an unplanned pregnancy, and doctors tend to be sympathetic when you are older. Deciding on a termination is never easy, especially if you feel that factors outside your control have forced your hand and you have no option. You only have the information available to you at the time, however, so trust your instinct. Becoming pregnant unexpectedly does not mean you are a careless or thoughtless person, and if termination is the only answer try not to judge yourself harshly.

On a more positive note, an unexpected pregnancy often turns out to be a blessing in disguise, confirming your fertility and relieving you of the burden of choice. Quite a few surprise pregnancies are half-planned and welcomed after the first shock. Life does not always work out the way you expect and maturity can make an unplanned pregnancy easier to deal with.

Many women have healthy babies with no preparation and others who prepare carefully fail to conceive or carry a baby to term. Although there are benefits to planning pregnancy, if you have not managed such foresight there is no point in worrying about not having improved your diet or taken folic acid to reduce the tiny risk of neural tube defects. Just start as soon as you can.

Older mothers' experiences

Elizabeth (42): 'For two or three years I thought about having a baby and the effect it might have on my career. I decided the risk was worth it, but my partner Michael wasn't keen. His work takes him away at a moment's notice and he likes the freedom, knowing I can look after myself. It caused a lot of arguments and eventually I forced the issue because I felt time was running out. If I have a baby I won't be so independent, but we have reached a stage in our lives when we're not short of money, and money can solve a lot of problems. I'm also quite realistic about life and prepared to knuckle under and get on with it.'

Q: Michael and I agreed to have an only child. What are the pros and cons of this?
A: Family units of two parents and a child are becoming more common and are well suited to contemporary life if you and your partner both want to work full-time. One child costs less, is easier to cope with and does not have to share living space, scarce resources or your attention. Only children tend to be confident, articulate and mature. They can also be lonely and over-serious, trying to live up to parental expectations. A hen with one chick watches it like a hawk, so you could deliberately turn a blind eye occasionally and let your child be herself, not the focus of all your hopes and dreams.

Only children miss out on lessons that are learned easily in the rough and tumble of family life: how to give and take and stand your ground. They never need to claim their share of the cake – it will still be there whenever they choose to eat it. You can encourage participation in group activities, however: football rather than solitary computer games, the recorder as well as the piano; choose holidays where there will be other children around, invite a friend for companionship and meet regularly with cousins to foster a feeling of belonging to a wider family.

Think about the provisions you make for the future, too, as there will be no brothers or sisters to share responsibility for you as you grow older.

Valerie (44): 'Barry is nine years younger than me and the decision to try to have a baby was easy – he loves children and is a good father to my daughters, Emma and Claire. I want to give him the chance to have a child of his own. I might have problems conceiving so we have never used contraception.

'I expect to feel more tired and have less stamina because I'm older, but my job is physically demanding and I know my body well. Barry manages a small factory and his job is reasonably secure, but if he was ever made redundant we could role swap. He'd love that, and as a trained nurse I can always find a job.'

Q: I was sexually abused as a child and it made Emma and Claire's births more difficult than they should have been. How can I have a more positive experience this time round?

A: Pregnancy and birth are such intimate experiences that they can stir long-buried emotions, although when they are handled well they can also heal deep wounds. The first step is to be ready to confront your past. You have taken this, so now ask your doctor (a woman doctor if you prefer) to refer you to a clinical psychologist or a trained counsellor, who could help you to resolve some of your feelings.

Midwives are increasingly aware of the effects of past abuse, so take courage and mention it at an early stage. You should meet with respect, support and special consideration during pregnancy and birth.

Lesley (36): 'We tried to have a baby soon after we married. We'd bought our house and our friends were all settling down, so it was hard when they started families and we couldn't. You never realise how much you want to be like everyone else until you can't! Eventually we put babies out of our minds and got on with life. Phil built up his plumbing business and became a voluntary youth leader. I put my energy into our nieces and nephews, but the longing was always there. Our new GP encouraged us, as infertility treatments have moved on in the last few years.

'Phil is afraid that if infertility treatment doesn't work I might get as upset as I was in my twenties. I want a baby very much but now I'm older I don't get my hopes up too high. If it happens it will be a bonus. At 36 I have a better chance than I will have in a few years' time, so we are giving it another try.'

Q: I've waited for so long that I worry about things like whether I would be a good mother. How can I tackle such fears constructively?
A: One of the things that gets you up in the morning is optimism and your belief that life is worth living. There is no such thing as a perfect mother or an ideal family; you only have to do your best. Like every other parent, sometimes you'll get it right and sometimes you'll get it wrong.

A practical way to handle worry is to have three imaginary boxes. Mark the first **ignore** and in it file worries that you really have no control over, such as the state of the world or the education system in five years' time. Label the second box, **store** and put in anything that you want to think about in the future, or that you might change your mind about, like going back to work. In the last box put things that you actively want to think about now. Mark it **explore**.

Shift items from box to box at will, but only think about the ones in the box marked 'explore'. Although it may sound contrived, this effectively sorts the wood from the trees so that you can tackle real concerns more constructively.

Sue (39): 'Age was the deciding factor before we had Jack, who is just four. Kenneth was already 54 and we felt that we could not delay having our first baby as I wanted a family while we had enough energy to enjoy bringing them up. The instinct to have children gets put aside while your job is exciting and new things are happening, but I'd reached a point where being able to please myself all the time was no longer satisfying.

'I was lucky to meet Kenneth when I felt that not to experience motherhood would be to miss out. After Jack was born we left it to nature, but a year later I had a miscarriage. This made us absolutely sure that we wanted another child. Once you know that you want a baby the longing becomes very strong.'

Q: I will be in my fifties and Kenneth will be over 70 when our children are teenagers. How does having older parents affect a child?
A: Children hate to be different from their peers so their view depends on whether their parents look and behave much the same as their friends' parents. At 20, 39 sounds old, but when you get there it seems quite young – so you shift the goal posts and decide that 50 seems over the hill. A child sees any adult as ancient, however, even a 20-year-old.

If you have developed friendships with other new parents regardless of age, and have met together right from the start, your approach to parenting, your attitudes and even your appearance are likely to be broadly similar. Energy levels partly depend on how fit and healthy you are and on how many things you are trying to do at the same time. Physical activity tends to decline with age but it is also easier to accept this and work round it. With an eye to the future, older parents often foster interests that do not depend on physical prowess, such as painting or solving crosswords, to enjoy with their child.

Teenagers sometimes resent having parents who have grey hair or are unable to keep up, but most go through a critical phase and find their parents embarrassing whatever they do and whatever their age. It is part of breaking away and becoming independent.

At-a-glance chart

This chart will help you to locate the main topics of interest to you more quickly.

You are planning to conceive. What are your interests?		
RELATIONSHIPS	FETAL ABNORMALITY	HEALTHY PREGNANCY
Your partner p.37 Your other children p.43 Your family p.42 Lesbian parenting p.41 Men and babies p.38 Communication and sharing p.48, 49	Evidence of risk to the baby p.56 Tests for fetal abnormalities p.58 Deciding about testing p.70 Options after a bad result p.74 Continuing a pregnancy p.74 Terminating a pregnancy p.75	Contraception p.81 What to eat p.82 Your weight p.88 Getting or staying fit p.90 Avoidable risks p.93 Pre-conception planner p.97

You are trying to conceive or are pregnant. What are your interests?

GETTING PREGNANT	PREGNANCY	PREPARING FOR BIRTH
Conception and your fertility cycle p.103 Help for infertility p.106 Stress and infertility p.107 Treatments for infertility p.108 Choosing a clinic p.113 Other ways of having a baby p.112 Miscarriage p.105	What happens in pregnancy p.124 Antenatal care p.127 Common pregnancy problems p.145 Twins, triplets or more p.126 Looking after yourself p.134 A difficult pregnancy p.156 Coping if you lose a pregnancy p.160 Pregnancy planner p.138	Your birth choices: natural, low and high technology p.168 Home or hospital birth p.172 Water birth or active birth p.169 Making a birth plan p.175 How to make birth easier p.178 Practical preparations p.180 Birth planner p.184

You are expecting your baby soon. What are your interests?

NORMAL BIRTH	HELP DURING BIRTH	THE EARLY MONTHS
What happens in labour p.191 Labour or false alarm? p.192 Labour pain p.198 Different labour patterns p.203 Episiotomy or tear? p.204 After the birth p.205	Induction p.211 Active management p.212 Assisted delivery p.213 Multiple birth p.216 Breech birth p.217 Caesarean section p.220 Coming to terms with birth p.224	Feeding and caring for a new baby p.231 Baby equipment p.233 Your health p.252 Relationships and sex p.262 Getting back to normal p.259 Sources of help p.268

Some other interests

WORKING LIFE	LONE MOTHERHOOD	FAMILY LIFE
Pregnancy and work p.270 Should mothers work? p.271 Full-time motherhood p.277 Full-time work p.274 Part-time work p.275 Childcare options p.278 Your return to work p.283	Your child's needs p.299 Your own needs p.300 Your child's father p.295 Money and budgeting p.296 Getting support p.301 Balance in your life p.303 Advantages of being alone p.293	What it is really like p.309 Family relationships p.312 Your other children p.314 Step families p.313 Juggling your life p.316 Coping with stress p.319

2 Relationships

CHILDREN ARE ONE OF THE ADVENTURES THAT LIFE THROWS AT you. It is impossible to fulfil their needs without change, so it does not take a crystal ball to see that having a child will affect every aspect of your life, including your relationships with your partner, your wider family and your friends.

A baby may bring you and your partner even closer together, and you may be in broad agreement about how to bring up a child. On the other hand, you may disagree over almost everything and have to negotiate continually.

Your parents or other children may be thrilled at the prospect of a new baby in the family, or they may react with misplaced sympathy, implying that at your age you are guilty of carelessness or could not possibly be delighted to be pregnant. People do not always behave as you hope or expect.

Whether you find parenthood easy or challenging depends as much on you and your baby as on the approach you take to child-rearing. Relationships are shaped by the personalities of the individuals involved and by other things that are happening in their lives. Personality is modified by experience of life, but basic temperament is probably inherited: genes influence whether a baby will claim all the time you are able and willing to give or be more self-sufficient. A demanding child with a strong personality can disrupt previously serene relationships, but life can also be more fun.

Children grow up best in a generally stable and loving environment. Total harmony is never necessary, but it helps to have realistic expectations and a strategy for dealing with differences of opinion.

You and your partner

If you have delayed having children until you found the right partner you are likely to have developed self-knowledge and a clear idea of what is important to you. Many couples discuss how they feel early in a new relationship and agree whether to start a family before making a long-term commitment. New partnerships demand a willingness to adapt to the other person's needs which often makes it easier to discuss such issues frankly.

Long-standing relationships face different challenges. Over the years many people adapt to their partner's needs so subtly that much passes unspoken between them. If you have been together for a long time without wanting children you may find it difficult to talk if one of you changes your mind. Your lifestyle and expectations of each other are more fixed and it may take patience to alter them. Even if you and your partner agree that the time is right to have a baby, it will be easier to adjust to the changes it will bring if you can discuss feelings freely, but this takes more effort when you think you understand your partner well. A stable, long-term partnership involves a considerable depth of caring between partners, however, and has usually developed strategies for surviving ups and downs.

Some couples create a strong relationship by having plenty of time for each other. Parents have less time, for themselves and each other, and cannot preserve the same degree of independence they had before a baby arrived. To sustain a good relationship with your partner when you have a baby you have to give it a high priority; making time for each other in the evening, for example, in preference to watching a TV programme or finishing the book you are reading. Older couples, especially in second relationships, often find this easier to take on board.

Although parenthood is hard work a baby can bring a healthy dose of anarchy to lives that may have become over orderly. Laughter often increases dramatically when you look at the world through a child's eyes and watch him learn things that you have long taken for granted.

Men and babies: Many men enjoy children and are delighted at the thought of becoming a father for the first time or having another child. Others stall for as long as possible. 'We'll think about it in a couple of years' or 'let's get the kitchen sorted out first', they say, hoping that the whole subject of children will quietly fade away.

Insecurities often surface when people try to balance what they have with what they feel they might lose. To many men, having a baby seems like an emotional and practical curtailment of life rather than an expansion. They do not find the idea appealing, nor do they find babies and young children engaging. This may change when they have a child of their own, but a man who has children from a previous relationship may feel no desire to have any more.

Some men are reluctant to share their partner, even with a tiny scrap of their own flesh and blood. In a long-term partnership you may have to face the painful reality that your partner does not want a baby because he likes the way that your relationship functions as a couple and a baby would intrude. Men who shy away from childcare can feel surplus to requirements; their partner is preoccupied for much of the first few months; and if the baby fulfils some of her needs for physical comfort and she is exhausted for much of the time, it is bound to affect their sex life.

Childhood memories are a powerful incentive to wanting a child of your own and a man who has few positive memories from his own childhood is likely to feel much less secure about fatherhood. Although he may explain his reluctance in terms of career, travel or domestic plans, he may actually doubt his readiness for the responsibility of parenthood or his ability to do the job well.

You may hesitate to brainwash a reluctant partner into agreeing to have a baby, but if your desire is strong the issue will eventually affect your relationship. Some men, brought up to believe it is natural for women to want children, agree because they are afraid of losing the woman they love and are prepared to go along with anything that makes her happy, despite their own doubts.

Some women gamble on an 'accident', hoping that their partner will change completely when a baby arrives, but this is taking a chance with a child's happiness. In the long run, honesty is more constructive and less likely to lead to resentment. It may mean facing some painful truths about your priorities as individuals and the nature of your partnership, but this is preferable to having a baby on the wrong footing.

Late fatherhood: A new father in his mid-forties or fifties has as good a chance of living to see his child grow up as a 30-year-old father had a century ago. Over the last hundred years physical health has improved, active life has lengthened, attitudes have changed and the gap between the generations has shrunk. Parents today behave very differently from the way their own parents behaved.

Older fathers are more likely to have shared the decision to have children, and they often relish being emotionally close and involved with their child. Less absorbed in career, sports or social activities than when they were younger, they put more into fathering and get more out of it. Redundancy or retirement can be an opportunity for role reversal and the chance to be a hands-on father at a time when new experiences are becoming less available.

Any financial or health worries tend to be balanced by greater confidence and readiness for emotional and personal commitment. Older men are more likely to seek financial advice, make careful pension and life insurance provisions and appoint a guardian for their child. They develop reserves of stamina and strategies for conserving energy to compensate for slowing down physically.

If your partner is much older than you, talk about having a child at an early stage in your relationship, before making a long-term commitment. Men sometimes underestimate the rewards of late fatherhood, but few relationships survive total disagreement over something as fundamental as whether to have children. If you let things drift and assumptions are made you may feel cheated as time moves on.

Marriage: Marriage is more important for some couples than for others when children come along, but unmarried parents are in a much less secure position than married couples. Unless they make a formal agreement with each other (or a court order is imposed) all rights and responsibilities for the child rest with the mother alone. This may pose no problems while the parents are getting along well, but it can lead to much bitterness if they decide to separate. Courts put the interests of the child first and try to recognise the value of shared responsibility, but the father is in a weaker position than the mother.

When a parent dies unexpectedly without having made a will their estate passes in a prescribed fashion to their next of kin. If you are not married this favours your parents, brothers or sisters, or even the partner of a previous marriage (if it has not been formally dissolved) over your current partner. You may want to see a solicitor about making a will and other legal arrangements, to ensure that your intentions towards your partner and child are upheld.

Although marriage may seem the next logical step, it can change the way you and the wider community see your relationship. All partnerships go through ups and downs and any major commitment can be unsettling. Some couples who have been together for many years experience problems or even separate within a short time of marriage, although this is less likely if they have talked honestly about what each other wants and expects. A good relationship can carry you a long way but it may need an extra spark to survive the commitment of marriage and parenthood.

If your partnership is under strain (after an infidelity, for example), having a baby can make things worse. When one partner feels let down, trust is lost and unconditional love is withheld. Unless you both want to repair the relationship, a baby will only provide a temporary diversion before putting you under even more strain. One advantage of maturity is that it may help you to reconcile differences successfully before having a baby. Counselling (see *Directory*) can enable you to discuss problems on neutral ground.

Lesbian parenting: There is no evidence that sexual orientation has anything to do with the ability to be a good parent. On the contrary, a good deal of research suggests that the children of lesbian parents are at least as healthy and well adjusted as anyone else's. Most couples who have children do so within a stable partnership and lesbians tend to be more conscientious than most parents in thinking the issues through and coming to careful decisions.

There is more involved, however, such as how to have a child in the first place, who to come out to and what the effect will be on the child and on friends and family. You need to be sure that a baby is something both you and your partner want as there are likely to be extra stresses. Society generally does not give whole-hearted approval to lesbian couples who decide to become parents.

If you feel indifferent about becoming a parent but your partner wants a child you may be tempted to go along with it as an expression of your love for her. Take your time, however. It is hard to remain detached from parenting when your partner has a baby, and a decision made in haste and regretted later can cause problems both for your relationship and for the child involved.

Talk to other parents so that you have a realistic idea of what parenthood entails if you and your partner are trying to decide whether to have a child. How you feel about the job description is likely to be more relevant than whether you are lesbian or heterosexual. More information is available today from book-shops and organisations for lesbians but some women come late to the realisation that their sexual orientation does not necessarily exclude motherhood.

Other relationships

Although you and your partner are likely to experience the greatest changes when you have a child, it will also affect other important relationships in your life, especially your family and any other children you or your partner may have.

Your family: One of the nicest things about having a late baby is the excitement and delight of most families. Your own or your partner's parents may be elderly, infirm and unable to offer much practical support, but a baby arriving in time for them to see or enjoy usually brings great happiness.

Families have to adjust their expectations, seeing you as a mother when they thought of you only as a career woman perhaps, or conceding that your new partner is here to stay. When you and your partner come from different cultures there may be two sets of parental expectations to fulfil. Some cultures are more tolerant and more supportive of pregnant women than others. Mixed-up generations (your new son is uncle to your grandchild, the offspring of your adult son or daughter, for example) cause amusement rather than confusion in most families, but for some it is seen as a disruption of the established order.

Change revitalises many families but threatens others and, faced with news that they were not expecting, some relatives react negatively at first and speak their mind with no regard for tact. Be prepared for unguarded comments if you have fended off hints about children for so long that it is assumed they are off the agenda, if you already have a baby only a few months old or if you start a second family after a long gap. You may imagine an unspoken 'at your age' in deflating remarks such as 'what on earth for?' or 'I can't see how you'll cope', so make it clear how you feel when you announce the news. Relatives, friends and colleagues will then know whether to offer sympathy because it was an accident, or congratulations because you are delighted.

Children or step-children: If you already have children you will want to take their feelings into account when planning a baby. Some couples allow their children to take part in the decision, but this needs caution as it may give a child more power than he or she is mature enough to handle.

Most children are relatively unaffected by pregnancy, unless you are repeatedly sick or have an illness that takes you away when they expect you to be around. Toddlers need time to adjust when a new baby takes up your attention, or later on becomes more active and demanding. A confident youngster who likes babies and feels secure in his or her world may react with delight, showing surprisingly mature thoughtfulness and concern during your pregnancy.

Teenagers sometimes find the thought of their mother becoming pregnant disturbing, not to say embarrassing, and the fuss made over a new baby can seem out of proportion when they are worrying about exams and the opposite sex. Adult children are often sufficiently independent not to feel threatened when a new baby is expected, although resentments may surface if an inheritance is involved or they feel that their own childhood was insecure.

Step-children have divided loyalties, whether they live with you or not. Their response to a pregnancy may be influenced by how well they get on with you, and the attitude of their mother or grandparents. Men who had different priorities when they were younger often take eagerly to fatherhood the second time around, and this can cause resentment; a child's behaviour can be affected by adult conflicts.

It is difficult to appreciate the needs of children at different stages until you experience them; and the pressures of a previous stage are forgotten when the next one arrives. You may feel that your partner lavishes too much time or money on his first family while his ex-partner feels that he ignored their children but is excited about his new family. She may resent money spent on a nursery that a baby soon outgrows, while she cannot afford the expensive trainers that her children want; and you may not understand why cheaper trainers will not do.

Children are quick to sense injustice and if they feel that a new baby will take the lion's share of attention a sense of shared commitment can easily turn into jealous resentment. With careful handling, however, a new baby can build a bridge, a half brother or sister to every child and special to them all.

Conception, pregnancy and parenthood

Having a child is not especially risky when you are older, but equally there are no guarantees that it will be straightforward. If your pregnancy or birth is complicated your partner and family will be affected as well as you.

Trying to have a baby: Statistics show that it is almost as common for a woman over 40 to have an unexpected pregnancy as for a teenager, which suggests that older women become pregnant easily. Many do, but it is a hard fact of life that the chance of conceiving decreases with age. On average it takes longer to conceive and the chances of early miscarriage are greater than they are for younger women. When you want a baby it is soul-destroying to see your period arrive month after month, or to become pregnant only to miscarry.

Older women face more hurdles along the way to motherhood than younger women and each can put a strain on their partnership. Once it surfaces, the desire to have a baby is usually strong. As time passes and you know that the choice will be taken away in the not-so-distant future, resentments that might normally be taken in your stride rise to the surface.

A woman who implicitly agreed not to start a family sooner may blame the decision entirely on her partner. Couples who have been together for a long time rarely make love as frequently as they did at the start of their relationship, and a man may resent having to 'perform' at certain times of the month, feeling that he is being used as a stud; or he may feel responsible for his partner's distress and lose confidence in his ability to respond in a way that would help. Infertility treatment may mean that hopes are built up and dashed over and over again, and with each treatment cycle the likelihood of success decreases.

Anger at life in general and the unfairness of it all can affect the strongest of relationships and many couples can only cope by temporarily switching off from their emotions, or from each other.

Neither you nor your partner should feel inadequate because you find the stress of trying to have a baby intolerable. If there is tension between you try to get support from elsewhere to set your relationship back on track. Friends or relatives may be able to provide a listening ear, or there are counselling services and support groups (see *Directory*) that could help.

Pregnancy: It has been said that up to the age of 30 women can cope with pregnancy, work and a frenetic social life; from 30 to 40 she can handle pregnancy plus either work or a hectic social life but not both; and after 40 pregnancy alone is quite enough! Many women in their late thirties or forties would argue that having a much wanted baby actually has a revitalising effect, but even a normal pregnancy adds a degree of extra physical exertion.

When you are generally used to running your own life you may be dismayed to find that pregnancy means other people suddenly want to take over. Well-meaning advice or uninvited criticism of your decisions is more likely if you are expecting your first baby or there has been a long gap between children.

Many people generalise from the links between chromosome disorders and age, wrongly assuming that pregnancy and birth are automatically hazardous for older mothers. The emphasis on fetal testing is especially hard as it focuses attention on relatively rare but genuine problems (see pages 58–73). Deciding to have tests is often far more upsetting than you anticipate, although it helps if you prepare the ground by discussing it with your partner before you become pregnant.

There are more complications of pregnancy among older women simply because they have had longer in which to develop general health problems that can affect it adversely, such as increased weight, diabetes or high blood pressure. Pregnancy is more stressful at any age if you have an illness, but if you are healthy, fit and of normal weight, your chances of problems developing once pregnancy is established are little different from a younger woman's.

Parenthood: Babies soon grow up and most parents feel that after the first few months the emotional energy they expend is returned with interest. Life is more complicated as a parent, however; inevitably your baby's needs conflict with your own. You cannot go anywhere without either taking him with you or making arrangements for him. This can seem daunting when you have never faced such restrictions, but the reality is little different from getting to work on time or feeding a pet. It becomes a routine and you get used to it.

Some couples worry that if they have a child they will stop being 'people' and turn into 'parents' who no longer talk about or do anything interesting, but the richness of life simply changes. Where you enjoyed a concert or the theatre you listen to your child's speech develop, watch his mind unfold. The park becomes an art gallery and you give a butterfly as much attention as a painting. You skim the newspaper but discover the excellence of children's literature. From the outside it can be hard to imagine just how fascinating watching a child develop can prove to be.

Trips to the park can be as boring as going to the same art gallery every day and feeding the ducks may lose its charm for you long before it does for your child, of course. If you are at home all day you may feel that life is passing you by and resent your partner, especially if his or her job appears more exciting and glamorous. Nevertheless, child rearing is more varied than many occupations; most jobs have an element of being what you make of them and, however stimulating, most include less attractive aspects or chores.

Sharing parental responsibilities

A baby gets in the way of work so one partner usually has to accept more responsibility for childcare and things like taking time off if a child is ill. Even if you and your partner want to, it is hard to organise equal parenting roles when earning a living is based on the notion of 'full-time' work and there are only a few snatched minutes between the commuter train and bedtime.

Weekends have to be planned carefully if the partner who is less involved on a daily basis is to develop a relationship with their child. Organising mealtimes, clearing up toys and getting cross when a child is naughty leads to a different quality of closeness, compared with reading a bedtime story or going to the swings. Men who want a closer relationship with their child than they had with their own father often find the demands of a career trap them into the role of 'playmate'.

As more women work outside the home they expect more of their partner domestically. A father who enjoys looking after his child more than his job may willingly take on day to day childcare, but many men would rather someone else did it. The nitty gritty of caring for a child may not appear to hold much interest.

A woman who has worked hard to achieve some success and cannot imagine life without her career may hold similar views before she has a baby. Often, however, she is genuinely surprised to find her priorities change and she does not want to invest the same level of commitment in her career. Such a change of heart has consequences if your lifestyle is based on two incomes. Children are an irreversible economic charge, and both partners may worry about the effects of losing one source of income, especially in times of uncertain employment.

Communication

Relationships work better when they are seen to be fair and resentment can be undermining if one partner feels that the other is not pulling their weight. The best solution is to sit down and negotiate who will do what; to be honest and work out satisfactory alternatives without feeling guilty. If you and your partner have different expectations about something important to one of you, and are unable to find some common ground or compromise, your relationship may flounder. Good communication can be surprisingly difficult within a family, however. It sounds so simple, but the pressure of day to day life makes it easy to put it off until tomorrow. And tomorrow never comes.

In many ways men and women communicate from different perspectives. Women often reach their own answers by talking something through, but they feel upset if nobody listens or what they say is dismissed. Men tend to look for the 'problem' and then provide practical solutions, and they feel upset when this 'help' is not accepted. Men are sometimes reluctant to listen as they feel they are a sitting target for criticism. For an employee a salary or wage is compensation for doing something they would rather not. Within a family the reward is a more subtle feeling that you are valued or your views are acknowledged.

If you find it hard to discuss something important without becoming upset a counsellor could help you to express difficult thoughts and move forward in your relationship by providing a neutral, non-judgmental background and by asking the right questions. Your doctor or a friend may be able to suggest someone, or there are a number of contacts in the Directory.

Talking to your partner

If something is important and you want your partner to listen, wait until any anger has subsided and prepare the ground first:

❑ Learn to judge when the time is right. Your partner may be more receptive if he is not exhausted at the end of the day or preoccupied with something else, or if he is left alone for half an hour to finish whatever he is doing.
❑ Set a time limit for the discussion so that he does not feel trapped.
❑ Tell him specifically that it helps you to talk something through and you only want him to listen; you are not criticising him or asking him to find solutions.
❑ Make it rewarding – appreciate his effort and thank him for it.
❑ If he resists, try again another time. It takes a while for some men to stop feeling pinned down and threatened when their partner suggests discussing something.

Older mothers' experiences

Elizabeth (42): 'Once we'd agreed to have a baby we planned to marry. Michael saw this as justifiable for the child's sake, but I was thinking of my mother, who always called me 'neither fish nor fowl'. As it happened she became ill and I spent a lot of time with her before she died. I'd always taken her for granted but I began to realise how much she meant to me. We put the wedding plans on hold and our relationship went through a difficult patch, with a lot of silly arguments. I cut myself off from Michael after my mother's death. He had an assignment abroad and things seemed better when he returned.

'I want to become pregnant as soon as possible. Michael would be supportive if I wanted to talk something through or there was a problem, but I don't expect to discuss everything because he's away so much. He would rather I handled the nuts and bolts of pregnancy and this suits me.'

Q: My relationship with Michael is very important. How can I make sure that a child will not come between us?
A: Keeping a partnership alive is relatively easy when you have only yourselves and each other to think about. Relationships withstand a certain amount of harsh treatment, but like house plants they die of complete neglect.

A baby's needs seem paramount and when you are exhausted and under stress it can be hard to think of anything else. Putting a baby first is necessary to some extent, but your relationship with your partner also demands attention. There is no magic formula for staying on course, but some couples find it helps to make a habit of sitting down regularly to plan family time, time for each of them and time as a couple, arranging babysitters as needed. As Michael goes away on long trips you could discuss and plan your time together each time he gets home.

Valerie (44): 'Barry and I have different views on bringing up children. It's easy to feel in control when children are little and you make all the important decisions. When they reach their teens you worry just as much, but you can't do anything about it and it's terrifying to let the reins go. When Emma goes off with her friends I need to know where she is, but Barry sometimes disagrees with the rules I make. Then everyone joins in the row.

'I like to think the worst so that if things work out better than expected I'm pleasantly surprised. Barry is an optimist who refuses to see any problems. I never feel able to discuss my fears with him as he just says it will be all right. He means well but sometimes it puts a lot of stress on me.'

Q: How should we tell Emma and Claire that we want to have a baby?

A: If the subject comes up naturally you could say that you and Barry would like to have a baby together some day. Otherwise, wait until you are pregnant. In general, the younger the child the later you can leave it before telling them.

Your girls are old enough to be told early so that they feel included and do not hear the news from someone else. You could take them to a restaurant to make it a special occasion. You will have their attention and can talk about it in a positive way, reassuring them that the new baby will help to bring you together as a family and you will still be there for them even though you may get more tired at times.

Having a baby is your decision. Your children will probably be pleased and excited, but they have to come to terms with it regardless of how they feel. It is not always easy to adjust to such news, especially for teenagers who have many pressures in their lives, so make allowances if necessary. If they seem worried about what their friends might think about their mother having a baby be tactful in the way you talk or dress when friends are around. There is no excuse for rudeness, however, so if an unkind remark upsets you point it out.

Lesley (36): 'Phil and I have learned over the years to accept each other's moods and ways of coping. Phil was sad when we couldn't have a child, but he carried on with life, whereas I was desperate and couldn't stop thinking about it. I conceived once, but miscarried. We cried and hugged a lot, but then I began to feel that I was responsible for Phil's happiness, so I stopped talking about what had happened because I felt it caused Phil more pain.

'Now we are older we are starting IVF treatment in a different frame of mind. Whatever happens we feel we can accept it. I'm optimistic and Phil is alternately happy about the decision and very wary. We have a large, close family and everyone is excited for us.'

Q: Our treatment will mean numerous hospital visits and we want to retain our privacy. How can we handle it so that nobody in the family feels left out?

A: Large, close families can be wonderful but they can also be overwhelming, and you have to be the ones to set the agenda. You could share the broad experience with them while keeping the intimate details private. Unless they have been through it people do not know what and what not to ask.

Politicians learn how to volunteer the information that they choose without giving anyone a chance to ask questions they might not want to answer. You could chat about the clinic decor, how many people were there, how pleasant the nurses were and when you have to go again; then if you are asked a question that you prefer not to answer say so, or move smoothly on to another topic of conversation.

Sue (39): 'Kenneth's son Robert and his wife Julie are in their twenties. They were sweet when I had a miscarriage the year after Jack was born and it can't have been easy because Julie was expecting twins at the time and getting bigger by the day. They were both very sensitive about our feelings, and we had to make it clear that we really wanted to share in the preparations for the twins.

'Kenneth and I became closer if anything after the miscarriage. I was more anxious than I was before Jack was born, because I was already 36. I worried about not getting pregnant and if I did whether it would all go wrong again. We can talk to each other easily so voicing my concerns always helped. Kenneth has a calming influence on me as he's much more philosophical than I am.'

Q: Kenneth feels that playing golf and running around with Jack keeps him young, but I worry about him as he is now 58. Should I get him to slow down?

A: Men who have successful careers often have a great deal of surplus energy and stamina when they retire. If your husband plays golf regularly and enjoys rough and tumble with the children he is probably quite fit.

Talk to him about your worries. Most older fathers take their responsibilities very seriously and are prepared to stop smoking, cut down on alcohol, give up dangerous sports and generally live a healthier lifestyle. They go for health checks and make adequate insurance provisions because they know how unpredictable life can be. Nobody can see into the future, but your husband has a new capacity to enjoy life and the children are a real incentive to look after himself.

3   Will the Baby be All Right?

PREGNANT WOMEN OFTEN HEAR THE MESSAGE THAT IF THEY TAKE care over their diet, do not smoke or drink, rest, exercise and take advantage of antenatal care, including pre-natal screening, they are guaranteed a high chance of producing a healthy baby. This is true, but it also suggests that the outcome of pregnancy is largely under your control, which can make it even harder for the small number of parents whose baby has a problem.

Ninety-six per cent of babies are born without defects and two per cent have a minor variation, such as an extra finger or toe, that does not affect their quality of life. Of the four per cent of babies who have an abnormality at birth, roughly half are structural malformations such as cleft lip and palate or a heart defect. Some of these can be treated by an operation after birth. About a quarter are rare single gene defects such as cystic fibrosis. Chromosome abnormalities, for example Down's syndrome, account for 0.6 per cent of all defects; that is six per thousand. Their link with age gets so much attention, however, that older mothers often see their risk of bearing a baby with any defect as greater than it really is.

For an older mother the risk of having a baby with a chromo-some abnormality is higher than for a younger mother. Risk is not entirely objective, however. It can be played up so that it seems more important or toned down to appear insignificant, according to your agenda.

If a hundred women aged 40 are pregnant, one baby will suffer from Down's syndrome. If a hundred women use the progesto-gen-only pill exactly as instructed for a year, one will become pregnant. Yet you probably do not think about the risk of preg-nancy if you take your pill carefully, while the risk of Down's syndrome probably worries you. Why are women encouraged to trust a pill but doubt their own body's ability to produce a perfect baby, when the actual risks are identical? It could change your life just as much to become pregnant accidentally as to have a baby with Down's syndrome.

The media and the medical profession barely mention pill failure but talk a lot about fetal abnormality in women over 35 and this affects your perception. The increased risk applies only to chromosome defects, which account for a small proportion (0.6 per cent) of all defects.

The evidence of risk

You have almost as good a chance of having a healthy baby as a younger mother. Most things that can affect a baby's health before birth are in no way linked to your age. A large study in Canada looked at forty-three non-chromosomal defects and found that forty of them were not linked to the age of the mother. The other three, congenital dislocation of the hip, patent ductus arteriosus (a congenital heart defect) and hypertrophic pyloric stenosis (a common narrowing of part of the stomach) were actually less common in babies born to women over the age of 35.

Studies in the past have often failed to separate out the risks to the baby that stem from the mother's age and those linked to factors such as her health and the number of pregnancies she has already had. Most non-chromosomal risks to the baby that were thought in the past to be linked with age have disappeared with better controlled studies. A study using uniquely detailed birth registers in Sweden showed that there is a slightly higher risk for older mothers of having a low birth-weight or premature baby, however, even when previous pregnancies, education, diseases and smoking habits were taken into account.

The risk of a woman over 35 suffering from a pre-existing medical disorder, such as diabetes or hypertension, that could affect pregnancy is about twice that of a woman under 30, but it is still only about 12 per cent and obstetric care for such disorders has improved greatly in recent years. It is not clear at present whether the risk of stillbirth increases slightly with age, but if it does it may be linked to the increase in illnesses that can affect both mother and baby.

Chromosome abnormalities often occur when a chromosome fails to separate normally. The most common is Down's syndrome (also called trisomy 21). Rare ones include Patau and Edward's (trisomies 13 and 18) and a few associated with the sex chromosomes, such as Triple X syndrome. They may be linked to the age of either parent. For example, it is thought that about a third of women's eggs at the age of 35 have a defect, but that up to a fifth of Down's syndrome may be the result of a sperm defect.

Some eggs and sperm are likely to be defective whatever your age, or your partner's age. Most embryos with a defect are lost within the first twelve weeks; many very early, before a pregnancy test has been carried out. The increase associated with age partly explains why older women are more likely to miscarry. The table on page 58 shows the number of babies with a major chromosome abnormality compared with normal babies at birth.

Age-Related Risk of Major Chromosome Defects			
Age	Risk	Age	Risk
35	1:335	41	1:75
36	1:270	42	1:60
37	1:215	43	1:45
38	1:165	44	1:35
39	1:130	45	1:25
40	1:100	46	1:15

Everything in life carries risks. Some are preventable while others are inevitable. A small proportion of the inevitable risk involved in having a baby is linked to age, but factors such as eating healthily and not smoking influence the preventable risks more than age. Older mothers tend to be more willing than younger ones to make lifestyle changes to avoid preventable risks and give a baby a healthy start in life.

Although in the past older women have been discouraged from having babies, in developed countries all risks start from low baselines. Taking everything into account, you probably do not need to lose much sleep over it. The average older woman has almost as good a chance of having a straightforward pregnancy and birth and a normal baby as the average younger woman.

Fetal testing

Fetal diagnosis is a great medical advance, giving the possibility of detecting certain defects before birth. The links between age and chromosome abnormalities tend to encourage the assumption that every older mother will automatically want tests, but in fact about one-fifth of women in western Europe, Australia and the USA prefer not to have them. You do not need to accept whatever you are offered, or let yourself be persuaded that you are taking a 'risk' if you refuse tests.

The attractions of tests come at a price, but as you may be encouraged to have them it is an advantage to think about the issues before you become pregnant. Decisions need to be made in the first few weeks of pregnancy, just the time when you need to be rational but may be feeling indecisive. Going through tests is stressful and mothers often say that they were emotionally unprepared for what lay ahead. It is easier to jump on to the testing bandwagon than to get off it, and it can be more scary along the way than you expect. You will be better able to take the reality of testing in your stride if you are sure that you really want the information it provides.

Broadly speaking, there are two types of test, screening and diagnostic. Screening procedures, such as ultrasound scans, identify babies who appear more likely to have a defect. They are non-invasive and low risk, but they can only make a prediction. Diagnostic tests, such as amniocentesis, take cells directly from the uterus and analyse them to detect defects with a fair degree of certainty. They provide more information and are more accurate. They are also invasive and carry an additional risk of miscarriage that can be worrying if you have taken a long time to conceive or fear that you might not be able to become pregnant again. The miscarriage rate at 16 weeks is about 1 per cent if you do not have tests.

If a screening test puts you in a high risk category (it is only a forecast so it may not be correct) you will be offered a diagnostic test; and if the result is still unclear a repetition of the same test, or additional investigations.

Tests cannot guarantee that a baby is perfect as they only detect certain problems. At present this excludes about 60 per cent of mental disability and most rare single gene disorders. They do not distinguish the degree to which a baby is affected by a condition, which may vary from slight to profound.

No test is 100 per cent accurate, and occasionally a baby is wrongly diagnosed as having, or not having, a defect. At present there is no remedy for many of the detectable defects, so termination is offered. New developments will increase the range of tests available but it is unlikely to substantially change their limitations.

The tests: Fetal diagnosis has made great strides in the past few years and by the time you read this new tests will already be available to help women who have a family history of a genetic defect or to provide information earlier in pregnancy. For example, a very few cells cross the placenta from the baby to the mother and at the time of writing a computer program has just been developed to identify them. If it becomes widely available, checking for chromosome abnormalities will involve a simple blood test instead of amniocentesis.

The following tables provide a guide to some established tests, with spaces to fill in additional information about new tests (pages 67–8). You may find out about these from media reports and magazines or from your doctor or midwife.

SCREENING TEST	**Nuchal scan**
WHEN IT IS DONE	About 10–13 weeks.
WHAT IT IS FOR	Predicts the likelihood of a chromosome defect by measuring a dark, fluid-filled space behind the baby's neck.
HOW IT IS DONE	Your abdomen is covered with gel to provide contact and a transducer is passed across it, allowing high frequency sound waves to build up a picture of your baby on a screen.
RISKS	Non-invasive; low risk.
PROS AND CONS	Results available immediately so that further tests (and termination if necessary) can be performed early in pregnancy. Not available everywhere and there may be a charge.
AVAILABILITY /COST (fill this in yourself with local details)	

SCREENING TEST	**Blood tests** (for example, AFP test, triple test, triple-plus test)
WHEN IT IS DONE	About 16 weeks, or earlier in some centres.
WHAT IT IS FOR	Predicts the risk of a baby having a neural tube defect or chromosome abnormality.
HOW IT IS DONE	A blood sample is taken and the levels of various chemicals in it are measured. If the results predict a risk higher than about 1 in 250 you are offered a diagnostic test. Age is taken into account, so the older you are the more likely a high score becomes.
RISKS	Non-invasive; low risk.
PROS AND CONS	Results available in one–three weeks, depending on the area and the test (ask when and how you will be informed before having the test). About 70 per cent of women aged 40 have a predicted risk lower than a woman of 35; this may reassure you so that you feel an invasive test is not necessary. Blood tests are not very accurate at present and can cause unnecessary anxiety; a large baby, a twin pregnancy or inaccurate dates can confuse the results. They were standardised on largely white populations so women of other cultures suffer poor detection rates and more false positives.
AVAILABILITY /COST (fill this in yourself with local details)	

SCREENING TEST	**Anomaly scan**
WHEN IT IS DONE	About 16–20 weeks.
WHAT IT IS FOR	Screens for visible anomalies of the spine or limbs and defects of organs such as the heart, bladder or kidneys. If anything looks unusual a more detailed diagnostic scan can be performed. A test such as amniocentesis may be offered for confirmation or to obtain additional information.
HOW IT IS DONE	Similar to a nuchal scan.
RISKS	Non-invasive; low risk.
PROS AND CONS	Results are available immediately, although you may be asked to discuss them with a doctor or midwife. The image can be hard to interpret especially if the baby is active; the technician may miss a problem or 'see' one in error.
AVAILABILITY /COST (fill this in yourself with local details)	

DIAGNOSTIC TEST	**Chorionic villus sampling (CVS)**
WHEN IT IS DONE	About 11–13 weeks
WHAT IT IS FOR	Detects similar abnormalities to amniocentesis, but is performed earlier in pregnancy.
HOW IT IS DONE	The baby and placenta are located by ultrasound scan; tissue is removed from the edge of the placenta, through the abdomen or cervix (neck of the uterus), and cultured or examined directly.
RISKS	In the best hands the risk of miscarriage as a result of the test is 1–3 per cent (as it is done early in pregnancy some miscarriages might have happened anyway). There are reports of limb damage if CVS is done before 11 weeks.
PROS AND CONS	Results available in one–three weeks. In about 3 per cent of samples the cells fail to culture, results are inconclusive or the cells come from the mother, not the baby. CVS carries higher risks than amniocentesis for similar information, but testing is completed earlier.
AVAILABILITY /COST (fill this in yourself with local details)	

DIAGNOSTIC TEST	**Amniocentesis**
WHEN IT IS DONE	About 16–18 weeks
WHAT IT IS FOR	Detects chromosome abnormalities such as Down's syndrome and genetic defects such as cystic fibrosis. Usually follows a blood test or scan, but women over about 40 sometimes omit these.
HOW IT IS DONE	The position of the baby and placenta are located by ultrasound scan and a sample of amniotic fluid is withdrawn through your abdomen. Cells from this are cultured or examined directly.
RISKS	In the best hands there is a 0.5–1 per cent risk of miscarriage as a result of the test. One per cent of babies have unexplained minor breathing difficulties at birth, possibly linked to the reduction in amniotic fluid due to the test.
PROS AND CONS	Results may take up to four weeks. In about 1 per cent of cases insufficient fluid is collected or cells fail to grow and the test has to be repeated. Occasionally the mother's cells are grown in error, giving false reassurance.
AVAILABILITY /COST (fill this in yourself with local details)	

DIAGNOSTIC TEST	**Fetal Blood Sampling (FBS)**
WHEN IT IS DONE	About 20 weeks, at a specialist centre.
WHAT IT IS FOR	Gives extra information following diagnosis by amniocentesis or CVS. Also detects infections such as rubella, toxoplasmosis, cytomegalovirus or herpes simplex.
HOW IT IS DONE	Guided by ultrasound scan a sample of blood is taken directly from the baby's cord where it joins the placenta (cordocentesis), or occasionally from the baby's liver or heart. The cells can be examined directly.
RISKS	In the best hands, 1–2 per cent risk of miscarriage as a result of the test.
PROS AND CONS	Results take less than a week. May provide reassurance after an unclear amniocentesis or CVS test, or contact with an infectious disease, but may also raise more questions than it answers.
AVAILABILITY /COST (fill this in yourself with local details)	

NEW SCREENING TESTS

TEST	WHEN IT IS DONE	WHAT IT IS FOR	HOW IT IS DONE	RISKS	PROS AND CONS	AVAILABILITY /COST

NEW DIAGNOSTIC TESTS

TEST	WHEN IT IS DONE	WHAT IT IS FOR	HOW IT IS DONE	RISKS	PROS AND CONS	AVAILABILITY /COST

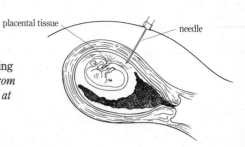

Chorionic Villus Sampling
(CVS). *Cells are taken from
the edge of the placenta at
about 11–14 weeks.*

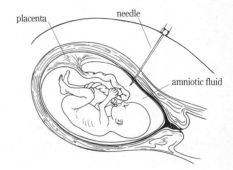

Amniocentesis. *A sample
of amniotic fluid is
withdrawn at about
16–18 weeks.*

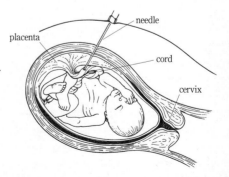

Cordocentesis. *A sample of
the baby's blood is
withdrawn from near the
placenta after 18 weeks.*

Deciding about testing: If you have an inherited disorder in
your family or already have a child with a disability you may
have no hesitation in having tests, or in confidently turning them
down. Otherwise, you need to weigh up how much you want the
information against the possible disadvantages of tests. When
you go for any test your doctor will be looking for an abnormality,
while you will be looking for reassurance. These are fundamen-
tally different attitudes to the procedure.

Some women have tests because they do not want to bring a
child with a disability into the world. Others refuse because they
want to avoid the drawbacks inherent in even the simplest procedure, or they feel that tests provide too little information to base
decisions on, and that children who are different enrich us all.

Maturity is an advantage when difficult choices have to be
made. You have probably had practice at thinking issues through
and facing the realities of life, and know yourself and what is
right for you better than when you were younger, but counselling
is sometimes offered as part of a fetal testing programme.

Ultimately, your decision will depend on your view of life, your
emotional and financial resources, your previous experience of
disability and the effects you feel having a child with a problem
would have on you, your partner and any children you already
have. The issues are complex and personal. Whatever you decide
may be applauded by some people and possibly condemned by
others.

Many men feel that such important decisions are best left to
the mother, but thinking about testing can be a more emotional
experience than you expect. Your partner, or a sympathetic friend
or relative if you are not closely involved with your baby's father,
can discuss the issues with you over days or weeks if necessary.
Your partner may be more detached and find it easier to weigh
up the pros and cons. Reaching a shared decision may help you
to handle the responsibility.

Some pros and cons of fetal testing:

❑ Tests give the option of termination if you feel strongly that you would not want to bring a baby with a disability into the world.

❑ They can forewarn you of a problem so that you can adjust, find out more about it, tell family or friends or alert specialist services to provide treatment at birth.

❑ A clear result may provide some reassurance, so that you can enjoy the rest of your pregnancy.

❑ Waiting for the results can be extremely worrying. You may feel unable to relax until testing is completed, which in some cases takes more than half of pregnancy.

❑ If a screening test puts you in a high risk category but later results are clear you suffer unnecessary anxiety and may never feel completely reassured.

❑ Once you start you may feel bound to carry on, leading to more dependence on doctors and medical technology. Repeating an invasive test or undergoing additional tests exposes you to the risk of miscarriage again.

❑ If you are under 40 the risk of miscarriage from a diagnostic test can be as great as the risk of a defect being detected.

Arranging to have tests: If you decide to have tests, talk to your doctor or midwife as early as possible in pregnancy, because the availability, cost and timing of tests vary from place to place. You may decide to accept whatever is available locally, arrange to have a test that is not usually offered in your area or refuse something that other people think is beneficial. One advantage of being older is that you will probably feel more confident about whatever you choose.

If you want a test that is not yet generally available your doctor can refer you to a specialist centre. You can also make a direct approach, although you might have to pay. Large numbers of volunteers are required to take part in trials when the initial results of a new test are promising. If this appeals to you, find out the benefits compared with existing tests; ask about the reliability and possible risks of the test, although this may be partly what the trial aims to discover.

If you are considering having an invasive test you might wish to ask about the level of expertise of the person who performs it. As a guide, a doctor who carries out at least fifty procedures every year is likely to be expert enough to minimise the risks attached to the test.

Questions to ask your midwife or GP
You may not get full information from a single source, but you only need enough to know what test is likely to give the best results for you.

❑ What tests are available routinely? Are they well established?
❑ When would they be carried out and what do they involve?
❑ How long would I have to wait for the results?
❑ How reliable are the results?
❑ What are the risks attached to the test?
❑ How often does a test have to be repeated?
❑ Are there any new tests I could have by travelling to another hospital?

Test results

Most women will be reassured by the results of their tests, but inevitably a few will learn that their baby may have a problem. This is a shock even if you have thought about the issues carefully beforehand. You never really think it will happen to you. Suddenly, opting for termination if the baby had any sort of defect may seem less clear-cut, and even a gentle reminder that this is one option may seem like pressure when you are in a highly emotional state.

Before deciding what to do, take enough time to let the shock subside; a few days will make little difference. You may want to find out more about the condition. Tests can pick up abnormalities that have few practical implications for the baby, and doctors feel bound to pass all the information on. There are probably many people walking around with an odd chromosome that they know nothing about, because it has no consequences or they are affected so slightly.

Unless the defect is common, non-specialist doctors may know little about it. Some conditions are so rare that they are unnamed; for others the doctor may only have a name and a discouraging text-book description. He or she may paint a bleak picture, assuming that you will want to terminate the pregnancy.

A specialist centre may have more information about a rare or ambiguous diagnosis, or you can ask to be referred to a genetic counsellor (see *Directory*). Self-help groups can also be a valuable source of information; other parents can tell you what day to day life caring for their child is really like. Talk to people who are close to you and to the experts. The outlook may be much more positive than you imagine.

Questions to ask an expert

Although it is not always easy to answer questions with any certainty, because even where a defect is well known there may be considerable variation, you will want to start somewhere. Here are some questions to ask:

- ❑ What is the usual lifespan of a baby with this disability?
- ❑ Are there likely to be other disabilities linked to the defect?
- ❑ If so, what would the likely treatment be?
- ❑ What is the child's quality of life likely to be?
- ❑ What facilities are available and what is the outlook for the child?

Making a decision after an adverse result

It is hard to take responsibility for deciding what to do, especially when you face the expectations, disapproval or thoughtless comments of people who have not had to make such a difficult decision themselves, or who chose differently.

Regardless of what other people think about the merits of continuing or terminating the pregnancy, you have to reach a decision that you can live with. You can only do what is right for you and your family. If you have done your best to make the right decision try not to judge yourself afterwards.

Continuing the pregnancy: You could continue the pregnancy even if your baby is only likely to live for a few days. You could seek foster or adoptive parents. Some agencies have a waiting list of couples wanting to adopt a baby with Down's syndrome, for example (see *Directory*). Many parents, however, accept their lot with grace and look forward to doing their best for their child.

The quality of life for disabled children and their families is affected by local facilities. Relatively few babies are born with severe disabilities each year, so your skill in finding your way around the system may determine the support you get. A self-help group could point you towards sources of assistance and help you to adjust your view of the future. Some parents hesitate to make contact, but once they do the future opens out dramatically. Having a child with special needs can bring a whole new range of experiences and friendships.

Testing tends to emphasise the tragedy of a baby with an impairment, not the potential for love; sticking a label on a child sets up expectations that take no account of personality. Outsiders focus on the disability first and the child second. Parents see it the other way round: their child is not abnormal but simply different.

Although maturity and stability are an advantage, the thought of bringing up a child with a disability can still be daunting, especially if the likely outcome is not known. People often delight in alarming any new parents, however: 'If you think she's a problem now just wait until she's a teenager!', 'Make the most of it – you won't have a good baby next time!' they predict gloomily. Yet every baby is different; every parent faces some problems and completely escapes others. This is the challenge of parenthood.

Terminating the pregnancy: If you decide to terminate a pregnancy you will probably do so with a heavy heart. You may want to maintain your privacy by telling only part of the truth: that the baby died. This can also be an explanation for other children, although close family and friends may be told more.

Knowing what may happen can make termination less intimidating. You will be admitted to a gynaecology or a maternity ward and probably given a single room. If you are less than about 14 weeks pregnant, the neck of the uterus is usually dilated under general anaesthetic and the fetus is removed. Between 14 and 18 weeks some obstetricians favour dilation and evacuation, while others induce labour using prostaglandin pessaries or a drip. After 18 weeks it is usually considered safer for you if labour is induced. As the uterus is not ready for labour it can be longer and more painful than a normal birth, but pain relief will be available and you can have your partner or a friend with you.

Inevitably a termination for abnormality causes great sadness. You lose your hopes and dreams and may also have to come to terms with feelings of anger that it was necessary, and guilt that it was you who made the decision.

Suppressing the emotional distress of termination sometimes causes it to surface later on, so it is better to face and live through it than to ignore it and try to get on with life. It can help to talk about your feelings to someone who accepts them without seeing them as a problem to be soothed away or solved with a bit of good advice. If you want to protect your partner or feel that he does not understand, a midwife, a friend or someone from a voluntary group (see *Directory*) may help.

The process of grieving takes time and generally passes through several stages (see pages 160–2 and 227) before you come to terms with what has happened. Only then can you move forward confidently to another pregnancy.

Older mothers' experiences

Elizabeth (42): 'I want to do what I can to avoid having a baby with a disability for the child's sake, although I'm surprised at the limitations of tests. I'd assumed that if I was given the all clear the baby would be perfect, which is unrealistic. Now I think about it, nature and man will always make mistakes.

'As soon as I have a positive pregnancy test I shall phone a hospital that specialises in fetal medicine and ask for details of all the tests they offer. Then I can discuss it with my doctor, find out what is offered locally to women of my age and make a decision. I like to be in control and I'm used to handling information.'

Q: Apart from my age, what would make me more at risk of having a baby with an abnormality, and could I be tested?
A: It is not known what causes most fetal abnormalities, but environmental and genetic factors are probably involved. If your family history suggests your baby could inherit a defect your GP can refer you to a genetic counsellor before or during pregnancy. About 5,000 single gene defects have been identified and tests on cells obtained by CVS or amniocentesis are available for a few hundred. They are not offered routinely as it would be like looking for a tiny diamond in a sack of sugar.

Many things could theoretically put a baby at risk, including toxic chemicals and deficiencies in some nutrients, but their effects are not always predictable. For example, carrying a gene that makes you susceptible to something does not mean you will encounter it; you might come in contact with an infection but be immune to it, or past the critical stage of pregnancy when your baby could be affected.

Individually, the risks are very small and the best approach is probably to be as healthy as possible before conception, avoid known hazards and have faith in your body's ability to produce a normal baby so that you can enjoy your pregnancy.

Valerie (44): 'I was under 35 when Claire was born so this is the first time I've had to decide about tests. I feel I owe it to Emma and Claire to have them as I want them to have better tests when they grow up and if we abandon them no progress will be made. I assumed Barry would be in favour of them and that I would have a termination if our baby had a defect, but he doesn't see disability as a disaster and he pointed out that even at my age I'm far more likely to have a baby who doesn't have an abnormality than one who does. I shall have tests, but I'm more relaxed now and we've agreed to discuss what to do if and when the need arises.'

Q: How can I handle the fear of having a baby with a disability?
A: Most parents who have a child with a disability say that once the initial shock subsided it was not the disaster that it seemed at first. It was a matter of changing their expectations over a period of time. Clearly it depends on the circumstances and the extent of the problem, but the outlook for many disabilities is better than it used to be. It could very easily open new doors and enrich your life.

This is not a worry to handle alone, however. Talk to Barry and to your daughters, if you feel they are old enough. They probably feel positive about the future, whatever it might hold, and will be able to support you at a stressful time.

Lesley (36): 'I'm not worried about having a baby with a disability because I don't think I'll be given a task that I can't cope with. Parenthood is a privilege after so many years of infertility and we have the economic and emotional resources to cope if we have to. We're probably in a better position than many younger couples to give a child with a disability extra attention. I have more time and patience now.

'Phil and I have decided to take what life throws at us and make the best of it. Everyone is afraid of the unknown but having tests would just make me more anxious as I feel that it draws attention to a few disabilities in a negative way. It would play on my fears and give me more responsibility than I want.'

Q: What causes Down's syndrome and what progress do the babies make?

A: Down's syndrome children have an extra chromosome 21, making 47 instead of 46. About 3 per cent of them inherit it from either parent, as the genetic material is exchanged between chromosomes from different pairs (translocation). About 1 per cent show mosaicism (some trisomy 21 and some normal cells); these babies are only mildly affected by the facial characteristics and mental impairment of Down's.

A happy family environment is one of the most important influences on any child. In the past, Down's syndrome babies were expected to be severely handicapped, but a better understanding of how their development is affected has led to early education programmes, with parents as teachers.

These programmes take considerable time and energy, but the children make more progress than would have been thought possible a few years ago. They learn to take care of themselves, integrate into the community and generally lead a fulfilling life. Many go into mainstream schooling, learning to read and write alongside their peers. The Down's Syndrome Association (see *Directory*) will send you further information.

Sue (39): 'When I was expecting Jack I had a blood test that predicted a high risk of chromosomal abnormality, although I was only 35. I decided to have an amniocentesis, but the cells did not culture properly and it had to be repeated. By the time I got the results of the second amniocentesis I was 21 weeks pregnant and had felt Jack moving. Fortunately all was well, because I couldn't have faced a termination at that stage. Everybody knew I was pregnant but all that time I was so anxious that I couldn't enjoy it.

'Having a miscarriage made me realise how much I want another child. If I were younger I might hope for the best, but I have Jack to think of so I shall grit my teeth and have tests again. I feel I'm more prepared this time.'

Q: Should I tell people as soon as I'm pregnant, or keep quiet until all the antenatal tests are over?

A: If you decide to have an amniocentesis do announce your pregnancy, because you may be nearly halfway through your pregnancy before you get the results and, like most women, you have an excellent chance of receiving good news. If you were the unlucky one, you would need sympathy and support. Denying your pregnancy, to the world or to yourself, would not make it easier to grieve and it would put a great strain on your husband if he was the only person who knew.

Many people prefer not to tell anyone other than very close family that they are pregnant until after the main risk of miscarriage is over at about twelve weeks, however. If you feel like this you could consider having early tests, for example a nuchal scan followed by CVS.

4   *Healthy Pregnancy*

NOT EVERYONE HAS THE OPTION OF PLANNING THEIR PREGNANCY three to six months in advance, but if you do it could have long-term benefits for your baby. There is growing evidence that a baby's health in later life is linked to the health of the mother, not only during her childhood but also around the time of conception.

Tipping the balance even slightly in favour of having a healthy baby by being careful for a few months around the time of conception seems well worth it. Older women often take several cycles to conceive so you may have a few months' grace. The advantage of thinking ahead is that you could get pregnant as soon as you try and an embryo is vulnerable before you know for certain, as its organs are forming in the first few weeks of life. If you are already pregnant when you read this there is no point in worrying about what might have been, but you could make your health and fitness a priority from now on.

A major pre-conceptual care campaign may not be necessary for most women, but forward planning can help you to maintain your fertility and reduce the risk of miscarriage. It is also easier to adjust your weight or treat a minor disorder when you are not pregnant, and you are likely to suffer fewer discomforts during pregnancy if your health is at its best.

Contraception

Taking the contraceptive pill does not appear to affect future fertility in the long term. Previously fertile pill-users are as likely to have a baby within two and a half years as women who do not use the pill. A few pill-users get a fertility boost just after stopping it, but on average they take between three and twelve months longer to conceive than women who used other contraceptive methods.

For example, 50 per cent of a group of older pill-users trying to conceive for the first time took a year longer than a similar group of diaphragm-users. It was six years before their conception rates were the same. You might want to take this into account if you hope to start a family in the future.

Your choice of contraceptive may affect how easily you conceive. The combined pill shuts off your ovaries and women sometimes fail to ovulate for a few cycles when they stop taking it. The progestogen-only pill disrupts the normal secretion of cervical mucus and carries a slight risk of ectopic pregnancy (where a fertilised egg implants outside the uterus, often in the uterine tube) which could affect future fertility. The intrauterine device (IUD) works in various ways, including altering the lining of the uterus to make implantation harder and affecting sperm movement and cervical mucus, so that it is harder for sperm to reach an egg; it carries a small risk of ectopic pregnancy and of pelvic infection.

Hormone methods of contraception deplete your body of essential vitamins and minerals, so stopping them a few months before you try to conceive gives your body a chance to recover. Some women use a barrier method such as a condom or diaphragm for a year or so before stopping contraception. Others learn the sympto-thermal method of natural family planning, which can be as effective as barrier methods when well taught. It also has the advantage of making you aware of your fertile time, as useful for trying to conceive as for trying not to. There are addresses in the Directory if you want more information about contraception.

Nutrition

Taking care over what you eat before and during pregnancy can reduce the chances of a fetal abnormality and help to ensure that your baby grows well. Your nutritional state around the time of conception is important in determining your baby's birth weight; babies who are of average weight (3,500–4,500 grams) tend to have fewer problems at and around birth.

A super diet is not essential, just the normal sort of healthy eating that would benefit everybody. This means food rich in vitamins, minerals and fibre, and not too high in sugar or fat. Natural sugars such as fructose are present in many whole foods, but refined sugar adds calories without nutrients.

Ideally, fat should provide no more than 30 per cent of your total daily calories, yet a check on food labels shows that many products, including some so-called health foods, contain well over this amount. The percentage of fat may be openly declared on the packaging of a product if the company is proud of it; otherwise you can work out for yourself: multiply the number of fat grams by nine (1g of fat = 9 calories), then divide by the total number of calories and multiply by 100. If the result is more than 30 per cent the product is high in fat.

Most of the fat in processed foods, sandwiches and snacks is saturated or hydrogenated. Ideally we should be eating more unsaturated fats, found in things like fresh nuts, oily fish, seeds and olive, walnut or sunflower oils. These contain essential fatty acids and although an embryo's growth will continue in the absence of some of them because your body will supply the next best ones available, development may not be as good as it could be.

Fibre is essential for the absorption of vitamins, minerals and other nutrients from food and for the process of digestion. On a practical level it also helps to prevent pregnancy discomforts such as constipation and haemorrhoids.

The easiest way to make sure you eat healthily before conception and during pregnancy is to select a variety of whole, fresh foods. Whole foods contain a range of nutrients that are often removed when food is highly processed. Go easy on products low in fibre and high in fat and sugar such as cakes and sweets as they may take away your appetite for more nourishing food. Here are two ways to look at your diet and decide whether you need to make any changes:

The Mediterranean diet pyramid: A Mediterranean-type diet is considered to be healthy as it is whole, fresh, low in saturated fat and high in fruit, vegetables and carbohydrates. If you want to see how your own diet compares, every night shade in a square in the appropriate section for each normal-sized helping you ate that day and see if the proportions roughly form a pyramid shape after a week.

FOOD   HOW OFTEN TO EAT IT

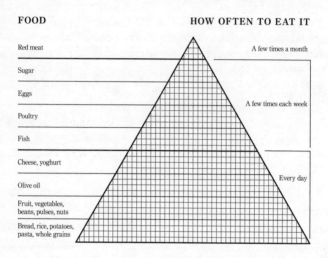

Red meat   A few times a month

Sugar

Eggs   A few times each week

Poultry

Fish

Cheese, yoghurt   Every day

Olive oil

Fruit, vegetables,
beans, pulses, nuts

Bread, rice, potatoes,
pasta, whole grains

Take five! Another way to balance your diet is to think of everything you eat as belonging to one of four groups. Aim to take at least five helpings of fruit or vegetables and five of complex carbohydrates each day, with five from the protein and fat or dairy produce groups together. The more variety you choose the better.

Other things to bear in mind are to eat some fresh, raw food (such as nuts, fruit or salad vegetables) every day, to store food only briefly and to keep the cooking simple, as fresh foods tend to lose nutrients along the way.

Fruit and Vegetables	Complex Carbohydrates
Carrots, broccoli, beans, cabbage, cauliflower, parsnips, mushrooms, peppers, spinach, Brussels sprouts, onions, leeks, celery, lettuce, tomatoes, apples, citrus fruits, pears, soft fruits, etc.	Wholemeal bread, pasta, rice, potatoes, whole grain cereals, muesli, porridge, buckwheat, couscous, pitta bread, noodles, pizza base, etc.
Proteins Meat, peas, beans, nuts, eggs, white and oily fish, seeds, etc.	**Fats and Dairy Produce** Olive oil, sunflower oil, safflower oil, walnut oil, cheeses, milk, yogurt, etc.

Everyone has individual nutritional requirements and different diets can be equally healthy. Vegetarians or vegans tend to be generally food aware, but if you cut out meat or dairy produce without replacing them with other sources of protein such as beans, nuts and seeds, you could run short of vitamin B12 and iron. If you need individual advice ask your doctor to refer you to a nutritionist or contact the Eating for Pregnancy helpline (see *Directory*).

After you stop taking the contraceptive pill your vitamin and mineral levels may take about three months to return to normal. The amount of folic acid, vitamin C, vitamin E and zinc in your blood is reduced, for example, while iron and copper levels are raised. There is no direct evidence that this harms a developing fetus, but it may reduce your fertility and there is concern that it might predispose a baby to things like high blood pressure or diabetes later in life. If you are already pregnant this is not worth worrying about; if not you may want to bear it in mind.

You may be eating healthily but have a gene that means you use folic acid less well, so every woman planning pregnancy is recommended to take a supplement (0.4 mg) for at least three months before and after conception. Folic acid deficiency impairs cell division and can prevent the baby's neural tube from forming, leading to defects such as spina bifida or anencephaly.

As a general rule, vitamins and minerals are better absorbed and used by the body in the natural combinations present in food. A poor diet plus a pill or a vitamin-fortified drink is not the same as a good diet. Supplements can be valuable in some circumstances but you need to know what you are doing; they may interact with other medications and too much of some of them can be harmful. Check with your doctor before taking any vitamin or mineral pills, other than folic acid.

Vitamins and Minerals

NAME	FOODS THAT CONTAIN IT	EFFECTS ON THE BODY
Vitamin A	Carrots, green leafy vegetables, broccoli, milk, cheese, salmon, halibut, apricots, peaches.	Bone growth, healthy eyes, skin and gums; helps the mucous membranes resist irritation and infections.
Vitamin B-Complex	Red meat, yeast extract, dairy produce, eggs, nuts, bananas, pulses, wholemeal bread, fish, rice, bran, potatoes, beans.	Healthy nervous system, tissues and skin; metabolise carbohydrates, fats, proteins, to release energy; helps produce red blood cells.
Vitamin C	Citrus fruits, blackcurrants, green peppers, broccoli, cauliflower, cabbage, potatoes.	Healthy skin, bones and joints; increases the absorption of iron; helps the body recover from stress; fights infection.
Vitamin D	Eggs, cheese, milk, margarine, butter, oily fish such as herrings, kippers, salmon, mackerel, sardines, tuna; sunlight also increases vitamin D levels.	Strong bones and teeth; regulates the absorption of phosphorus and calcium.

Vitamin E	Almonds, Brazil nuts, olive, sunflower and safflower oils, eggs, dairy produce, whole grain cereals, broccoli, carrots, celery, apples, avocados.	Healthy circulatory, nervous, reproductive systems; strengthens muscles, aids endurance, helps lower blood pressure; prevents break-down of fatty acids.
Vitamin K	Lean meat, broccoli, spinach, tomatoes, nuts, oatmeal, avocados; also manufactured in the gut by bacteria.	Produces a blood-clotting substance that prevents haemorrhages.
Folic Acid	Dark green leafy vegetables, yeast extract, nuts, oranges, eggs, cheddar cheese, bananas, lettuce, broccoli, Brussels sprouts, haddock, salmon.	Important for cell division and reproduction and for the formation of red blood cells; deficiency can cause neural tube defects.
Calcium	Milk, yogurt, cheese, green leafy vegetables, oranges, bread, sardines, soya, wheat-germ, yeast extract, molasses, raisins, prunes, almonds, Brazil nuts.	Healthy immune system, bones and teeth; helps muscles to contract, blood to clot, energy production and the release of hormones.
Iron	Red meat, molasses, sardines, dried fruit, asparagus, whole grains, beans, lentils, almonds, wholemeal bread, cocoa, potatoes, broccoli.	Combines with protein to form haemoglobin which transports oxygen through the body; helps muscle contraction; helps prevent fatigue and breathlessness.
Zinc	Cheddar cheese, oysters, chicken, turkey, lamb, pork, tuna, eggs, peas, carrots, wholemeal bread, sweetcorn, oatmeal, seafoods, whole grains.	Essential to over 100 enzymes that process nutrients in the body.
Magnesium	Nuts, seafood, meat, eggs, dairy produce, dried apricots, almonds, Brazil nuts, green leafy vegetables, whole grains, hard drinking water.	Healthy tissues, muscles and nerves, helps absorption of other vitamins and minerals; deficiency may contribute to miscarriage and premature birth.

Your weight

Weight has a habit of creeping up almost unnoticed as you get older, and you will conceive more easily and be less likely to suffer problems such as high blood pressure or diabetes during pregnancy if you are within the normal range.

The body mass index (BMI) is an internationally accepted standard, based on the discovery that there is a more or less constant relationship between weight and the square of a person's height, regardless of their age or build. Your BMI is usually calculated at your first antenatal check – 20 to 25 is ideal for optimum health (see chart). A little higher or lower does not matter, but if it is under 17 or over 30 you may want to do something about it before conceiving.

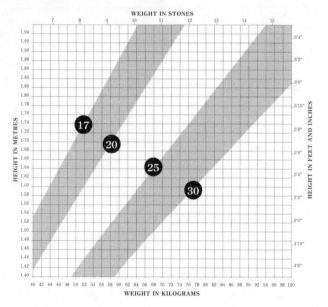

For a safe, steady weight loss of a pound or two per week, increase the amount of exercise you take and aim for a daily energy intake of 1,200–1,500 kcals, choosing food high in nutrients and low in empty calories. Ask your doctor to refer you to a nutritionist if you need individual advice.

You could also check whether you are an 'apple' or a 'pear'. With your body relaxed take your waist measurement and your hip measurement (round your bottom at the fullest part). If your waist measurement divided by your hip measurement is 0.85 or less you are a 'pear'; 'apples' have a waist to hip ratio over 0.85 (see chart).

'Apples' put on fat around their stomach and several problems including some heart conditions are linked to it, so it may be more important for them to keep their weight under control. 'Pears' store fat on their hips and thighs. This seems to be safer and they also tend to conceive more easily than 'apples', although the reason for this is unknown. For example, in a study of 500 women receiving artificial insemination over 12 cycles, 63 per cent became pregnant when their waist to hip ratio was under 0.7 and only 32 per cent when their ratio was greater than 0.85. As the ratio increased the proportion of women who conceived fell.

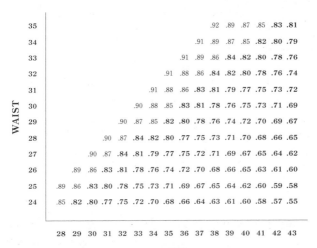

WAIST	28	29	30	31	32	33	34	35	36	37	38	39	40	41	42	43
35											.92	.89	.87	.85	.83	.81
34										.91	.89	.87	.85	.82	.80	.79
33									.91	.89	.86	.84	.82	.80	.78	.76
32								.91	.88	.86	.84	.82	.80	.78	.76	.74
31							.91	.88	.86	.83	.81	.79	.77	.75	.73	.72
30						.90	.88	.85	.83	.81	.78	.76	.75	.73	.71	.69
29					.90	.87	.85	.82	.80	.78	.76	.74	.72	.70	.69	.67
28				.90	.87	.84	.82	.80	.77	.75	.73	.71	.70	.68	.66	.65
27			.90	.87	.84	.81	.79	.77	.75	.72	.71	.69	.67	.65	.64	.62
26		.89	.86	.83	.81	.78	.76	.74	.72	.70	.68	.66	.65	.63	.61	.60
25	.89	.86	.83	.80	.78	.75	.73	.71	.69	.67	.65	.64	.62	.60	.59	.58
24	.85	.82	.80	.77	.75	.72	.70	.68	.66	.64	.63	.61	.60	.58	.57	.55

HIP

Exercise

Regular exercise has a number of beneficial effects on the body and helps you to take pregnancy, birth and everyday life with children in your stride. Talk to your doctor before starting an exercise programme if you have had a miscarriage or have high blood pressure, or you smoke and your BMI is over 30.

What sort of exercise?

The three main elements of physical fitness are stamina, muscle strength and suppleness. The table gives you a rough idea of what ten popular forms of exercise can contribute to fitness when performed actively (for example, a brisk walk not a stroll). The more stars the greater the contribution.

	STRENGTH	STAMINA	SUPPLENESS
Aerobics	**	***	***
Athletics	***	***	**
Badminton	**	**	***
Cycling	***	****	***
Dancing	**	****	***
Jogging	**	****	**
Swimming	****	****	****
Tennis	**	**	***
Walking	**	***	*
Yoga	**	**	****

If you are very physically active and underweight you may need to reduce your training level and let your weight rise a little to improve your chances of conception. Otherwise, which of these groups best describes you?

A: Normal weight, very active, exercise or play competitive sport regularly.

B: Moderately active lifestyle, have young children or an active job.

C: Sedentary job and lifestyle; a little overweight; no regular exercise.

If you are in group A, think about taking up a moderate form of exercise that you can continue to enjoy throughout pregnancy. If you are in group B try to fit three 15 to 20 minute sessions of moderate exercise each week into your life. If you are in group C you will really benefit from taking up regular mild exercise, such as walking, so that you can aim to take moderate exercise during pregnancy.

Safety guidelines for exercise during pregnancy suggest that you keep strenuous activity to a maximum of fifteen minutes per session, and that your pulse rate does not exceed 140 and your temperature stays below 38°C. Your body has many physical changes to accommodate, so moderate, low-impact exercise is more suitable than competitive sport or activities where you risk overstretching or have to work hard to keep up. It may be

Walk to fitness

Walking provides good aerobic exercise, helping your lungs take in more oxygen with less effort. To find your maximum safe heart rate in beats per minute, subtract your age from 220 and multiply the result by 0.6 and 0.85 for the lower and upper ends of your range. Walk for ten minutes and check your pulse. If it is near the lower end of your range your walking speed is about right; if not, slow down!

This is a good way to check that you are exercising within safe limits whatever your activity. As your fitness improves your heart rate will go down while you walk at the same speed or maintain the same level of activity.

Age	Pulse Rate	Age	Pulse Rate	Age	Pulse Rate
35	111–157	41	107–152	47	103–147
36	110–156	42	106–151	48	103–146
37	110–155	43	106–150	49	102–145
38	109–154	44	105–149	50	102–144
39	108–153	45	105–148	51	101–143
40	108–153	46	104–147	52	100–142

better to start a new form of exercise before rather than during pregnancy.

Your pelvic floor

Your pelvic floor consists of two rings of muscles, overlapping like a figure of eight to form the hammock that supports your internal organs, including your uterus and growing baby. It also controls the openings to the front and back passages.

Like all voluntary muscles your pelvic floor can be strengthened to perform its work more effectively, and will benefit from exercise throughout your life. Weak muscles often result in stress incontinence – a tendency to leak when you cough, laugh, jump or run. Strong muscles can improve your sex life and they help turn your baby's head so that it passes more easily through your pelvis during birth.

You can identify the right muscles if you sit on the edge of a firm seat and lean forward with your knees about 18 inches (45 cms) apart. Without using your abdominal or buttock muscles, tighten the muscles between your legs as though you wanted to stop urinating. Alternatively, try to stop the flow when using the toilet and notice which muscles you contract.

Once you are aware of the right muscles, strengthen them by tightening and releasing them several times in quick succession. Then draw them in slowly and let them out in two stages (which is harder). Progress to six or seven stages, both in and out, as the muscles become more responsive. Aim to do six repetitions, several times a day. Finally, try to distinguish and then work with the muscles around your front and back passages separately.

Preventable risks

Every generation finds new sources of worry. It's easy to forget that the risks to your baby are tiny compared with those you would have faced a hundred years ago, when women were poorly nourished and overworked and medical knowledge was primitive to say the least. However careful you are around conception and in pregnancy, nature gives no guarantees and perhaps you should not expect them.

Nevertheless, it is sensible to tackle dependency on anything known to delay conception or increase risks for the baby before you become pregnant if possible. Talk to your doctor or contact the Health Information Service (see *Directory*) for details of organisations that can help you.

Alcohol: If you drink heavily you double your risk of miscarriage and have a higher chance of having a baby with a major abnormality. Fetal alcohol syndrome is marked by distinctive facial features and mental retardation. The risks start to rise at the equivalent of four measures of spirits or glasses of wine, or two pints of beer or cider per day, increasing steeply at about three times these amounts.

For unknown reasons, babies of women over 35 fare worse than those of younger women, and black babies are seven times more vulnerable than white ones. Individuals respond differently to alcohol so nobody can state that a particular limit is safe or otherwise; what is fine for one person may be damaging to another, possibly for genetic reasons. Statistically, however, you are no more likely to have a baby suffering from fetal alcohol syndrome if you have a glass or two of wine each week, or even one a day, than if you abstain entirely.

Alcohol-related risks are greater if you drink heavily on most days, or your diet is poor or you smoke. Consuming enough to feel drunk in a short time also increases your risk, whether you

normally drink or not. It makes sense to avoid binges and tackle
a drink problem before you become pregnant.

Ways to reduce your alcohol consumption
- ❑ Only drink alcohol on certain days and choose fruit juices on
  the other days.
- ❑ Adopt the French habit of diluting your wine with mineral
  water.
- ❑ On social occasions stick to a glass of wine and drink it slowly.
- ❑ Choose low-alcohol drinks for preference; check the bottle –
  some lemonade or fruit-based drinks contain more alcohol than
  you might think.
- ❑ Choose long drinks rather than shorts and make them last.

Drugs: Drugs alter the chemistry of your body and should be
treated with great caution around the time of conception and
during pregnancy. Check with your doctor, pharmacist or a qualified alternative practitioner before taking any that are not
essential to your health. This includes over-the-counter remedies
for minor ailments, aromatherapy oils which are absorbed
through the skin and can have powerful effects, homeopathic and
herbal remedies and slimming pills.

Street drugs are known to increase the risk of abnormality,
miscarriage and poor fetal growth. Ecstasy is an amphetamine
derivative that has been linked with cleft palate and heart problems; marijuana and cannabis have been linked with low sperm
count in men and with premature birth. Cocaine increases the
likelihood of abnormality, bleeding and premature birth; it
also constricts blood vessels and reduces the baby's oxygen
supply. Heroin reduces fertility, trebles the risk of miscarriage
or stillbirth and raises the risk of premature labour and low
birth weight.

Sudden withdrawal during pregnancy (especially of drugs

such as heroin and cocaine) can cause miscarriage or premature labour. If you are addicted to any street drug it is important to seek help before conceiving or as soon as possible during pregnancy. People offering rehabilitation do not judge their clients and the programmes are especially effective when you are well motivated.

If you have a condition that requires medication (including asthma if you use an inhaler) tell your doctor that you plan to become pregnant. Your medication may have no known problems, or there may be alternative approaches that can be tried. If your condition requires treatment with drugs that could pose hazards, talking it through with an expert will at least help you to decide what to do.

Smoking: Smoking during pregnancy is associated with miscarriages, vaginal bleeding, premature births and low birth weight babies. If you are over 35 there is also a significant increase in the risk of your baby having a minor malformation and five times the risk of low birth weight (a major cause of infant illness) compared with a younger smoker.

❑   If you give up before you conceive your baby will have the same chance of good health as a non-smoker's baby, even if you have smoked for many years.

❑   If you give up before the fourth month of pregnancy you protect your baby from the worst effects of smoking, which occur between the fourth and ninth months.

❑   For every cigarette that remains unsmoked your baby escapes a dose of nicotine and carbon monoxide.

❑   Even quitting in the ninth month may make your uterine muscles work more effectively and help preserve your baby's oxygen flow during labour.

Quit smoking

Books or voluntary groups (see *Directory*) can offer support and ideas if you are trying to give up, or your doctor may be able to refer you to a local quit group.

Acupuncture or hypnosis, alone or with group therapy, may help. Pregnancy is a good motivation, however, so even if you have tried before and failed you may find it easier than you expect to give up on your own. Nausea in early pregnancy often provides reinforcement.

If you want to give up slowly keep a diary of the times you smoke each day. When a pattern emerges distract yourself from the cigarettes that are least important to your routine. Have some early nights so that you are not overtired and use the money you save on cigarettes for some treats as a reward.

More people succeed by stopping completely than by cutting down, however. If you were a heavy smoker the worst craving may last for a couple of weeks. Here are some distractions that women have found helpful:

❑ Change your routine. Go for a short walk, make a coffee, count to a hundred.

❑ Take a few deep breaths, pausing between each one. Practise relaxation (see page 109). Turn your attention to visualising a pleasant scene.

❑ Eat a spoonful of yogurt, an apple, stick of celery or raw carrot (instead of chocolate or fattening snacks). Chew on some gum.

❑ If smoking helped you concentrate fiddle with a paper clip, a rubber band, worry beads or a ball of blu-tack.

Other risks: You cannot avoid exposure to all substances that might possibly prove harmful, but you can use common sense. For example, you could:

❑   Avoid unnecessary exposure to chemicals, especially those that have toxic warnings on the packaging or remind you to keep them off your skin.

❑ Ask local farmers to tell you when crop spraying is due to be carried out and stay indoors. Some people may be more susceptible to their effects than others.

❑ Query the need for an X-ray, but if it is essential tell the operator that you may be pregnant so that your pelvic area can be shielded to reduce any risks.

❑ Get your microwave oven serviced to make sure the seal is good and follow the manufacturer's instructions on usage.

❑ Avoid all excess – most things are safe in moderation. Have one or two cups of mild coffee a day, not ten strong ones, or soak in a warm bath rather than one so hot that it might raise your temperature, for example.

Pre-conception planner

❑ If possible stop using the pill, hormone injections or implants, or an intrauterine device with progestogen about three months before trying to conceive. This will restore your mineral and vitamin levels which are altered by the hormones, let your natural cycle reestablish and make dating your pregnancy easier.

❑ Tackle fitness or a weight problem and improve your diet if necessary.

❑ Take a folic acid supplement (from your GP or chemist).

❑ If you are worried about drinking, drug or smoking habits tackle them now.

❑ Check you have immunity to rubella (German measles) and ask your GP to treat a persistent infection or adjust any medication you're taking.

Older mothers' experiences

Elizabeth (42): 'I tried and failed to give up smoking on my own several times. What finally worked was making a pact with my friend Anne to give up together. She got pregnant by accident and was distraught thinking of all the things she should have done or not done, so I gave up smoking to keep her company.

'It was hard for the first fortnight, being with other people who were smoking, but I didn't want to be the first to give in. Now after several weeks we both consider ourselves non-smokers. I'm still tempted sometimes at a party but it's embarrassing not having cigarettes to return and that stops me from accepting any. I do feel pleased that I did what I've been saying I wanted to do for so long.'

Q: Michael's job takes him to exotic locations and I want to join him as much as possible before we have a baby. What should I do about immunisations?

A: In general it is best to avoid immunisation with any live vaccine (for example, rubella, measles, yellow fever and BCG for tuberculosis) around the time of conception and during pregnancy, as there is a small risk to the baby. If you need these have them beforehand and use contraception for 1–3 months afterwards.

Inactive vaccines, such as diphtheria and cholera, generally pose little threat to the fetus, although they are usually avoided during pregnancy unless the benefits of having them clearly outweigh the risks. Decisions have to be made individually, so make a list of the places you might visit and talk to your doctor.

Valerie (44): 'My weight has always been a problem as I used to eat for comfort. I've tried diets but ended up putting the weight back on. Since I met Barry I've felt more confident, and more motivated to lose weight slowly so that it stays off.

'Deciding to have a baby gets you in the right frame of mind to sort yourself out when you're older. I took everything for granted when my daughters were born but not any more. I know my body isn't in very good shape and I really want to do something positive about it before it's too late.'

Q: I injured my back so I'm not working and we have to watch the pennies. How can I lose weight and improve the health of the whole family on a budget?

A: Small changes in the sort of foods you choose can make a big difference, although it needs more thought when you cannot spend freely. Your local library will have books to give you ideas for eating healthily on a budget. Staples like wholemeal bread, potatoes and brown rice are relatively cheap, filling and full of nutrients. Shop for fresh vegetables every day or two if you can, and cook them briefly or serve them raw where possible to improve their nutrient value at no extra cost. Serve yourself slightly smaller portions to lose weight slowly and steadily.

You will soon see an improvement in your fitness if you walk for 20 minutes three times a week and keep a record of your pulse. The whole family could enjoy walking at the weekends, or you could swim together at your local leisure centre.

Sue (39): 'It's hard to keep everything in proportion and not feel that it's all your responsibility to make sure your child is healthy. I have to accept that I can't control everything and there is no point in worrying about things like traffic pollution that I can do nothing about.

'Kenneth and I are taking Jack on a farm holiday soon as he loves animals. It's only common sense to pay attention to hygiene when you're around animals, but I want us to enjoy ourselves as a family without putting everything on hold because I might be pregnant. There's an infection called *chlamydia psittaci* that causes sheep to miscarry and it can have a similar effect on women, so Kenneth will have to show Jack the lambs while I keep well clear.'

Q: Would it be wise to ask my GP for a pre-conception check-up?
A: It's not imperative, unless you want to discuss something with your doctor or have been putting off seeking treatment for a problem. It is sensible to get any chronic illness stabilised and to check with your doctor before trying to conceive if you use any medication. You might also want to discuss any reasons for your miscarriage. Fibroids become more common as you grow older and if you have any you could discuss getting treatment because they can cause complications during pregnancy for about one in ten women (see page 132).

A check-up could make sure that your blood pressure is normal and you do not have a hidden vaginal infection. You could also get tetanus jabs up to date as you are visiting a farm, and have a blood test to screen for anaemia and immunity to infections such as toxoplasmosis or rubella that could harm a developing fetus.

Anne (47): 'My pregnancy was a complete surprise as I thought I was starting the menopause. I was on holiday, enjoying my first taste of freedom after the hard work of being a single parent, and I was devastated. I felt irresponsible and slightly embarrassed to be caught out and couldn't think how to tell everybody.

'My partner is not one to play at happy families but my older children have been a great support and I've caught some of their excitement. My mother made slightly acid comments, but even she has started to look forward to another grandchild. The whole experience looks like being a revelation.'

Q: I did not take a folic acid supplement before conceiving and had no chance to stop smoking. Could I have harmed my baby, not knowing that I was pregnant?
A: Women who are well nourished before conception have

reserves to draw on when their baby's organs are forming. This is probably nature's way of making sure that a baby develops well, even if a mother cannot eat much because she is sick in the early weeks. Your chances of having a healthy baby are high.

Although it is ideal to take a folic acid supplement before and during early pregnancy the chances of your baby having a neural tube defect are small, especially if you normally eat things like green leafy vegetables that contain folic acid. Ask about having an anomaly scan (see page 63) if you are concerned about it, however.

It is better to do what you can, such as giving up smoking as soon as you realised you were pregnant, than to waste time worrying about things you failed to do in the past. Life is far from perfect and many women find themselves in your situation. An unhealthy 25 year old is more likely to have problems than a fit woman of 40 something, so try not to let anxiety overshadow what could otherwise be an enjoyable pregnancy.

5   *Trying for a Baby*

IF YOU HAVE CONVINCED YOURSELF OVER THE YEARS THAT ONE
act of unprotected sex would lead to pregnancy you may be dismayed to find that this is far from the truth. The chances of
conceiving in any one menstrual cycle are thought to be less
than 30 per cent, even for the most fertile of couples. About a
quarter of women under 25 take more than twelve months to
conceive, rising to about 45 per cent for women over 30. For
every woman over 35 who conceives in less than twelve months
another, with no reproductive problem, will take longer than a
year.

In one study, pregnancy rates for women aged 35–40 using
artificial insemination (to exclude sperm-related problems) were
roughly 54 per cent over twelve ovulation cycles. In another study
just over half the women aged 41–44 who were ovulating regularly conceived over four cycles.

You have the best chance of conceiving if you ovulate regularly
and have sex at least three times a week (even if your partner has
a low sperm count). Some older women fail to conceive because
they are not having intercourse sufficiently often. It may help to

remind yourself how your fertility cycle works, although it could be less stressful and more productive to have sex frequently throughout your cycle, as deliberately timing it for your fertile period often causes tension.

Your fertility cycle

Your periods, plus changes in your temperature, the position of your cervix (neck of the uterus) and the consistency of your cervical mucus indicate where you are in your fertility cycle. After your period glands in the cervix secrete sticky mucus; as a new egg ripens this becomes stretchy to allow sperm to swim through.

At the same time your cervix becomes softer, rises in your body and opens slightly and when an egg is released your temperature rises. If it is not fertilised your cervix closes, becomes firmer, drops lower in your body and produces the sticky mucus again. About two weeks after ovulation your next period starts.

Sperm can live in your body for 5–7 days and an egg for 24–48 hours, so you can only get pregnant on about 7 days in your monthly cycle. If you have a longer or shorter cycle than average (28 days) you will not release an egg at the mid point of your cycle. You can learn to recognise ovulation using fertility awareness techniques (see page 82), or buy an ovulation prediction method (such as *Persona*) from the chemist. Most women occasionally have a cycle when they do not ovulate at all, but if you have two or three consecutively talk to your doctor.

At 35 your chance of conceiving in any one cycle is about half that of a woman of 30, and at 38 it is halved again. This may be because the pituitary gland starts to increase the levels of the hormones FSH and LH to stimulate the ovaries as you get older, and as a result eggs are lost more rapidly. Once you are down to your last thousand or so menopause sets in. Even so, it may not be too difficult to get pregnant but it helps to be realistic about how long it could take.

Conception: When an egg ripens and is released from your ovary your cervical mucus alters so that sperm can swim easily through it and are nourished on their journey. At the same time the lining of your uterus becomes thick and spongy. If the egg is fertilised it drifts down your uterine tube for several days, growing and dividing. A week after conception (about the third week after your last period) there are sixteen cells. These multiply rapidly to form a cluster and by the time you miss a period they are a fluid-filled sphere, with an inner layer that will form the embryo and outer cells that will become the placenta and amniotic sac. This nestles into the lining of your uterus, developing fine blood vessels, or villi, to anchor and nourish it. At this stage your baby is the size of a grain of rice and as fragile as jelly.

Genes and inheritance: The nuclei in an egg and sperm each contain twenty-three chromosomes. Threaded within, like two strings of beads twisted round each other (the double helix), are thousands of genes too small to be seen under a normal microscope. They contain molecules of DNA, giving instructions for the design of every part of your baby.

Every egg contains one X chromosome, and every sperm either an X or a Y chromosome. An egg fertilised with an X sperm (X + X) becomes a girl. One fertilised with a Y sperm (X + Y) becomes a boy. More boys are conceived than girls so the numbers of X and Y sperm may not always be equal. Other factors, such as the length of time between ovulation and fertilisation, may also play a part in determining a baby's sex.

When a sperm penetrates an egg the nuclei lie side by side and in a few hours their contents combine to form a new nucleus with forty-six chromosomes arranged in twenty-three pairs. Each pair is joined at a single point, one half from the mother and the other from the father. When the egg divides the pairs break apart and develop new 'halves' to duplicate the originals.

Early miscarriage: Miscarriage is a normal part of the human reproductive experience, so common that it can almost be less daunting than some rarer events. Most occur in the early days or weeks of pregnancy (see page 159 for symptoms and what to do). The most common cause is a chromosomal abnormality, nature's response to a genetic error. A hormone imbalance that prevents implantation or fails to sustain pregnancy is the next most common cause. Auto-immune or antibody problems and vitamin or mineral deficiencies are occasional causes.

Overall, 20 per cent of unconfirmed pregnancies miscarry, and 1 per cent of women suffer three or more in a row before a successful pregnancy. A study in America shows that the risk for confirmed pregnancies rises gradually from just over one in ten at age 30 to about one in six at age 38, and to almost half by age 45.

In another study, more than half of women over 40 who conceived with IVF lost their babies, which is more than would be expected from the increase in the number of chromosomal abnormalities that is linked to age. It is thought that the uterus may also play some part in the increased number of early miscarriages among older women.

These facts are unwelcome when you desperately want a baby and feel the pressures of time running out, but it is better to be realistic; and even the most gloomy forecast suggests that your chances of *not* miscarrying an individual pregnancy are better than even.

Infertility

Infertility is referred to as 'primary' if you have never been pregnant and 'secondary' if you have had a child or a miscarriage.

About 35 per cent of fertility problems are traced to the man and 35 per cent to the women. Twenty per cent involve both partners and for about 10 per cent something is amiss but with present knowledge it is not possible to find out what.

Possible causes of infertility that can affect men or women include stress, ill-health, blocked tubes and hormone imbalances. Women may fail to ovulate or have a defect of the uterus, endometriosis (tissue resembling the lining of the uterus develops outside it) or fibroids (thickened tissue in the uterus or, occasionally, the cervix).

Men may produce too few sperm to fertilise an egg, or sperm that are abnormal or do not move vigorously. A sub-fertile sperm count may be affected by overheating (the scrotum has to be slightly cooler than the rest of the body to manufacture sperm), excessive exercising, a diet that provides insufficient zinc or vitamin E, and high coffee or alcohol consumption. Research suggests that a man who is sub-fertile has a one in two chance of increasing his sperm count if he stops drinking or smoking for three months.

Success rates after sterilisation reversal can be over 50 per cent for women and even higher for men, depending on the skill of the surgeon and the length of time since the original procedure. The increased chances of ectopic pregnancy and lowered sperm counts can affect pregnancy rates, however.

Infertility may appear to be increasing because its profile is raised. The rate for couples has been a steady 14–17 per cent for the past thirty years, but as more treatments become available more couples hear about them and come forward.

Seeking help: If you cannot conceive when you want to the sense of personal failure can be immense. Individual fertility is partly determined by genes and environmental factors that were present before you or your partner were born, but you are likely to feel inadequate, powerless and excluded from what most people take for granted.

The older you are the sooner it is sensible to check out your fertility. If frequent intercourse fails to produce a pregnancy after a few cycles you may not have a problem, but talk to your doctor. A blood test to check your hormones and see if you are ovulating and a sperm test for your partner could reassure you. Further investigations may take about a year, including waiting time. Treatment could take another year or two and the chances of success decline with age. Accurate diagnosis is vital to avoid inappropriate or unnecessary treatment.

Basic tests are more complex for women than for men, who may get away with providing a sample of semen. A laparoscopy and dye test, for example, involves passing a minute telescope through a small cut below your navel under anaesthetic and injecting harmless dye into your uterus to see if it flows through your uterine tubes. Your ovaries may be examined for cysts using a vaginal scanner and your uterus checked for fibroids or thickening of the endometrium (lining) by scan, by an X-ray and dye test (hysterosalpingogram or HSG) or by hysteroscopy, which involves passing a miniature telescope through your cervix.

Infertility denies you choice in a way you never really expect. It can be especially stressful for an older woman because there is less time to sort it out. At least a diagnosis tells you where you stand, however, and you can seek treatment or come to terms with it in your own way. Unfortunately about one couple in ten are left in a state of uncertainty.

Stress and infertility: Relatively little is known about the effects of stress on reproduction, but ironically, failing to conceive may trigger a vicious circle that makes pregnancy less likely. Stress is a vague term, but it contributes to male impotence and it seems likely that a sensitive woman might involuntarily switch off the delicate mechanism of conception if she is anxious, over-worked or, for some other reason, not in the best condition to have a baby. Women who long to be pregnant often experience hormonal chaos, with unpredictable moods and other stress-related symptoms.

The body cannot tell the difference between stress caused by wanting to be pregnant or any other reason, but there is some evidence that the changes it produces can suppress ovulation and shorten the post-ovulatory phase of your menstrual cycle, so that even if you conceive the pregnancy is not sustained. If you feel stress may be a factor for you, do whatever experience tells you may alleviate it. Take a holiday, ease up in your job, join a yoga group, try hypnotherapy, aromatherapy or acupuncture. Letting go seems to help some women to conceive.

Monthly periods seem like so many lost chances and can put great pressure on your relationship at a time when you need mutual tolerance and understanding. You may become so focused on having a baby that your partner distances himself for fear of upsetting you further and eventually you stop communicating. If you are not too wrapped up in each other's emotional distress a sense of humour can help.

Counselling can also help you to refocus your relationship if you experience tensions, and some voluntary organisations (see *Directory*) offer sympathetic general support to anyone undergoing investigations or treatment. If you lose confidence, or find yourself becoming depressed or obsessive, talk to your doctor.

Treatment for infertility

The success of infertility treatment depends on your age, your problem and how long you have been infertile, and the expertise of the clinic you attend (see page 113). A course of antibiotics to

Learning to relax

It is well worth improving your ability to recognise and release tension. Practise this exercise every day, sitting in a chair or lying in bed:

❑ Tense and release the following groups of muscles, focusing each time on the contrast: one leg, then the other; your abdomen; your lower back and buttock muscles; your shoulders; one arm, then the other; your neck, jaw, lips, cheeks; the muscles around your eyes, then those in your forehead.

❑ Go round your body in the same order a second time, but on this occasion release the tension the instant you become aware of it.

❑ The third time round simply check each group of muscles and release any tension that you recognise. When you are fully relaxed observe how gentle and quiet your breathing is.

❑ After a week or so check your shoulders, hands and face at intervals during the day without going round your body three times, although the whole ritual may still help you to get off to sleep at night.

clear up an underlying infection or drugs to correct a hormone problem may be all that you need.

About two-thirds of ovulation problems are caused by ovarian cysts. These can be treated with fertility drugs which stimulate your ovaries to produce eggs, although one in twelve women under 40 and one in three over 40 does not respond. Blocked uterine tubes, which account for about a fifth of female infertility, can sometimes be repaired by micro-surgery, but success rates are low.

Before you embark on infertility treatment decide how much you and your partner really want to invest in time, money and especially emotional energy.

Most treatments are stressful at best. Some treatments are also expensive and only available privately, and success rates for older women tend to be low. Nevertheless some women do succeed in having the baby they long for. To make sure you are as prepared as possible for whatever lies ahead, consider the consequences at the outset and decide how far you want to go.

Here is a brief guide to some treatments available at present. The addresses in the Directory can provide more information.

Egg or sperm donation: It is rare for women between 40 and 45, and rarer still for anyone over this age, to conceive with IVF using their own eggs. Younger eggs are more likely to succeed, but the process of retrieving them is demanding and there is a shortage of donors. Most are white women and you could wait 2–5 years, or longer, if you are non-white. If you manage to recruit a donor you go to the head of the queue, although you usually receive an anonymous donor's egg.

Artificial insemination can be carried out using your partner's sperm (AIH), or donor sperm (AID). At a licensed clinic egg and sperm donors are screened for medical disorders including HIV, and they have no ongoing legal responsibility for the baby. Health and other details such as interests, hair and eye colour, but not the donor's identity, are kept so that the child can request them in adulthood.

Clinics are not supposed to discriminate against single women or lesbians, but in practice some make it more difficult for them (see *Directory*). Some women ask a friend to donate sperm; self-insemination is not technically difficult (you use a needleless syringe, or a turkey baster in the USA). A private arrangement needs careful thought, however. You would have to screen the donor's health yourself and obtain at least one HIV test. Even if you have a signed agreement, the father might change his mind and make a claim on his child. As the legal father he could be liable for maintenance if you receive welfare benefits at any time, and your child might also want to know about or search for him in the future.

In vitro fertilisation (IVF): Requests for IVF are judged on merit, with no restrictions on age, marital status or sexual preference, although the welfare of the child must be considered and doctors must satisfy themselves that it is likely to be born into a stable environment.

Your ovaries are stimulated to produce eggs and these (or donor eggs) are mixed with sperm in a test tube. You take a series of drugs to a strict timetable over several weeks and are monitored closely to make sure they are working. Although additional embryos can be frozen and stored, no more than three may be implanted into your uterus in any one treatment cycle, to reduce the chance of multiple births. About 20 per cent of assisted conceptions lead to twins and 3 per cent to triplets.

At any stage in the process your body might not respond and you could have to start all over again, so the process can be emotionally distressing. For this reason you should be offered counselling; it can help you to cope if your hopes are repeatedly dashed.

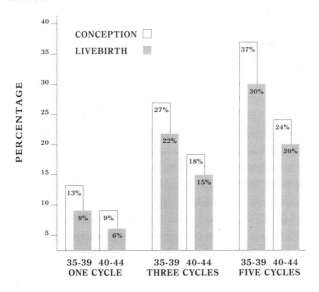

Well-established, large infertility centres tend to have higher live birth rates, although the rates in some clinics seem high because they include each baby in a multiple birth. The chart on page 111 shows roughly how many women conceive after one, three and five IVF cycles *and take a baby home*. About 5 per cent of women over 45 conceive, but sadly it is rare for a pregnancy to succeed.

Other methods of assisted conception: Gamete intra-fallopian transfer (GIFT) and intra-cytoplasmic sperm injection (ICSI) are similar to IVF in that drug regimes are used to collect an egg and support a pregnancy. GIFT can be used if you have undamaged uterine tubes. Up to three eggs and fresh sperm are placed in the end of your tube nearest your ovary, using laparoscopy. Fertilisation takes place within your body so you do not know immediately whether it has succeeded.

ICSI, where a single sperm is injected directly into an egg, can help if your partner has a low sperm count. If the egg is fertilised successfully it is replaced in your uterus two days later. The technique works well, but there is concern that the reason why some men do not produce enough sperm may be because part of the Y chromosome is missing, and ICSI may pass this defect on to their sons.

Post-menopausal pregnancy is possible using drugs to replace lost hormones and eggs donated by a younger woman, although shortage of donors is a major stumbling block. The proposal is usually put to an ethics committee with a variety of independent views. For women over 50 pregnancy tends to be arduous and the risks are greater, but some clinics will consider each case on its merits.

Infertility clinics: You may find it quicker and more convenient to attend your local hospital, or you may prefer to attend a specialist infertility unit with more facilities for diagnosis and treatment. Many private and semi-private clinics have sprung up in response to the demand for infertility treatment, and the quality of service offered will affect your chances of taking a baby home.

A good clinic will co-operate with your GP, review your records and make sure you have had full investigation before discussing treatment. It will offer a range of tests and treatments, continuity of care (you see the same staff on each visit) and an independent counselling service. The staff will be honest about your chances of conception – sadly, for some women treatment may be a waste of time.

Choosing a clinic

As the experience and expertise of a clinic is an important factor in the success of treatment, discuss where your doctor intends to refer you and why. Consider the general atmosphere of a clinic and its convenience, too, as you will have to visit regularly for monitoring. Here are some questions to ask:

❑ What tests could be carried out and what treatments offered?
❑ How many visits will be necessary? How will your partner be involved?
❑ What happens if you become pregnant? And if you don't?
❑ How long has the clinic been established?
❑ What is its multiple birth rate, and its live birth rate per pregnancy?
❑ What information and counselling is offered? Is there a patient support group?
❑ How much is it likely to cost and how long is the waiting list?

When you can't have a baby

Unfortunately, infertility treatment may not provide the baby that you long for, but it is hard to stop when you feel that the next cycle might just be the one that works. Treatment offers hope, leaving you with no focus for your sadness and nothing tangible to mourn when you finally reach the end of the road.

You may feel guilty, inadequate, less of a woman. You may blame yourself for something you did or failed to do in the past; but infertility is not a judgment of your value as a person or a modern punishment for past indiscretions. You are still a real woman, you have not got a life-threatening disease, and you do not have to be unhappy for the rest of your life. Nor does your life have to be without children.

Having a special relationship with a child can bring the greatest joy. When you have come to terms with your sadness, perhaps after many months, you may want to look at other options.

Surrogacy: Surrogacy arrangements are not enforceable in law and the baby has to be formally adopted, but they are becoming more acceptable. The British Medical Association now supports it, and it can be carried out using IVF techniques; or the surrogate, who might be a relative, a friend or someone introduced by an agency (see *Directory*) could be inseminated with your partner's sperm. Commercial transactions are not allowed, but the host mother is normally paid expenses. It may seem like the answer to your prayers if you and your partner can produce eggs or sperm but you cannot become pregnant. There are pitfalls, however, so consider everything carefully before going ahead.

Adoption at home or abroad: In America private adoption arrangements are legal, but in Britain they can only be carried out by a local authority social services department or by a voluntary organisation such as Barnardo's.

The process involves a medical and police check, followed by a home study during which social workers find out about all aspects of your life. Many hopes and expectations are attached to parenthood. People want children for personal fulfilment, to carry on the family line, to give and receive love, for the joy of bringing a child up or not to be the odd one out, for example. The aim of an adoption service is to see whether your needs and those of a child can be realistically fulfilled.

Cases should be judged on merit, but the shortage of healthy newborn babies available for adoption in most developed countries means waiting lists are long and preference tends to be given to younger couples. Some adoption agencies have an upper age limit of 35 or 38 for taking couples on.

As a result, older couples often consider adopting a baby from abroad. The process of adoption and the safeguards for overseas children are similar, but you have to do the groundwork yourself and pay legal and travel expenses. Overseas adoption is better regulated than it used to be, but tales of duplicity still occur, so get all the information and advice you can before you start.

The first step is to contact your local social services department. Some local authorities give international adoptions low priority, so there may be a long wait for a home study to assess your suitability for adopting. There is often a charge for the home study report, which most countries require and which includes a medical and police check. In addition you will need birth certificates and usually a marriage certificate, a financial statement and an employer's reference.

You write to a designated adoption agency, or to orphanages, maternity hospitals, government departments, doctors and lawyers in your chosen country. When you have found a child, you apply to adopt. A medical check is carried out on the child and a birth certificate and parental consent form, or a signed certificate of abandonment, should be available.

International figures suggest that about one in thirteen national adoptions and one in four or five inter-country adoptions break down. The reasons for this include over-high parental expectations, inadequate preparation (especially if the parents already have a child) and lack of post-adoption support (see *Directory*).

Adopting a hard-to-place child: Children need stability and consistency to develop healthily, so generally the younger a child is at the age of adoption the better. Widening your sights to consider an older child, or one with a disability can be rewarding, however, if you are realistic.

An older child who has been moved frequently, has experienced physical or sexual abuse or has been kept in an institution (something to bear in mind if you plan to adopt a baby from abroad) will inevitably have suffered emotionally. The longer it has gone on, the more damage adoptive parents may have to cope with. A child who is emotionally needy is likely to be more demanding and challenging.

If the child you adopt has a disability you should be given information about the likely progress and the support available locally. The more you know the more successful any placement is likely to be, so check out voluntary agencies, too.

Adopting a child who is hard to place can be an especially satisfying and positive experience if you go into it with your eyes wide open and preferably with the support of your wider family and of the experts.

Caring for other people's children: Most people remember a teacher, an aunt or a neighbour who had no children of her own but was unforgettable and special. With no day to day responsibility for raising a child she may have brought something unique to the relationship that was lacking in the hurly-burly of family life: tolerance, fun, an ability to make a fancy dress costume or chocolate cakes; the time or patience to listen carefully and not judge.

Para-parenting is a relatively new idea based on the ties of neighbourhood and friendship rather than blood. Childless women or couples build up a close relationship and become 'honorary parents' to a child who lives nearby. Such a relationship develops slowly, taking effort and commitment in the same way as those that can bring such delight to grandparents, godparents, aunts and uncles.

Some women sponsor a child from another country; a portfolio of such children can bring great satisfaction and interest. Others work with children in a professional or voluntary capacity. Paediatric nursing, teaching, fostering, running a playgroup or dancing school or writing children's books have great potential for developing special and satisfying relationships with children. Such ties can never be quite the same as having a child of your own, but they can bring great pleasure. There is a special art in loving other people's children.

Older mothers' experiences

Elizabeth (42): 'I saw my doctor just before my fortieth birthday, after we had tried to have a baby for about six months. Emotionally it felt like an admission of failure. I had various investigations over several months and keeping all the appointments while making up for lost time at work was physically exhausting. When I was told that everything seemed to be working normally I found it depressing as there was nothing to "fix". I considered adoption, but realised that what I really wanted was Michael's baby.

'Looking back, one of the reasons it took me so long to conceive was probably that Michael was away so frequently!'

Q: I had an abortion in my twenties. Could it have affected my ability to conceive?
A: Probably not, as research now shows it is rare for an abortion to cause infertility. A ten-year trial involving 1,500 pregnant

women found no difference in the time it took them to conceive again compared with those who had not had an abortion.

Circumstances do not always allow a free choice about abortion, but for some women, painful memories and guilty feelings can be buried deeply. If a woman has not been able to grieve adequately (see page 227) she may not be able to let go of the past and move forward; then it becomes easy to interpret failure to conceive as a punishment. It can be helpful to talk to somebody about such feelings, even if the abortion happened a long time ago.

Valerie (44): 'I have given myself two years to conceive so that instead of worrying about my age I can concentrate on increasing my chances of getting pregnant. Seeing it as a long-term project has helped me not to get upset each time my period comes. It seems to have taken the desperation out of trying to conceive and turned it into a part of my life, not the whole purpose of it.

'Our diet has improved considerably, although we have had so many complaints from Emma and Claire that we've had to make some compromises. I take more exercise and Barry and I usually go for a long walk together every weekend. As a result I'm losing weight steadily and feel better for it. People are beginning to say how well I look.'

Q: Apart from diet and fitness, what could affect my chances of conceiving?
A: Smokers are more than three times as likely as non-smokers to take a year or more to conceive, and the effect increases the more you smoke. Cotinine is a breakdown product of nicotine and a study has shown that when women having infertility treatment had cotinine in their ovaries their eggs were less likely to be fertilised. If you smoke, give up: it may help you to conceive and it will certainly help avoid problems when you are pregnant.

Drinking a lot of coffee or cola may also delay conception. The effect of caffeine on reproduction is not fully understood, but an American study of nearly 2,000 women showed that drinking more than three cups of regular strength coffee per day (two cans of cola contain about as much caffeine as a cup of coffee) more than doubles your chance of taking over a year to conceive.

Although of no concern to you at present, breastfeeding can delay ovulation and it affects your hormone balance so that if you do conceive the pregnancy is not sustained. If you intend to breastfeed but want to have another baby without too long a gap this may be something to bear in mind.

Lesley (36): 'Once we were accepted on an IVF programme Phil organised every detail of my treatment. The drugs I took to stop ovulation made me irritable and produced some irregular bleeding. Then I had a daily injection to stimulate my ovaries, and when the hormone levels were right the eggs were collected through the vagina and mixed with Phil's sperm.

'Three embryos were replaced in my uterus, and it was a bit like having a smear test. I had progesterone for two weeks by injections and vaginal pessaries to help the embryos implant, but the treatment failed and so did the next cycle. The third time I knew it would work as I felt different right from the start. We are expecting twins and it's such a miracle that I skip about with a grin on my face!'

Q: How can I relax when my pregnancy is so precious to me?
A: Remind yourself that although you took more trouble to conceive than most women, a successful IVF pregnancy is no different from any other pregnancy. You do not have to prove that you are worthy of the honour of having children just because you had a little technical help to get pregnant; nor do you have to be better or more careful than the average parent.

You are likely to have extra medical attention because you are expecting twins but in every other respect this is a normal pregnancy. Take care in a common sense sort of way, without wrapping yourself in cotton wool. Let other people lift things you know are heavy, eat healthily without worrying about the odd lapse, rest if you are tired but never miss an outing that sounds fun. Relax and enjoy it in every way you can, because when you have done your best the rest is not down to you.

Sue (39): 'My second pregnancy was a surprise as I was breast-feeding Jack. I was thrilled to have conceived again so easily, and miscarrying at twelve weeks was devastating. I didn't realise how common it is among older women, so I felt very alone and fearful that I might never get pregnant.

'When I conceived again people thought that because I was pregnant everything was fine and the pain had gone away, but I was still very vulnerable. Every time I felt the normal vaginal secretions of early pregnancy I rushed to the toilet, terrified that it was another miscarriage. Later on I had some bleeding, but I now know that even this doesn't always mean there is a problem.'

Q: What hope is there for women who have recurrent miscarriages?
A: A miscarriage proves that you are able to conceive, which is encouraging. Ninety-five per cent are one-off, which means that whatever causes them is unlikely to recur. Even if you have had six or more miscarriages you have roughly a one in two chance of going on to have a normal pregnancy, unless a specific abnormality such as an immunological or a genetic problem, or one of a number of previously unrecognised conditions, has been discovered.

Chromosome abnormalities often result in miscarriage so you would expect more as you grow older, but they would be one-off, not the result of an underlying problem. It seems hard to wait for three consecutive miscarriages before investigations are set in motion, but this is really a message of hope: you have probably been unlucky and do not have a fundamental problem.

Nutritional deficiencies may contribute to miscarriages, so ensure that your diet contains plenty of vitamins and minerals. In Britain, the charity Foresight (see *Directory*) claims to reduce the miscarriage rate dramatically for women who follow their pre-conceptual care programme. Some authorities advise waiting for three months after a miscarriage, to give your body a chance to rest, although for older women others say wait until you have a normal period and then try again.

6 *Pregnancy*

HOWEVER WELL YOU CONTROL THE REST OF YOUR LIFE, HAVING A baby is a different sort of adventure. Many older women regard motherhood as a privilege and are delighted to be pregnant; most look back on it as one of the most positive experiences they have ever had. Pregnancy does not always come at an ideal time, however, and it is likely to be only one of a number of important things in your life. It has never been safer, whatever your age, but it changes your future and the way you see yourself. Change involves individual growth and is rarely stress-free.

First-time mothers are often apprehensive about losing their freedom and coping with the reality of parenthood. Women who already have children may be equally nervous about adding to their work load, or returning to nappies and pushchairs after a long period without them. An unexpected pregnancy may be initially unwelcome, so that you struggle to decide what to do and dread people finding out. If you are going through a bad patch at work or in your relationship with your partner, or if there are other sources of stress in your family, you may worry that having a baby could make things worse. The pleasure and excitement of being pregnant may be tinged with fear if you have had trouble conceiving, or problems in a past pregnancy, and find it hard to trust your body.

Doubts and negative thoughts feel like a uniquely personal burden, but it is a rare woman who never has any, however positive she feels about having a baby. Give yourself time to adjust to your pregnancy – then relax and enjoy it.

How your baby grows

Pregnancy is dated from the first day of your last menstrual period, which in an average 28 day cycle occurs about two weeks before you conceive.

Months one to three: In the first month your baby develops arm and leg buds, a simple brain and a spinal cord. By the end of the second month (week ten) he is about the size of a peanut, but his internal organs, nervous system and main muscles are almost complete. His heart beats and he can move, although you do not feel it. In the third month his major organs, blood vessels and hormone glands develop and he swallows, digests and makes breathing movements using amniotic fluid. His skeleton turns from cartilage (like the tip of your nose) to bone, and his delicate facial features make him look human. By 14 weeks the placenta and all the baby's major systems are formed; he is about 3 inches (8 cms) long and weighs 15 grams.

Months four to six: The next three months are a period of growth. Your baby doubles in length and quadruples in weight, the fastest he will ever grow. Unique fingerprints appear and blood vessels show through his skin, giving it a pinkish tinge. In the fifth month nails, sweat glands, lanugo (fine body hair) and vernix (a creamy substance that keeps his skin soft in the amniotic fluid) develop, and he can detect light and darkness. By 28 weeks he weighs almost 1 kg.

Months seven to nine: In the next three months your baby's ability to cope with the outside world improves. His brain continues to mature, developing specialised functions like hearing and speech centres. At eight months babies show personality differences in the way they move or respond to music. They all have blue eyes (the iris needs exposure to light over a few weeks to darken) and light skin; colour is literally only skin deep. From now on they gain about 225 g a week, building up fatty layers under the skin so that they look plump. As they fill the space available in the uterus they become less active. A baby born after seven months (and sometimes before) has a fighting chance of survival, and this improves with each day that passes.

Your placenta: Your placenta carries oxygen and nutrients from your bloodstream to your baby, and receives waste products in return to be processed by your body. It filters out harmful bacteria but allows viruses, gases and certain drugs to pass through. It produces oestrogen and other hormones to maintain your pregnancy and prepare your body for breastfeeding. Resistance to infection is vital for your baby in the first few months after birth, so your placenta passes your antibodies to your baby while his own immune system matures. In the last few weeks of pregnancy it produces immunoglobulins (natural blood substances) to further boost his immunity, and to ensure that you are as healthy as possible before the birth. By the ninth month the placenta has almost completed its job and your baby is ready to be born.

What happens in pregnancy

Early pregnancy: A feeling of bloating, tenderness in your breasts or extreme sensitivity in your nipples may be just some of the early symptoms of pregnancy. Vaginal secretions may increase, your periods may stop or become light and you may feel very tired.

The excitement of knowing you are having a baby, planning for the future and feeling special often competes with exhaustion, nausea and fears about what may happen and how you will cope. Hormone changes and the effort of adjusting to pregnancy can lead to bickering with your partner at a time when you most need to feel supported. If you feel caught up in emotional rapids and are having a rough ride hang on tight; the fourth month usually brings calmer waters.

Many women hide their pregnancy in the first three months and try to lead a normal life. When it becomes public knowledge your family, friends and colleagues may assume that it was an accident, or focus on the negative side of being older with unwelcome frankness. Some people are shocked when someone they accept as childless or having completed their family suddenly announces a pregnancy, but most people react with delighted support.

Mid pregnancy: This is the most enjoyable part of pregnancy for many women. You start to look pregnant instead of feeling fat, and at around 18 weeks, or earlier if it is not your first baby, you may feel movements. Rhythmical knocks indicate that your baby has hiccups. Many women blossom physically and emotionally as sickness has usually diminished and they have more energy. You may feel more confident and get on especially well with your partner; pregnancy hormones may make sex especially rewarding.

Some men suffer minor symptoms often associated with stress, like stomach or headaches. Others feel out of their depth and withdraw to ground that feels safer, spending extra time at work or on leisure activities. Adjusting to parenthood does not happen to a timetable.

Late pregnancy: If you are fit and healthy late pregnancy can be most enjoyable. People tend to be interested and look after you when they see a sizeable bump. You may feel a new sense of fulfilment, and there is the stimulus of making plans, preparing for a positive change in your life and perhaps making new friends at antenatal classes.

As your bump grows your body tends to slow down. Working, and especially travelling in the rush hour, may be increasingly stressful (pregnancy and work are discussed in Chapter 13). Babies usually turn head down in the ninth month and engage: your ligaments soften, your pelvis expands and your baby's head fits into it. This usually improves breathlessness, but trips to the toilet become ever more frequent! Your breasts enlarge and may leak colostrum, a creamy substance that precedes milk production.

Towards the end of pregnancy you may feel Braxton Hicks or practice contractions. These are usually painless in a first pregnancy but can be strong in later ones. You may sleep badly and dream more or feel anxious about giving birth. A few days before labour starts you may lose a little weight or have diarrhoea.

Twins, triplets or more

There are more multiple births to mothers over 35. One reason may be that older women produce higher levels of gonadotrophin hormones such as FSH (follicle stimulating hormone) and this causes more eggs to ripen and be released. Another may be that proportionately more women undergo fertility treatment when they are older; hormone therapy and the transfer of up to three embryos increase the chance of implantation but can lead to a multiple birth.

For the first six months, the babies develop in much the same way as a single baby, although you will grow faster and probably feel more tired. In the last three months, space is at a premium and the babies' growth may slow down. On average quads are born at 31 weeks, triplets at 34 weeks and twins at 37 weeks, although some go to 40 weeks or more. Most women give up work at 6–7 months.

Carrying more than one baby can be uncomfortable and tiring. It does not help any pre-existing illness you have and it increases the chances of developing a problem like pre-eclampsia or intrauterine growth retardation (see page 156). You will probably be treated with extra care at least in the later stages of pregnancy, or throughout if it is your first or you have had any difficulty conceiving. At least 90 per cent of multiple pregnancies are successful, however.

Here are some ways to avoid problems:

❑ Pay attention to getting fit – walk or swim regularly, for example.
❑ Eat an excellent diet. This can make a big difference to your energy levels and to your babies' growth. You need larger portions and should expect to put on more weight when you are expecting more than one baby.
❑ Watch your posture right from the start to avoid unnecessary aches and pains.
❑ Attend all your antenatal checks and take to heart any advice to rest.
❑ Organise extra help in the last three months.

Your care during pregnancy

In Britain most women are cared for by an NHS midwife. Some receive maternity care from their GP, or a consultant obstetrician if the pregnancy is unusual. Your GP can tell you about local provisions and arrange for you to see a midwife, or you can contact one directly. If you prefer not to involve your GP phone the supervisor of midwives at your local hospital. Routine care may be in hospital, at home or a local clinic, or shared between them, but the conveyor-belt style of routine care is making way for a more individual system based on actual need.

Types of antenatal care
Your choice will depend on what is available, where you choose to have your baby (see page 172) and what is important to you.

Team care: Many areas have teams of about six midwives, but there are also larger groups who work in hospital, rotating between the antenatal clinic, labour and postnatal wards so that you see some familiar faces as you progress.

Domino scheme: Your midwife cares for you at home or at your GP's surgery during pregnancy, takes you to hospital when you are in established labour, delivers your baby and cares for you at home afterwards.

Caseloads: In some areas midwives look after all women on a one to one basis, working in the community in partnerships of two or three and covering for each other according to their own wishes. Your midwife is responsible for your antenatal care, delivery (in hospital or at home) and postnatal care.

Drop-in clinic: Some areas have a drop-in clinic where you can see a midwife (or the consultant, in late pregnancy) in addition to your routine antenatal visits.

Private care: You will not necessarily get better care going privately but it offers more certainty if you want a particular sort of experience. Personal service and continuity are more or less guaranteed, and antenatal care can be at a place and time that suits you, especially helpful if you have a demanding job.

Your GP can refer you to an obstetrician who accepts private patients. He or she will be more used to dealing with complications of labour and is unlikely to stay throughout if labour is normal. Ask what the fees include as there may be extra costs for things like tests, a night in hospital or an anaesthetist for an epidural.

You contact independent midwives directly (see *Directory*). They are often highly experienced at achieving a natural birth. Ask what the fees include, what insurance is carried and what would happen if there was a complication.

Your midwife: A midwife is trained to check your progress during pregnancy, detect any illness such as diabetes, monitor your baby's growth and refer you to a specialist if she finds anything out of the ordinary. She can arrange tests for fetal abnormalities and offer advice to help you handle minor discomforts. It is part of her job to give you unbiased information and help you make decisions but she cannot decide for you and you are not obliged to take her advice.

Like policemen, midwives seem to get younger as you grow older, but what they lack in age they often make up for in dedication and enthusiasm. When you get to know each other your midwife may become a trusted friend, providing up-to-date knowledge and sharing responsibility for your wellbeing during pregnancy in an equal partnership with you. Ideally you should feel able to contact her for advice or to discuss anything that concerns you without waiting for a visit.

Your antenatal care: Antenatal care distinguishes pregnancy symptoms that are important from ones that are not. Healthy women with normal pregnancies have fewer routine checks these days, whatever their age, but you can seek advice whenever you need it. If a problem occurs or you are considered high risk you will be seen as often as necessary.

At your first visit your midwife will take your history to get to

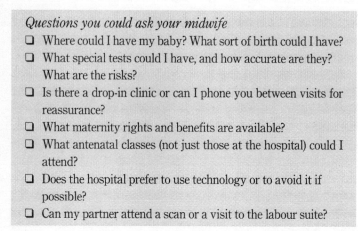

Questions you could ask your midwife

❑ Where could I have my baby? What sort of birth could I have?
❑ What special tests could I have, and how accurate are they? What are the risks?
❑ Is there a drop-in clinic or can I phone you between visits for reassurance?
❑ What maternity rights and benefits are available?
❑ What antenatal classes (not just those at the hospital) could I attend?
❑ Does the hospital prefer to use technology or to avoid it if possible?
❑ Can my partner attend a scan or a visit to the labour suite?

know you and note anything that might be relevant to your pregnancy. She will check your body mass index (see page 88) and ask about things like your health, your job, lifestyle and previous pregnancies, including terminations. She might ask about past sexual abuse, domestic violence or your use of street drugs. All information is confidential, but if you do not want to answer a question or have something recorded just say so.

You may have a physical check-up but an internal examination is rare these days. Your height and weight may be recorded and blood samples taken to check your blood group and rhesus factor, to see if you are anaemic (this is usually checked again later in pregnancy) and to test for glucose, syphilis, rubella and possibly hepatitis B. You will be offered tests for abnormalities (see pages 60–8) and individual tests may be performed if you are at risk from a disease that needs special care in pregnancy, such as diabetes.

You will probably not be weighed at each visit, but your midwife will check your blood pressure and test your urine for sugar and protein, to monitor changes that could indicate the onset of something like gestational diabetes (see page 154), that needs treatment. From about the fourth month she will listen for your baby's heartbeat and feel your abdomen to check the size of your uterus and later your baby's position.

Antenatal care should be reassuring and older women are generally more confident about asking questions. Misunderstandings, poor communication or a reluctance to bother staff who seem very busy can leave you worried when there is no need, however. Here are some common examples:

❑ **Your midwife says your baby is big (or small, or lying awkwardly).**

She is feeling through your abdomen and making a guess; some midwives are better at judging than others. There is no cause to worry unduly as a big baby can be just as easy if not easier to deliver, provided you have enough room in your pelvis. A 'small' baby could turn out to be a good size, and a baby lying awkwardly will probably move into a better position before the birth. Wait and see.

❑ **Your feet are small and your midwife mentions a caesarean section.**

Shoe size relates to overall frame size, but gives no clues about the size of your pelvic cavity or the position of your baby, which are what really matter. A small woman may have a large pelvic cavity, and vice versa. Even someone with size nine feet might need a caesarean section and a normal-sized baby who is well curled up is easier to deliver, whatever the size of your pelvis.

❑ **You want to breastfeed but have inverted nipples.**

Evidence shows that the rolling and stretching that used to be recommended for inverted nipples make no difference. Women who do nothing before the birth are just as likely to breastfeed successfully. Borrow or buy a book on breastfeeding so that you know how to position your baby at your breast and then ask for as much help as you need after the birth.

❑ **Your doctor says you have fibroids.**

These thickenings of the muscle of the uterus affect 2–5 per cent of women. There is a slightly increased risk of miscarriage and of premature labour if you have several, and a fibroid growing low in the uterus occasionally obstructs labour, requiring a caesarean section, but for most women they make no difference. High oestrogen levels in pregnancy enlarge them in about 20 per cent of cases. Unless the risk of fetal abnormality is high some doctors suggest avoiding amniocentesis, but they are not removed as they rarely interfere with a baby's development. Occasionally a fibroid growing on a stalk twists, causing abdominal pain and fever. This is called 'red degeneration' and it may be painful but is not usually harmful.

❑ **Your blood test results indicate that you are rhesus negative.**

If your partner is rhesus positive and your baby inherits his blood group your baby's blood will contain a D antigen while yours does not. Traces of rhesus positive blood could pass into your bloodstream during birth, miscarriage or termination and if this happens your blood will develop antibodies against the D antigen. These could attack the blood cells of a future rhesus positive baby.

You will have extra blood tests to check your antibody status as 2 per cent of women need treatment in pregnancy because cells from their baby's blood leak across the placenta. Most women simply have an anti-D injection within a day or two of the birth, however, to destroy any cells from the baby's blood before antibodies to them can develop.

What your notes mean

You may carry your own notes, so here are some common abbreviations. Ask your doctor or midwife if you are not sure what something means.

BP	Blood pressure.
US or USS	Ultrasound scan.
NAD	Nothing abnormal discovered.
Alb/Tr Prot+	Albumin/trace of protein found in your urine. + indicates the amount.
FM	Fetal movements felt (F), or not felt (NF).
FH	Fetal heart heard (H), or not heard (NH).
Vx/Ceph	Vertex or cephalic, meaning 'head down'.
Br/Tr	Breech (bottom down), or transverse (lying across the uterus).
E/Eng	Engaged (head has entered your pelvic basin).
NE/NEng	Not engaged.
=	The height of your uterus is equal to your dates.

Symptoms to report

If you are not sure whether something is important, mention it. You may want to query many things, especially during your first pregnancy and although most symptoms are not serious a few could be. Your doctor or midwife would always want to know if you have any of the following:

❑ Vaginal bleeding (often no problem, but it's always best to check).

❑ Abdominal pain, increasingly severe cramping, or bad pain just below your ribs.

❑ A high temperature, fever symptoms or vomiting.

❑ A bad headache that doesn't respond to simple remedies.

❑ Visual disturbances such as blurring or flashing lights before your eyes.

❑ Sudden swelling of your hands, face or feet.

Food precautions
To avoid potentially damaging infections, store cooked
meat separately from raw meat (your fridge temperature
should be below 4°C), cook food thoroughly (especially if it
is reheated) and wash all fruit and vegetables before eating
them. You are also advised not to eat the following:
❑ Foods that have been cooked and then chilled
❑ Soft and blue-veined cheeses
❑ Unpasteurised milk or cheese
❑ Raw egg, for example in desserts and home-made mayonnaise
❑ Pâté
❑ Undercooked meat
❑ Liver
❑ Shellfish
❑ Peanuts and other nuts in large quantities

Looking after yourself

Most of the discomforts that are considered part of pregnancy,
such as backache and heartburn, are caused by hormone changes
or by your baby taking up space that would otherwise be available for your internal organs. You can avoid some of them by
looking after yourself and simple remedies can minimise others
(see pages 145–50). Save some treats for the last few weeks to
make up for those discomforts you cannot avoid.

Hormones affect your whole body during pregnancy but the
discomforts they cause are linked to their beneficial effects. For
example, high levels of human chorionic gonadotrophin (HCG)
help to maintain your pregnancy in the early weeks, but may
cause nausea until the placenta takes over hormone production
at about 14 weeks. Another hormone, relaxin, contributes to
backache because it softens your ligaments to make giving birth
easier. A third, progesterone, relaxes smooth muscle fibres to

protect your baby from over-strong uterine contractions but also causes constipation; when the levels fall before the birth you get stronger contractions, and often some diarrhoea.

Posture: Poor posture can cause backache and other problems such as heartburn during pregnancy. Hold your spine naturally, with a small hollow below the waist and your head up and forward, not thrust out or pulled back.

Slumping makes heartburn after a meal worse as it puts pressure on your stomach when relaxin has softened the valve that closes it. Lengthen and widen your back instead of rounding your shoulders which will squash your internal organs and make you more breathless. If you lift a child or a heavy bag, bend your knees and hold the weight close to your body, transferring it from one place to another by moving your feet instead of twisting.

Exercise: It is easier to cope with the physical effort of pregnancy and birth when you are fit (see pages 90–2). An older body may not bounce back as easily as it used to, but exercise can reduce stiffness and improve your circulation to help avoid varicose veins. You could attend a pregnancy exercise class (look on the notice board at your local leisure centre or hospital), or a general class if the teacher has experience with pregnant women; or you might prefer to use a pregnancy exercise video at home (your local library may have one to lend). Pelvic floor exercises (see page 92) are especially important, and you can improve the flexibility of your pelvis by rocking it back and forwards and rotating it slowly in circles, as though you were belly-dancing. These movements may be easier if you bend your knees slightly.

Conserving energy: It can be frustrating not being able to do as much as usual but it is a useful preparation for the constraints of having a new baby. Pace yourself if you want to get through the day more easily or complete a task more effectively:

❑ Slow down! Rushing wastes energy.
❑ Never stand when you can sit, never sit when you can lie down.
❑ Never refuse an offer of help (write down all offers for after the birth).
❑ Pull your shoulders towards your knees and let go to release shoulder tension.
❑ Relax your jaw and face muscles consciously, and keep checking them.
❑ If you feel tired stop and rest. Relax completely for ten minutes (see page 109).
❑ Leave any task that is not essential until tomorrow – or the next day.
❑ Pause before taking on a new commitment. Consider how easily you can cope with it. Put it off if necessary.

Coping with tiredness

❑ Tiredness makes everything worse so rest after lunch and get some early nights.
❑ Listen to your body and try not to push yourself too hard.
❑ Ask for a seat on public transport and put your feet up in your lunch hour.
❑ Eat your main meal at midday and ask your partner to make a snack in the evening.
❑ Take a brisk walk in the fresh air every day.
❑ Try acupuncture, herbalism, hypnotherapy, homeopathy or aromatherapy.

Getting a better night's sleep

❑ Re-establish a sleep habit by winding down slowly before

bed for several nights: have a warm bath and a milky drink (not tea or coffee, which are stimulating); avoid anything exciting, be it a gripping book, a TV programme or an argument.

❑ Get comfortable in bed using plenty of pillows and light bedclothes; put a duvet under the bottom sheet if your pelvis aches; prop yourself up to avoid heartburn.

❑ Listen to soft music on a personal stereo; practise a relaxation exercise (see page 109).

❑ If you go to the toilet during the night, open the duvet to cool the sheets.

Maternity clothes: Maternity wear is designed so that the hemlines of skirts and tops stay straight instead of rising as your abdomen expands, and waistbands are adjustable. In a first pregnancy you may be comfortable for several months in loose ordinary clothes a size larger than usual, so that you can use them after the birth and before you return to your pre-pregnancy size. Women who have already had a child tend to swell sooner and often wear maternity clothes from the third month.

Your breasts will enlarge in the first few weeks and most women wear a supportive bra for comfort and to avoid over-stretching breast tissue. Maternity bras sometimes look hefty, but a flimsy bit of lace does not generally offer much support. The NCT (see *Directory*) and local department stores sell a range of maternity bras.

If your job involves standing you may also prefer to wear support tights to help avoid varicose veins (see page 151), and medium or low heeled shoes as your balance may be worse than usual.

The range of maternity wear in high street shops and mail order catalogues advertised in baby magazines such as *Practical*

Parenting has improved, so it's a matter of choosing clothes that are easy to wear and suit your lifestyle. Unless you have a size-able wardrobe your maternity clothes will get heavy wear in the last few months of pregnancy and you are unlikely to want to wear them after the birth.

Pregnancy planner

Months one to three

- ❑ Improve your diet if necessary and continue to take folic acid tablets.
- ❑ If you feel sick eat what you can even if it is not ideal. Make up for it later, when you feel better.
- ❑ See your GP or approach a midwife directly. Ask about the choices for antenatal care and antenatal tests (some must be performed early in pregnancy).
- ❑ Take firmer action now if you have not managed to give up smoking or if you have concerns about your alcohol or drug use.
- ❑ Send for maternity wear catalogues and choose clothes that are easy to wear and will keep their shape.

Months four to six

- ❑ Ask your midwife or friends to recommend antenatal classes. Book well ahead if you prefer a small class as they fill up quickly.
- ❑ Improve your fitness and stamina, especially if you do not get much exercise.
- ❑ Write the cut-off dates for telling your employer that you want to return to work (see page 272) on your calendar so that you do not miss them.

☐ If you want to carry on working after your date for maternity leave find out if your employer needs a letter from your GP.

☐ To save energy later in pregnancy try to complete major projects such as moving house, decorating and buying baby equipment (see pages 233–5).

☐ Eat a varied diet (see page 82) to help to maximise your baby's development.

Months seven to nine:

☐ If you change your mind about where you want to have your baby, tell your GP or midwife. There is still time to change your booking.

☐ Pack your hospital bag (see page 180) about six weeks before the birth and write a birthplan, outlining the approach you prefer and any special points (see pages 175–7).

☐ If you have other children plan their care during the birth, with back-up. Write a diary of your toddler's day to help whoever looks after her.

☐ Fill your freezer or store cupboard with basic ingredients for simple meals and check supplies of soap, detergent or pet food to make life easier after the birth.

☐ Arrange outings for after your due date in case you go overdue.

☐ Record a message on your answering machine to give callers information and you a respite from phone calls.

☐ Borrow or hire a TENS machine for pain relief (see page 201) or a radio pager to contact your partner.

Older mothers' experiences

Elizabeth (42): 'Motherhood does not have much status in the world of work and it's been surprisingly hard to ask people to recognise that I have different needs because I'm pregnant. The only person who always fetches a chair for me is a colleague whose partner has just had a baby. Everyone else expects me to carry on as usual.

'I was looking forward to leaving work early, taking some holiday entitlement before my maternity leave to travel abroad with Michael, but as the date draws nearer I have mixed feelings. I shall miss the excitement and variety of my job, and the mental stimulus of working to a deadline. Projects are already being discussed that I won't take part in. I wonder how I will adjust to such a different rhythm to life.'

Q: What should I bear in mind when travelling abroad during pregnancy?

A: Before making plans, check the dates of your antenatal appointments as timing is crucial for screening tests (see pages 58–68). Some airlines and cruise liners refuse to carry women over 26 weeks pregnant. Others will carry you up to 36 weeks on short journeys, if you have a letter from your doctor confirming you are fit to travel. You may be refused medical insurance if you take out a policy after pregnancy is confirmed, or the last few weeks of pregnancy may be excluded.

The middle months of pregnancy tend to be most comfortable for long haul travel, as you have not reached the stage when walking, long car journeys, rough roads or climbing out of a boat become difficult. In some regions it may be hard to avoid foods that carry a risk during pregnancy (see page 134).

Heat can be debilitating and you will need to drink plenty of water to avoid dehydration. Even a stomach upset can be alarming when you are pregnant, so take care over what you eat or drink. Take your antenatal notes, and perhaps a pregnancy book for general reassurance. Your pharmacist can suggest suitable preparations (including travel sickness pills) for minor ailments.

Pack lightly as you may find it difficult to carry heavy suit-cases, and bear growth spurts in mind – a scarcely visible bump can swell dramatically over a couple of weeks.

Valerie (44): 'This is Barry's first baby. It's a new experience for him and the girls and I want them to enjoy it. Emma and Claire are fascinated by how a baby grows so we borrowed books and a video from the library. I shall go to the antenatal classes as I don't want Barry to feel that because I've had children I'm an expert!

'Pregnancy makes me feel younger. I've staved off the menopause and extended my life, but I'm also more aware of the process of ageing. My father has just died unexpectedly so the new baby will not have a grandfather to spoil him as Emma and Claire have had. That makes me very sad. You depend on your parents for so long and you never really expect them not to be there for you.'

Q: Could a trauma like losing my father affect the baby?
A: Hormones cross the placenta and your baby may have been briefly affected – some kick strenuously a few hours after any sort of shock, for example. Physical and emotional development take place over a long period of time, however, much of it after birth so a baby is well protected. He needs to reach the right stage of maturity before he is touched by emotional events that affect other people. While it is unlikely that your baby will have been affected adversely you may take some time to come to terms with your loss (see page 227).

Lesley (36): 'I started reading books as I didn't know anything about pregnancy with twins, but they worried me so I put them away. Now that I've reached 30 weeks I feel more confident and want to know more about pregnancy, so I'm returning to them. I've had extra antenatal checks, mainly for reassurance as these are IVF babies, but no problems at all except for heartburn.

'The first time the babies moved I fell over! It was such a strange feeling that my legs just wobbled from under me. I'm much bigger than the other women at my stage of pregnancy and the babies wriggle like a basketful of puppies inside me. I certainly know that I'm pregnant at long last.'

Q: Is it really possible to have a baby without knowing about it?
A: Yes, if the symptoms are not very obvious and pregnancy is the last thing on your mind. A woman may have been sterilised or think she is menopausal. She may have been told that blocked tubes or some other condition make it unlikely she will ever conceive, and have given up all hope years ago. She might be taking the contraceptive pill and have light, irregular bleeding throughout pregnancy, and think that it is normal. The movements of a small, physically gentle baby can feel like commonplace intestinal activity.

Muscle twinges and extra tiredness may be put down to a new job, decorating, gardening or taking up aerobics to reduce the extra weight that seems to have crept onto hips and thighs. Even doctors occasionally fail to spot an advanced pregnancy, sending a woman complaining of abdominal pain to hospital to have a possible kidney infection or an ovarian cyst investigated.

Sue (39): 'This pregnancy has not been easy. I worried about losing the baby early on and now Jack is into everything and I haven't got any energy when he wants me to play. He gets upset when I can't do what he wants. I understand his frustration but tantrums are very wearing and it's hard to be patient with him.

'I blame my age, but younger mothers who are expecting second babies seem to be exhausted too, so it may have more to do with having a little boy who has been used to having my attention. I tell myself not to be so pathetic as this will be my last pregnancy. I should enjoy it, and in a funny way I do because I know that having a baby at the end will make up for everything.'

Q: How can I handle a lively child and save energy at the same time?

A: If you have more energy in the mornings, try to do everything essential, such as washing, shopping or preparing an evening meal, before lunch. Teach Jack to do things like sorting washing into light and dark colours and pressing the right buttons in the right order on the washing machine. You can judge his capabilities if you let him take on new tasks under supervision. He can probably do more than you expect. Children like to learn new skills and be given responsibility and his co-operation and genuine help will more than compensate for the extra time it takes at first.

Make a cardboard play clock with movable hands. When there is a task you have to do alone teach Jack that when the hands of the real clock match the play clock you will be free to come to him. The intervals should be very short at first. After lunch establish 'quiet time' for an hour, while you put your feet up. Tell him he can play on his own, watch a video, do a jigsaw or read a book with you, but you have to rest. Set the play clock, and when the real clock's hands match it, tell him quiet time is over and you will visit a friend, go to the library, take a walk or whatever. He will get into the routine if you are consistent.

Look out for activities where you can sit down with little active participation while he entertains himself. For example, if water fascinates him let him play in the bath while you sit beside it. Borrow videos and audio tapes from the library or record children's programmes on TV and save them up, or teach him how to use a tape recorder and play his own voice back.

7   *Handling Problems in Pregnancy*

IF YOU ARE FIT AND HEALTHY THERE IS NO REASON TO EXPECT your pregnancy to be anything other than normal. Nevertheless, very few women sail through without experiencing any side effects, although these are usually of a tiresome rather than a serious nature. Aches and pains become more common with age, and older women are more likely to be heavier or have several children, factors that contribute to common problems such as varicose veins.

If you are in any doubt about a symptom check with your doctor first. The everyday problems of pregnancy that are not considered serious tend to attract neither interest nor sympathy, but they can often be managed effectively using self-help or an alternative therapy. What you lose on the swings of an older body you often gain on the roundabouts of confidence and willingness to look after yourself.

Common pregnancy discomforts

Although not scientifically tested, these remedies for common problems are worth a try as they have been found to help some women. Alternative therapies can be powerful and some are not recommended for use in pregnancy so consult someone qualified (see *Directory*), with experience of treating pregnant women.

SYMPTOM AND CAUSE	SELF-HELP	ALTERNATIVE THERAPIES
Abdominal Aches: the ligaments supporting the uterus stretch, causing aches at the side of your tummy; often triggered by sudden movements.	Move more slowly; try gentle massage using the flat of your hand – vary the pressure to find what works best; consult an obstetric physiotherapist about wearing a maternity belt.	Aromatherapy.
Backache: softened ligaments and altered posture contribute to back strain.	Stand up straight; use a small cushion for support when sitting; lift with a straight back, keeping the weight close to your body; move your feet instead of twisting.	Chiropractic, osteopathy.
Breathlessness: hormones relax chest muscles and dilate respiratory tract capillaries; uterus presses on diaphragm, preventing lungs from expanding.	Sit-up – slumping restricts your lungs even further; breathe slowly and deeply; take your time when moving or climbing stairs.	Alexander technique.
Carpal Tunnel Syndrome: numbness, tingling or pain in your hands, caused by pressure on a nerve in your wrist, usually from swelling.	Rotate your hands, wriggle your fingers or spread them wide for a few seconds; hold them up in the air or hang them over the edge of the bed at night; ask your GP about a wrist splint to wear at night; check your diet for vitamin B6.	Acupuncture, chiropractic, homeopathy, osteopathy, shiatsu.

SYMPTOM AND CAUSE	SELF-HELP	ALTERNATIVE THERAPIES
Constipation: waste matter is processed less efficiently as hormones relax the smooth muscle of the gut and your uterus compresses it.	Eat fibre-rich foods; drink more water; try natural laxatives (liquorice, prunes, figs); use the toilet as soon as necessary and avoid straining – put your feet on a stool and flop your legs out. If taking iron tablets ask your GP for different ones.	Homeopathy.
Cramp: sharp pain in leg or foot; may be caused by greater blood volume and less efficient circulatory system or a dietary imbalance such as too much or too little calcium. It should improve within a week if an imbalance is the cause.	To improve circulation, roll each foot twenty times over an empty bottle before bed; on waking, flex toes upwards instead of pointing them; during an attack massage the area firmly or lean forward with your hands on the wall and stretch the affected calf behind you, pressing your heel to the floor and bending your other knee.	Herbalism, homeopathy, shiatsu.
Fainting: hormones relax your blood vessels, lowering blood pressure; your blood sugar level drops; your uterus demands extra blood which temporarily starves your brain.	Eat regularly; avoid overheating: wear several layers of loose clothing and peel them off; carry a fan or mineral water spray; shift your feet when standing; press down hard on balls of feet to return blood to your brain; if you feel faint, lie on your side or sit with your head between your knees.	Acupuncture.
Flatulence: progesterone relaxes smooth muscle so food and waste are processed slowly and wind builds up; you may be swallowing air unconsciously to relieve nausea or heartburn; alkaline food may react with stomach acids.	Relax and eat slowly to avoid gulping air; avoid gas-producing food like beans; sip peppermint or chamomile tea.	Aromatherapy, herbalism, homeopathy.

SYMPTOM AND CAUSE	SELF-HELP	ALTERNATIVE THERAPIES
Food Cravings: altered sense of taste; dieting, nausea or vomiting; drop in blood sugar level; need for extra nutrients such as calcium, vitamin C or iron.	Eat little and often, including complex carbo-hydrates such as pasta and bread; avoid sugary foods; a nutritionist could help correct any dietary problem.	Acupuncture, herbalism, homeopathy.
Gum Problems: hormones soften your gums so that scratches or food particles trapped around your teeth lead to infections and gum disease.	Brush teeth margins well using a soft toothbrush; rinse with a mouthwash; use dental floss gently; visit your dentist for advice.	
Headaches: hormones, stress, hunger, sinusitis, tiredness and dehydration can affect the frequency or severity of headaches.	Massage your neck where it joins the base of your skull; consciously relax and ask your partner to massage your face, neck and shoulder muscles; avoid dehydration by having a glass of water between meals and one beside the bed at night.	Acupuncture, homeo-pathy, osteopathy for painful sinuses.
Haemorrhoids (piles): painful or itchy swellings around the anus. Pressure from the uterus restricts blood flow, causing blood vessels to swell.	Check vitamins B6, C and E (see page 86–7); witch hazel or haemorrhoid cream from the chemist; gently insert a peeled clove of garlic and retain overnight; avoid constipa-tion and hot baths.	Herbalism, homeopathy, shiatsu.
Heartburn: a burning sensation in your chest and a sour taste in your mouth. Pressure from your uterus restricts space in your stomach and hormones soften the sphincter that closes it, so acid spills out and burns.	Neutralise acid at once with yogurt or milk; eat small, frequent meals, avoiding fatty or spicy foods, or any that seem to trigger it; don't bend over or lie flat after eating; prop yourself up with pillows for several nights to allow a burn to heal; your pharmacist may suggest an antacid.	Herbalism, homeopathy.

SYMPTOM AND CAUSE	SELF-HELP	ALTERNATIVE THERAPIES
Itching and Rashes: itching could be caused by overheating, tiredness or dry, stretched skin in late pregnancy; a rash may be caused by allergies to food, soap or detergents, or it may develop in moist, damp areas such as under your breasts or between your legs.	Drink plenty of water; use aqueous cream instead of soap which may make itching worse; apply vitamin E cream, Rescue ointment (from health food shop), calamine or baby lotion kept cold in the fridge; avoid overheating; keep skin folds dry and dusted with mild talc.	Aromatherapy, herbalism.
Nasal Congestion: extra oestrogen softens and thickens mucous membranes, leading to more mucus, a 'blocked nose' feeling and possibly nosebleeds.	Blow your nose gently; inhale the steam from two drops of eucalyptus oil in a bowl of very hot water; if the atmosphere is dry smear Vaseline inside your nose.	Acupuncture, aromatherapy, herbalism.
Nausea and Vomiting: hormones (human chorionic gonadotrophin (HGC) and later on, oestrogen and progesterone) may be responsible. It is more common in first and in multiple pregnancies.	Slow down and rest more; eat whatever you can, little and often; make tiny sandwiches to nibble, or try boiled sweets, ice lollies, ginger in any form; sip water, fizzy drinks or fennel tea; keep dry biscuits beside the bed in case you wake at night (eat some 20 minutes before getting up); carry a polythene bag inside a paper bag for emergencies.	Acupuncture, herbalism, homeopathy.
Night Sweats: increased blood supply makes your blood vessels dilate and radiate warmth.	Wear cotton nightclothes and use light bed covers; keep a fan or mineral water spray beside the bed; include potassium-rich foods (raw vegetables, bananas, nuts, dried fruits) in your diet.	Acupuncture, aromatherapy, herbalism.

SYMPTOM AND CAUSE	SELF-HELP	ALTERNATIVE THERAPIES
Pelvic Pain: may be caused by strain on ligaments that are softened ready for the birth; sharp pain deep inside may be your baby pressing on a full bladder.	Keep your bladder empty; try a maternity girdle to support the ligaments; put a duvet or sleeping bag under the sheet to soften a firm mattress; use pillows under your bump or between your knees; bend your knees and roll over slowly to avoid twisting; rock your pelvis before rising.	Acupuncture, aromatherapy.
Rib Pain: an ache across your back or sharp pain under one breast (costal margin pain) caused by your expanding uterus pressing on your ribs.	Try a larger bra or extension hooks and eyes; sit up straight to give your ribs more room; stretch your spine to relieve pressure: sit on the floor with your arms above your head and ask your partner to gently pull each arm upwards in turn.	Chiropractic, osteopathy.
Sciatica: pain low in your buttock or shooting down one leg as the baby presses on a nerve. It may pass when your baby changes position.	Try gently tightening and relaxing buttock muscles, or hold on to the back of a chair and swing the affected leg sideways up to 45° and back several times a day; avoid movements that trigger the pain so that the nerve does not become inflamed; if it does, bed rest will help it settle down.	
Stress Incontinence: your kidneys remove more fluid than usual as blood flow is increased; hormones also soften your pelvic floor making bladder control harder, so urine leaks when you lift, cough, laugh or sneeze.	Drink plenty of fluids to dilute your urine; use the toilet as soon as necessary; lean forwards to empty your bladder completely; use your thigh muscles when lifting and brace your pelvic floor before coughing or laughing; strengthen your pelvic floor muscles (see page 92).	Acupuncture, herbalism, homeopathy.

SYMPTOM AND CAUSE	SELF-HELP	ALTERNATIVE THERAPIES
Swollen Feet: oestrogen alters your potassium-sodium balance so that your cells retain fluid; blood volume increases and your growing uterus compresses major blood vessels.	Wear comfortable shoes and avoid hold-up socks or stockings; put your feet up whenever possible; lie on your left side to reduce pressure on the major blood vessels; put on support tights before getting up; swimming in deep water may relieve swelling.	Acupuncture, aromatherapy, herbalism, homeopathy.
Thrush: sore, itchy vagina with flaky white discharge; hormones prevent insulin from controlling sugar as well as usual, resulting in increased glycogen levels in cells; extra oestrogen favours the overgrowth of yeasts.	Wear cotton underwear, and skirts instead of trousers or leggings; avoid swimming pools and perfumed soap; wash gently with cool water and a shower spray on low power; wipe from front to back after using the toilet; eat a small tub of 'live' yogurt every day; ask your GP for creams or pessaries.	Acupuncture, herbalism, homeopathy.
Vaginal Discharge: increased secretions that are not offensive or irritating; caused by extra hormones.	Wash with warm water twice a day (avoid perfumed soaps) and change into fresh cotton knickers; use pantie liners or sanitary pads; avoid tight underwear, jeans or leotards.	Acupuncture, herbalism, homeopathy.

Preventing varicose veins

These look like soft blue knots in your legs (or vulva) and they make your legs ache. They are caused by extra blood volume, pressure from the uterus on your pelvic veins and vein walls that are softened by hormones, and they tend to run in families. It is easier to prevent them occurring than to cure them, so if you have had them during a previous pregnancy or suspect you may develop them try these measures:

❑ Watch your weight, increase your intake of vitamins B, C and E (see pages 86–7) and improve your circulation with brisk walking (see page 91).

❑ Avoid standing for long periods, crossing your legs and wearing tight elastic, hold up stockings or any restrictive clothing.

❑ Put on support tights before getting up, or after lying down with your legs and hips raised for ten minutes.

Leg exercises: Before you get up, push back the bedclothes and circle each foot separately, then stretch it up and down and side to side, feeling the movement in your ankle and calf. Start with 10 repetitions, working up to 30.

Lie on your back (if comfortable) with bent knees. Lift one leg vertically and gently shake it. Tense the muscles, drop the leg from the knee and kick it up again five times. Bend and lower it slowly. Repeat with the other leg.

Other pregnancy problems

Any problem during pregnancy can be worrying, but often the cause is simple and the treatment effective. Some of these problems are more serious, but with good medical care the majority of mothers and babies come through safely.

Bleeding: About one woman in five experiences bleeding at some stage of pregnancy, ranging from light spotting to a heavy period-like discharge. Often the cause is never identified and everything continues normally.

Early in pregnancy bleeding may be caused by a miscarriage, an ectopic pregnancy (one that develops outside the uterus) or a hydatidiform mole (see page 159). Less seriously, it could be linked to implantation, hormone changes, tests for fetal abnormalities, a cervical ectropion (erosion) or a polyp. Later in pregnancy bleeding could be caused by premature labour (see pages 215–16) or by a problem with the placenta:

Placenta praevia: The placenta partially or completely blocks the cervix instead of implanting higher in the uterus. This causes a potentially serious problem that can be avoided with good care. It may be suspected during an early scan, but when the lower segment of the uterus has developed fully another scan may show that the placenta is in the normal position. Placenta praevia affects about ten women in a thousand, and three of them can expect a normal delivery, while the other seven will have a caesarean section to avoid severe bleeding as the cervix opens.

Placental abruption: Occasionally a normally sited placenta separates prematurely from the uterus, causing severe pain without bleeding, or bleeding without pain. This is more common in women who smoke or who have had several children, and a small separation may be treated with bed rest. A larger one may resemble a heavy period with cramps or clots. The baby is not usually affected, although a few show signs of distress. Very rarely, however, bleeding is so severe that the mother becomes shocked and tragically the baby does not survive.

What to do if you experience bleeding

Your midwife or doctor would rather reassure you that bleeding is nothing serious than miss something important. If you can describe the bleeding it will help them to decide whether treatment is needed.

Seek help immediately if you have:

- ❑ Vaginal bleeding in early pregnancy and a history of miscarriage, or nausea, vomiting and lower abdominal pain on one or both sides.
- ❑ Any vaginal bleeding later in pregnancy, especially if you also have a 'show' of blood-streaked, jelly-like mucus.
- ❑ Any heavy vaginal bleeding, especially with abdominal or back pain.
- ❑ Blood in your sputum when you cough.

Seek help that day (or next morning if it starts at night) if you have:

- ❑ Slight vaginal spotting or staining in early pregnancy with no other symptoms.
- ❑ Bleeding from your nipples or blood in your urine.
- ❑ Bleeding from your back passage or from piles.
- ❑ Any other bleeding that concerns you.

Questions that may help you describe bleeding:

- ❑ When did it start? Does it come and go or is it continuous?
- ❑ Is it definitely from your vagina, not from your back passage or in your urine?
- ❑ What colour is it – bright red, dark red, brownish, pink?
- ❑ How much is there? Would it soak a sanitary pad in an hour, or a few hours, or is it more like spotting or staining?
- ❑ Is there anything distinctive about the bleeding, such as unusual smell, clots or tissue fragments in it?
- ❑ Is there any pain, and if so where and how severe? Did it start before or after the bleeding?
- ❑ Are there any other symptoms such as fever, weakness or nausea?

Gestational diabetes: About 50 per cent of pregnant women have sugar in their urine at some stage during pregnancy. Insulin controls the amount of sugar in your blood and gets rid of the excess. During pregnancy anti-insulin hormones allow extra sugar to circulate to meet your baby's needs. If there is too much sugar your body produces more insulin, but sometimes the adaptive mechanism is very efficient and prevents this. Treatment includes a good diet and extra monitoring to keep your blood sugar at normal levels.

The condition differs from 'ordinary' diabetes, where you cannot produce enough insulin even when not pregnant. If you normally suffer from diabetes the outcome for you and your baby is good, provided you are under the supervision of a specialist during (and preferably before) pregnancy.

Pre-eclampsia: This used to be called toxemia. It can develop at any time after 20 weeks but is more common in the last three months of pregnancy. If you have raised blood pressure, protein in your urine (a particular cause for concern, even with no other symptoms) or fluid retention (oedema) you will have more frequent antenatal checks. The disease can be difficult to diagnose as the absence of a symptom does not rule it out and the presence of one does not always indicate it. For example, newly raised blood pressure could be an early sign of pre-eclampsia or it could reveal underlying hypertension brought out by pregnancy.

Pre-eclampsia tends to run in families and affects one pregnancy in ten to some degree, but only about one in 2,000 women develop the more serious form, eclampsia. It is associated with conditions like kidney disease, diabetes and multiple birth, and may originate in the cells that become the placenta before you even know you are pregnant. It is more common in a first pregnancy, but rare in a second or later pregnancy with the same partner. Women who conceive in the first four months of a new relationship are more likely to get it than those who have been with a partner for a year or more, so exposure to your partner's semen over a long period may help your body to cope with proteins that trigger pre-eclampsia.

If your blood pressure rises to about 140/90 and your urine contains protein (a '+' or more – see page 133) you may be advised to go into hospital for closer monitoring. Although you may feel perfectly well, the disease is progressive and can be unpredictable after a certain stage. You might have several weeks in hospital feeling a complete fraud, but equally it could flare up over a few hours so that your baby needs to be delivered quickly by caesarean section.

Help your midwife spot early signs of pre-eclampsia

❑ Tell her at your first antenatal visit if your mother or sisters had pre-eclampsia.

❑ If you are at risk ask if low dose aspirin would help, or a Doppler blood flow scan early in pregnancy to see whether the placenta has embedded properly.

❑ Never miss an antenatal check – rearrange one if necessary.

❑ Tell her about any of these symptoms, which might indicate pre-eclampsia:

    ❑ sudden weight gain – more than 1 kg per week over two or three weeks.

    ❑ visual disturbances such as blurring or flashing lights.

    ❑ severe headache that does not respond to your usual remedies.

    ❑ severe pain or tenderness just below your ribs, with or without nausea.

    ❑ swelling of your hands, face or feet (so that you cannot get your shoes on).

    ❑ a feeling or instinct that something is wrong.

Fetal growth problems: A baby suffering from intrauterine growth retardation (IUGR) fails to grow as well as expected. Some causes are unknown, but factors that contribute to it include pregnancy complications, chronic illness, smoking, a poor diet and overwork. It is more common in older mothers, first pregnancies and in fifth or later ones. Development in the uterus is thought to affect both a baby's ability to cope successfully with the early months of life and health in adulthood.

If your midwife suspects IUGR when she measures your stomach or feels your baby, it can be checked. A scan may show normal growth (your baby may appear small for your dates because you are long waisted, for example) but if there is genuine cause for concern you may be advised to rest more or given medication to improve placental blood flow.

Your baby's progress can be checked by a series of scans and if necessary she can be delivered prematurely (see pages 215–16) to catch up outside the uterus. Many IUGR babies make normal progress once they are born.

High risk pregnancy

Women over 35 have more high risk pregnancies; they have had longer to develop illnesses and are more likely to have had a previous loss or problem in pregnancy, to suffer fetal growth problems or to be expecting more than one baby. Nobody chooses to have a high risk pregnancy; it happens by chance or it may be an unavoidable part of the deal if you want to have a child.

Most women are willing to accept any hardship that allows them to have a baby successfully. Nine months is a long time, however, if your activities are restricted or you have to follow a daunting medical regime. You may resent losing your independence and feel 'taken over' by doctors and obliged to follow every bit of advice. Extra medical attention may be reassuring, but it can also increase the stress of a high risk pregnancy. Sometimes only a successful outcome actually reduces your anxiety.

Such a pregnancy imposes a physical and emotional burden on you and your family, often for several months. You may walk a tightrope between hope and despair, or feel somehow inadequate when other women manage to have normal pregnancies; your partner may feel responsible for your suffering. You may worry about the financial effects of stopping work, or feel you are a nuisance to friends and family who look after you or your small children. It can be difficult to receive help gracefully, but it is easier for everyone if you approach the situation positively and accept the way it is without blaming yourself.

Coping with a high risk pregnancy
- ❑ If you are housebound or confined to bed invite friends to play a board game such as Trivial Pursuit or watch a video. Order a takeaway and suggest they collect it on their way.
- ❑ Take up a new pastime such as painting or embroidery. Borrow audio-tapes from the library, learn a language, write letters to magazines, read best-sellers.
- ❑ Use the phone to keep in touch with friends and to shop from catalogues.
- ❑ If you have to miss a special occasion send a message using a tape recorder or a camcorder, or get your partner to record the atmosphere for you to enjoy later.
- ❑ Think about your partner's needs. He will be anxious on your behalf and will miss out on the normal pleasures of life in your company, such as outings and fun. Other people may ignore him while they worry about you.

Losing a pregnancy

Sadly, some women will lose a baby during pregnancy. This is slightly more common as you get older, as it is linked to things like high risk pregnancy and chromosome abnormality.

Ectopic pregnancy: In about one in 200 pregnancies the egg implants outside the uterus, often in a uterine tube. The first sign is usually severe abdominal pain low down or to one side, which may be worse when you move. Brownish spotting or light bleeding may occur. Although the pregnancy cannot continue, early diagnosis and treatment can save the tube and help preserve your future fertility.

Early miscarriage: This is the loss of a baby between conception and 12 weeks. If it is threatened or thought to have occurred you may be offered a vaginal scan, using a probe rather like a vibrator covered with a condom. This can give a better picture of what is going on than an abdominal scan. Although such scans are being used increasingly frequently, some women prefer to avoid them; they feel that the information they could provide has no benefit unless there is the possibility of treatment. The choice is yours.

Some doctors advise bed rest for a threatened miscarriage. It may reduce bleeding and help you feel that you have done everything possible, but if you have to carry on working or caring for other children there is no evidence that *not* resting makes miscarriage more likely; some cannot be prevented no matter what you do.

There is some controversy as to whether it is always necessary to perform a D & C after a miscarriage, but it is offered in many hospitals. The neck of the uterus is gently stretched and the lining scraped or aspirated to make sure that nothing remains that could cause an infection. Afterwards you may be advised to wait for one normal period before trying to conceive again.

When you have invested a great deal into a pregnancy, and lose it, you may feel that it must be your fault and search your memory for something you did or failed to do. Miscarriage is rarely caused by any normal activity, however, including sex, lifting a toddler, minor falls or emotional upsets. If you miscarry before many people knew you were pregnant it may help to tell family and friends so that you receive sympathy, support and acknowledgement that you were pregnant.

Possible signs of miscarriage

Many women get aches and pains or light bleeding during pregnancy without there being any problem. Some have bleeding on and off for most of their pregnancy and still go on to deliver a healthy baby.

Seek help urgently from any doctor or hospital if you have:

❑ heavy vaginal bleeding, especially if you are passing clots or other material.

❑ severe pain, especially if you have a history of miscarriage.

Contact your own doctor if you have:

❑ bleeding that is as heavy as a normal period.

❑ light spotting or staining that goes on for two or three days.

❑ cramps accompanied by bleeding.

❑ pain that is moderate or lasts more than 24 hours without any bleeding.

Hydatidiform mole: This affects only about one in 2,000 pregnancies, but the risk increases with age, and it may be linked to a chromosome defect. Some women explain it simply as a miscarriage to friends and family.

The trophoblast, or outer cell layer of the fertilised egg, develops partially or completely into small grape-like cysts instead of forming an embryo and a healthy placenta. It is usually diagnosed by scan, often after severe nausea, intermittent fresh bleeding or a continuous brown discharge. The pregnancy is never viable and has to be removed under general anaesthetic.

In about 10–15 per cent of molar pregnancies the cells continue to grow, so you will be monitored for up to two years to make sure that it has completely gone. You may be advised not to try for another baby during this time, although the time limit can often be more flexible for older women, as monitoring advances. For most women there are no further consequences, but the chances of it happening again are about 2 per cent so you will be watched carefully when you become pregnant again.

Late miscarriage: Overall, 1–2 per cent of pregnancies miscarry after 12 weeks but before the baby has a chance of independent life. This risk doubles for women over 35 who are pregnant for the first time, but not for older women having a second or subsequent baby. Late miscarriage is rare where there are no other complications and serious mishaps such as a fall or a car accident seem to play little part. It is not usually linked to the baby but to problems with the placenta, the cervix or the mother's health, and good antenatal care can reduce risks such as untreated chronic illness. In many cases a cause can be established so that action can be taken to prevent it happening again.

Coping if you lose a pregnancy

Losing a pregnancy is especially distressing for an older mother who cannot always comfort herself with the belief that if this baby was not to be there will be another one. What is an inevitable part of life's reproductive tapestry can also be a personal crisis that changes the way you feel, turns a normal desire to have a baby into an obsession and makes the longing to be pregnant again unbearable.

In the first week or two you will need practical help making meals, lifting things or answering the phone. Many women feel guilty or responsible for losing a baby during pregnancy, even though they know it was not their fault. Some feel they have failed as a woman by not producing a perfect baby, especially if the pregnancy has been terminated for an abnormality. It is isolating to feel that nobody really understands this, and you may start to lose confidence in your body or become anxious about your ability to carry a baby in the future. Many women are shocked and ashamed by the strength of their anger towards other pregnant women, although such feelings are not unusual.

Men experience the loss of a baby during pregnancy differently and often find it easier to be philosophical. They cannot always put emotions into words, however. A partner who has taken an active interest in your pregnancy or attended scans may be as deeply upset as you are, but he may see his role as supportive and struggle to work normally and shoulder the depth of your grief while denying his own. Women often interpret this as lack of feeling rather than the lack of expression that it really is. If your partner cannot provide the reassurance you need both now and during another pregnancy, talking to women who have had a similar experience may help. Voluntary groups (see *Directory*) can offer information and support to help you cope.

Losing a much-wanted child is a tragedy at any time, but if it happens before anyone had a chance to get to know the baby as an independent person it is often regarded as somehow less traumatic. People who have not been through such an experience may fail to understand that comments like 'you'll have another one', or 'it's just nature's way', can be deeply hurtful as they appear to devalue your baby or make light of your ordeal.

Coming to terms with the despair, inadequacy and uncertainty that losing a baby during pregnancy can bring may take several months (see page 227), and most women need extra support during their next pregnancy.

Older mothers' experiences

Elizabeth (42): 'My midwife remarked on my stretch marks, measured my stomach with a tape measure and said I was rather small for my dates. She thought that my baby was not growing properly. I went for a series of scans over a few weeks before everyone decided that it was a false alarm.

'Although I'm glad it was picked up and monitored, it caused me a great deal of anxiety at the time. As soon as someone suggested there might be a problem I became instantly irrational. Some of the medical staff didn't seem to realise the impact their words had on me but it brought home to me that I'm not as strong as I appear.'

Q: Is there anything I can do about my stretch marks?
A: Stretch marks (thin, purplish lines that appear on breasts, thighs or abdomen) are caused by natural steroids produced by your body to combat stress and disease. They affect the proteins that support and give elasticity to your skin and when sudden growth in pregnancy stretches your skin and thins it the deepest layers tear.

Stretch marks cannot be prevented, but a steady weight gain and a varied diet helps avoid them. Creams enriched with vitamin E or Retin-A have been used to assist the body's healing process, and homeopathy or aromatherapy may also help. After the birth, pulsed-dye or carbon dioxide pulse lasers (normally used in cosmetic surgery for the removal of scar tissue) can treat them, but at a cost and with varying levels of success. Eventually stretch marks fade to silvery white.

Lesley (36): 'I've reached 36 weeks and am quite big now. I get tired and uncomfortable, but it seems such a small price to pay for having a child. I've been lucky that my pregnancy has been completely straightforward and I'm enjoying it, although Phil fusses round me as though I'm a china doll.

'It's touching that so many people take an interest in my welfare, but some tend to focus on problems. One lady told me that surgery had been carried out on one of her daughter's twins before they were born, which worried me. I can't get it out of my mind. You tend to latch on to what people say.'

Q: If a baby has a problem diagnosed during pregnancy what sorts of treatment can be carried out before birth, and are there any disadvantages?

A: Well-established treatments include blood transfusions to the baby through the mother's abdomen to solve a clotting or rhesus problem, or giving drugs which cross the placenta, such as antibiotics for an infection or steroids to mature a premature baby's lungs.

A growing range of operations are being attempted in the uterus, however, in order to solve rare problems. A precise diagnosis is essential because some conditions, such as those that are linked to certain chromosome abnormalities, may involve other impairments. If an operation goes ahead the baby may not survive or more surgery may be needed after birth.

Certain procedures are only offered to older mothers because of worries that future fertility might be affected, and by its very nature pioneering work may not produce benefits in the short term. The chances of failure can be high and the long-term effect on a developing baby unknown.

The decisions always need careful thought. Some mothers may feel that any chance is better than none, and bravely hold on to hope however slight the odds. Others may decide it would be a tragedy to intervene before birth and have a baby who survives but dies in childhood.

Sue (39): 'Everything seems fine now, but at 14 weeks I started bleeding. My GP suggested going to bed, which reduced the bleeding. After a few days it stopped so I got up – and flooded again. My GP arranged a scan but by the time I got to hospital I'd soaked two sanitary towels and wasn't optimistic. The scan technician said the baby was fine and a blood clot might be causing the bleeding. I was so relieved I burst into tears.

'I went back to bed and Kenneth looked after Jack, but after a couple of weeks I felt Jack needed me so I got up. I continued bleeding for several weeks. Nobody really knew why so there was a new drama at every scan, but eventually it simply tailed off and I had no further problem.'

Q: Chickenpox is going around our neighbourhood. If Jack catches it is there any risk to the baby in mid-pregnancy?
A: It is unlikely that your baby would come to harm as you would have to catch the infection first and most adults are already immune to it. If you have not had it and he catches it talk to your doctor. It is extremely rare for a baby to be affected after about 20 weeks and even in the first half of pregnancy fewer than one baby in ten will be harmed by a mother catching chickenpox. The risk rises if you catch it around the time of delivery when up to three babies in ten are born with the infection (before you passed on antibodies) and may be seriously ill.

Women who come into contact with children as part of their job often worry about picking up a virus during pregnancy, but the risks are small. Most have acquired immunity to common viruses such as mumps, measles, toxoplasmosis or cytomegalovirus (CMV) during childhood, naturally or through vaccination. If you catch something for a second time you (and your baby) already have antibodies to fight it. So if you catch shingles, the reactivation of the chickenpox virus, it does not usually affect your baby because antibodies are already present.

8   *Preparing for the Birth*

LABOUR IS A POWERFUL, EMOTIONALLY INTENSE EXPERIENCE AT any age, but it can also be profoundly satisfying when you are well prepared and it is managed in a way that feels right for you. Until a few years ago a woman having a baby was expected to submit to whatever the medical staff thought best for her; today she expects to share the decisions about her care. This tends to suit older women who are used to running their own lives and taking responsibility.

If you hope your baby's birth will be special, if you feel you may not be in a position to repeat the experience or you simply do not want to take anything for granted, time spent planning is especially worthwhile.

Approaches to birth

Births are like dresses – different styles suit different women. A normal labour can be completely natural, actively managed throughout, or something in between. One approach is not safer

Where to find out about birth

You need to know your choices before you can make decisions. Here are some sources of information.

❑ Your doctor or midwife has local knowledge, and can answer questions individually.

❑ Books and magazines give general information. You can look things up, learn at your own pace and find the addresses of self-help groups.

❑ Videos and TV programmes cover specific topics in depth.

❑ Friends or relatives can speak from individual experience.

❑ Voluntary organisations (see *Directory*) can help if you have special circumstances or an unusual query.

❑ Antenatal classes can provide information, confidence and practical advice, although some assume that everyone will use drugs or technology. Look for a small class if you want to ask questions, learn techniques to help you cope with labour or meet other parents to share experiences; friends or your midwife may be able to recommend one.

or better than another; just different. Certain things go together, however: you are more likely to achieve a natural labour at home than in hospital, and to get an epidural on demand at a large hospital rather than a small one, for example.

The amount of intervention depends on what you and your midwife prefer, unless there is a complication, but it is easier to progress to using more technology than to go in the other direction. If a woman is healthy and has had no problems in pregnancy it is rare for a totally unforeseen crisis to occur during birth. Labour is likely to be normal, calling mainly for patience and loving care.

You might be encouraged to go to hospital on the grounds of age or for your first baby, but there is no evidence that this is safer. A hospital birth may be safer if you have an illness or complication during pregnancy, if you are expecting twins or your baby is in a breech position, or if your baby is likely to be premature or need special care. An experienced midwife might conduct a water birth or deliver a mother at home after a previous caesarean section, whereas another midwife might feel less confident – so the decision depends on the circumstances. No particular choice is either obligatory or not available to you.

It is the responsibility of your midwife or doctor to make a booking according to your wishes; ideally they should try to achieve the approach you prefer in the place that you choose. Take your time to make the right decision, although if your feelings alter as pregnancy advances you can change your booking at any time.

Think about the basic approach to labour that makes you feel most comfortable, discussing the options with your partner or family if you like; then consider where to have your baby.

Different types of birth

Some of these approaches can be used together; for example, if you prefer a natural birth you can also be active or use water.

Natural birth: Labour starts spontaneously at its own pace provided you and your baby are fine. Your midwife relies on vigilance, experience and skilled hands rather than routine examinations or technology. Intervention is avoided unless strictly necessary, so labour is not speeded up just because it is taking a long time, for example. You cope with pain using self-help or natural remedies, plus support and encouragement.

Location: Most achievable at home and least likely in a large consultant unit. This approach is open to any woman if labour proceeds normally. Choose a hospital carefully – some claim to support natural birth but rapidly resort to technology.

Supporters say: 'Women are designed for giving birth. Natural birth gives you a sense of achievement and avoids the disadvantages associated with technology.'

Verdict: Technology or drugs can always be used if a problem arises. If you want a natural birth prepare in advance and ask your midwife to help you achieve it.

Active birth: You stay upright and active during labour and birth, using positions that work with gravity and help your pelvis to open. You can attend classes to learn the positions and need to practise daily if you want to be fully active.

Location: Home or hospital – no special facilities are needed. Anyone can have it unless a complication requires intervention. Some midwives actually encourage it, others leave it up to you.

Supporters say: 'You help your baby to be born instead of being passive. It makes labour easier, so you're less likely to need pain relief or intervention.'

Verdict: It can be tiring if labour is long, but many women are active to some extent during labour. Unless you practise you may be too stiff to make full use of it.

Water birth: Part of your labour (and sometimes the delivery) takes place in a birth pool where deep warm water helps mobility and relieves pain. You can use gas and air but must leave the pool if you need anything else.

Location: Some hospitals or GP units have a pool installed (although staff are not always keen to use it) or you can hire one to use at home or in hospital. Water births have taken place in caravans and council flats, on ground and upper floors, even out of doors. Most women can use water for at least part of their labour. In hospital there may be rules about entering and leaving the pool, what essential oils you may use and the temperature and depth of the water.

Supporters say: 'Water is buoyant, comforting and relaxing and you can move freely. A pool gives you personal space that nobody invades without an invitation.'

Verdict: A safe, relaxing option, especially helpful if you do not want to use drugs for pain relief. Persevere if a midwife does not actively encourage you.

Low tech birth: Technology is used when it is considered necessary. You might have a fetal monitor for 20 minutes to get a base reading of your baby's heartbeat in early labour, then walk around or stay in bed as you wish. A slow labour may be speeded up using a drip (your baby will be monitored and you may not be able to walk around). You use whatever pain relief you prefer, from self-help through to an epidural (although not usually on demand).

Location: This takes place in hospital and is the most common approach to labour, although the amount of intervention depends as much on hospital protocols as on how you feel about it or how your labour progresses.

Supporters say: 'You can discuss the need for intervention with the midwife or simply follow her advice. You don't feel you are being demanding or making decisions without knowing enough about it.'

Verdict: Most women have this sort of birth, but you do not automatically get what you want. If something is important to you write a birth plan (see pages 175–7).

High tech birth: This may be essential if you have a complication, but it can also be used to actively manage a normal birth (see page 212–3). Labour starts spontaneously or is induced, your contractions are speeded up with a drip if you fulfil certain criteria and you stay in bed throughout. Your baby's heartbeat is continuously monitored and you have an epidural on request.

Location: Most likely in a large consultant unit or teaching hospital. Anyone can opt for it if the service is offered, but small hospitals may not have the facilities.

Supporters say: 'Technology is reassuring. Labour doesn't go on for hours so your partner does not see you suffering.'

Verdict: It takes some of the uncertainties out of giving birth, but you cannot change your mind once it is set in motion. The chances of other interventions, such as an episiotomy, assisted delivery or caesarean section are higher (see chapter 10).

Technology and safety

Technology is more likely to be used for an older mother and although many women feel more secure if it is used just in case, this is not always advantageous. It may cause a problem that has to be solved by using more technology, leading to interventions that would not otherwise have been required.

Compared with women under 25, twice as many women over 35 expecting first babies have a caesarean section. Three times as many women over 35 with one or more children have one.

This increase is not linked to the actual number of complications so there are other factors involved, such as anxiety on the part of mothers or doctors. A caesarean section can be life-saving, but it takes longer to get over and is associated with more problems postnatally than a normal birth (see page 230). Illness or a complication may need the help of technology, but for a healthy woman having a normal labour there is no evidence that it improves safety.

Where to have your baby

The sort of labour you have will depend to some extent on where you decide to give birth. The choice is yours.

Home birth: Your midwife brings everything used for normal birth in hospital, and stays at your home once labour is established. She delivers your baby, clears up, leaves her phone number and visits frequently for several days (see page 197).

Advantages: You can relax and do as you like in your own home so labour may be easier. You are likely to know the midwife who delivers your baby and you do not have to leave your other children.

Disadvantages: Emergency treatment might take longer to get, although if a problem arises you can expect to be transferred to hospital in plenty of time.

Who can have it? Anyone, regardless of medical or other circumstances, including your age or having your first baby. Some doctors do not mention it and hope you will not ask, but midwives are increasingly positive.

Verdict: Research shows that it is as safe as giving birth in hospital. It is relaxing and empowering – a great help if you want a natural birth.

Hospital birth: You go to hospital when your waters break or when labour is established (you have strong, regular contractions). You have a single room for labour and may give birth there or be moved to a delivery room for the birth, and you stay for a few hours or days after the birth (see page 196).

Advantages: It may reassure you knowing that medical help and emergency facilities are on hand. You meet other mothers, your meals are made for you and midwives are there to help you care for your baby or answer questions.

Disadvantages: Women tend to have more interventions, need more pain relief and catch more infections than at home. If the staff are rushed off their feet you may not get enough help with breastfeeding, for example.

Who can have it? Anyone can be referred to any hospital although, depending on where you live, your choice might be limited by practical considerations.

Verdict: The majority choice, but hospitals vary considerably (see *Choosing a hospital*).

GP or midwifery unit: A separate building or one ward in a hospital, offering a low technology approach to normal birth. Supervision is usually by community midwives and some units have a birth pool or facilities for the disabled.

Advantages: Generally more homely than hospital. The

midwives tend to be confident about natural birth and have more time to help after the birth.

Disadvantages: If a problem arose you would be transferred to a consultant unit.

Who can have it? Anyone may deliver there or transfer from hospital postnatally, provided there is a bed available. Ask about it if your GP does not mention it.

Verdict: Informal, friendly, personal, well-liked by mothers who have the choice.

Disability

Women with a disability are sometimes made to feel different when they have a baby; access to clinics can be poor and facilities less than ideal. Some women also say that they would cope better if it was not for the prejudices of other people, or that they know more about their condition than the midwives or doctors caring for them. Many hospitals, midwives and antenatal teachers make great efforts to offer support and devise an individual approach, however. It may be up to you to ask for what you want.

Some women feel under pressure to have a high technology birth even though their disability is not relevant to labour. You may need special facilities to make your labour easier, such as a water birth, a home birth or an independent midwife who can adapt to your circumstances more easily. If you can demonstrate that your needs cannot be met by the local services offered, you may be able to negotiate an *extra contractual referral,* so that all or part of the cost is met by your local health authority.

Voluntary organisations and self-help groups have useful leaflets about pregnancy and birth, and contacts for you and your medical advisors are listed in the Directory.

Choosing a hospital

Hospitals differ in their approach to women and in the facilities they offer. Some are more open-minded and welcoming than others, so try to visit those you are considering personally. When you have thought about the approach to labour that you would prefer here are some questions you might wish to ask:

- ☐ Will I know the midwife who delivers me and see the same midwife after my baby is born?
- ☐ How long could I stay in hospital, and could I move to a GP unit if I wish?
- ☐ Can I labour without intervention so long as my baby and I are fine?
- ☐ How long would it be before my labour was speeded up?
- ☐ When is fetal monitoring considered necessary?
- ☐ Can I be examined or deliver in any position that feels right for me?
- ☐ Could my labour be actively managed at night or at the weekend?
- ☐ Is there a 24-hour epidural-on-demand service? If not, what determines whether I can have one?
- ☐ How many caesarean sections do you perform? (The World Health Organisation suggests 10–15 per cent is a maximum rate.)
- ☐ What is your episiotomy rate? How many mothers have no stitches?

Making a birth plan

Whatever sort of labour you prefer, small details will be important to you. For example, one woman disliked her abdomen being touched unnecessarily and another hated to be addressed as 'my dear'!

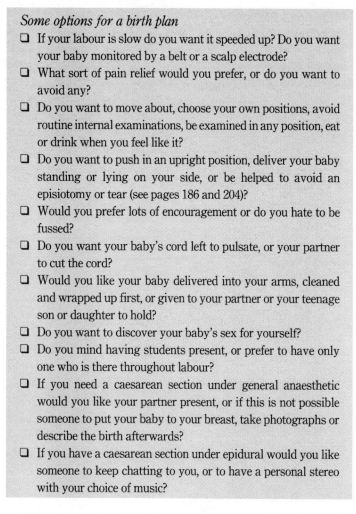

Some options for a birth plan

❑ If your labour is slow do you want it speeded up? Do you want your baby monitored by a belt or a scalp electrode?

❑ What sort of pain relief would you prefer, or do you want to avoid any?

❑ Do you want to move about, choose your own positions, avoid routine internal examinations, be examined in any position, eat or drink when you feel like it?

❑ Do you want to push in an upright position, deliver your baby standing or lying on your side, or be helped to avoid an episiotomy or tear (see pages 186 and 204)?

❑ Would you prefer lots of encouragement or do you hate to be fussed?

❑ Do you want your baby's cord left to pulsate, or your partner to cut the cord?

❑ Would you like your baby delivered into your arms, cleaned and wrapped up first, or given to your partner or your teenage son or daughter to hold?

❑ Do you want to discover your baby's sex for yourself?

❑ Do you mind having students present, or prefer to have only one who is there throughout labour?

❑ If you need a caesarean section under general anaesthetic would you like your partner present, or if this is not possible someone to put your baby to your breast, take photographs or describe the birth afterwards?

❑ If you have a caesarean section under epidural would you like someone to keep chatting to you, or to have a personal stereo with your choice of music?

A birth plan is a letter setting out your wishes. You could discuss them if you know the midwife who will care for you throughout labour, but many women do not. Writing a birth plan can help you to be realistic and to feel more in control even if your plans have to be changed. Make three or four points, wording them flexibly: if you write 'I do not want an epidural', you may not be able to change your mind!

Your baby's position

Labour will be easier if your baby is lying curled up in a ball with her back towards your front (anterior) so that the crown of her head enters your pelvis first. If she lies with her back against yours (posterior) your contractions will have to work to improve her position, often leading to a longer labour. If her head perches on the brim of your pelvis it cannot mould to fit under your pubic arch. Anterior, posterior and breech positions are illustrated on page 218.

When women scrubbed floors on hands and knees and were constantly on the move, as they had little leisure time and no labour-saving devices, most babies settled naturally into an ideal

Help your baby adopt a good position
- Put a couple of pillows on an upright chair and sit with your knees apart. Lean on a table to watch TV, or sit facing the chair back, resting on a pillow.
- Support the small of your back with cushions to tilt your pelvis forward in an easy chair. Avoid crossing your legs, which gives your baby less room to turn.
- Make a virtue of all-fours to pick up toys.
- Use a posture chair where weight rests partly on your knees.
- Make a hollow in a beanbag for your bump and lean forward onto it. Some women find this comfortable for sleeping.
- To encourage a breech (bottom first) baby to turn, lean forward so that your bottom is higher than your chest, supporting your knees and chest on cushions. Relax your stomach muscles and vividly imagine your baby turning head down.

position. Today women often sit at work, drive to the super-market and lean back in an easy chair to relax.

Movement and leaning forward will encourage your baby's spine (her heaviest part) to turn towards your front instead of your back. You can affect her position if you are generally active in the last two months of pregnancy and sit with your pelvis tilted forward, so that your knees are lower than your hips.

Preparing for an easier birth

Anything that reduces tension or helps you to handle pain will make labour easier. You have probably discovered ways of coping with things like headaches or period pain in everyday life, and similar techniques can be helpful during labour. They may not come automatically when you are under stress, however.

Here are some effective self-help methods of pain relief to practise:

Labour positions: Find positions that help you to relax. Try kneeling with your knees apart, leaning onto a bean bag or with your arms around your partner's neck; sit reversed on a kitchen chair resting over a cushion on the back; put a thick towel on the rim of a bucket and sit on it; stand with your legs wide apart and lean onto a table.

In labour: Switch between positions that are as comfortable as possible but also produce strong contractions to dilate your cervix effectively.

Delivery positions: Gravity can help your baby move down the birth canal if you adopt upright positions, such as kneeling or semi-squatting with support from your partner or midwife. When your baby's head is ready to be born, lying on your side with your partner supporting your top leg can make a tear less likely.

Practise with your partner to find comfortable positions. If you give birth semi-reclining on a bed your pelvis cannot open, you cannot tilt your hips back to straighten your birth canal and gravity will increase the pressure of your baby's head on the delicate tissues of your perineum, increasing the chance of tearing.

In labour: Keep your pelvis flexible and try various positions until you get an urge to push.

Relaxation: Relaxing during and between contractions saves energy and helps your cervix dilate, especially useful if labour is slow. Practise relaxing consciously (see page 109) until you are confident you can recognise slight tension and release it at will. Check that your shoulders are loose (pull them down towards your waist and let go so that they spring into a naturally relaxed position) and that your hands and your jaw are not clenched.

In labour: Check that you are relaxed at the start and end of *every* contraction so that tension does not build up.

Visualisation: To help you relax, rehearse a favourite image such as lying on a beach in warm sunshine, letting waves wash over your body taking tension with them. Or visualise each contraction helping to open your cervix smoothly; then visualise your baby moving easily through your birth canal.

In labour: Use the images to help you relax and imagine your labour progressing well.

Distraction and focusing: Plan activities for early labour (baking, writing letters, looking through family photographs, watching a video, listening to music or story tapes). Later on, choose something to focus on such as an image, an object or a sound; or use a task such as counting slowly.

In labour: Take your mind off contractions by keeping busy. As labour progresses focus on your chosen task.

Massage: Ask your partner to practise face, back, shoulder or foot massage to help you relax; try a wooden back massager or practise stroking round under your bump using light pressure until an ache disappears.

In labour: Use massage for distraction or to help you relax in early labour. If you have backache ask your partner to press firmly on your lower back.

Breathing: Notice exactly how you breathe naturally when deeply relaxed so that you can consciously breathe this way in labour. Practise emphasising the 'out' breath and letting air flow naturally into your lungs until it becomes automatic. Pause at the top and bottom of each breath and watch your tummy rise and fall.

In labour: Check that you are relaxed and concentrate on keeping your breathing slow and gentle. Sigh out at the start and end of each contraction.

Practical preparations for the birth

If you intend to have your baby in hospital it is wise to pack your bag about six weeks in advance, as some babies decide to arrive early. You will be given a list of things to take, such as toiletries, sanitary towels and clothes for you and your baby, and you may like to add some things from the checklist on page 182. In hospital or at home the progress of labour is uncertain and it is easier to cope if you are comfortably dressed, not too hot or cold and have refreshments and something to pass the time.

At a home birth everything does not need to be sterile and there is surprisingly little mess or disruption. Your midwife will bring what she requires and ask you to provide simple things like a flat surface for her equipment and a torch or anglepoise lamp. In addition to things for your comfort you may want to

Thoughts about giving birth

Giving birth is challenging. A first birth can be daunting, but it is equally hard to face labour if a previous experience was bad, or you believe you were just lucky last time. One of the secrets of having a positive birth experience lies in the way you think about it. Some women avoid reading or asking questions, decide not to go to antenatal classes and concentrate their preparations for the baby on choosing nursery equipment. This temporarily sidesteps uncomfortable feelings, but the thoughts that produce them can be difficult to suppress, as they keep on surfacing until you deal with them. Here are some ways to handle them:

❑ Face your fears. Every experience is a mixture of good and bad so try not to magnify the negative or focus on what *might* happen.

❑ Take control. Find out the options and decide what *you* prefer.

❑ Share responsibility for the way your birth goes. The staff are not completely in charge, nor is every problem your own fault.

❑ Ask for what you need without taking a refusal personally. A single incident is not likely to happen repeatedly.

❑ Set no 'rules' about how you should or should not give birth. Then you cannot feel guilty if you break them, or upset if other people do.

❑ Find the middle ground: nobody is *either* perfect *or* a failure and no birth is completely awful or completely wonderful.

❑ Remind yourself of all the positive things about giving birth.

obtain plastic sheeting (from a builder's merchant or DIY store) to protect your mattress or carpet, and an extra room heater in winter.

A home birth often has an intimate, celebratory atmosphere. You might like to prepare bulbs, flowers or autumn leaves to brighten your home, or candles or an aromatherapy burner for your bathroom or the birth room. Herb teas or fruit juices, or flavoured ice cubes to suck, are refreshing and snacks or special treats for you, your birth partner, your midwife and anyone else with you will be appreciated.

If you plan to have a water birth at home, or at a hospital without one, the hire company will advise you about siting the pool. If the pool has a soft liner put an old duvet underneath or mould a beanbag into a seat shape before filling it. At home you could set it up well before the birth to enjoy with your family (be vigilant if you have young children of your own or visiting).

You need plenty of towels, a towelling bath robe and a plastic stool to sit on or climb in and out of the pool. Wear a T-shirt (have dry ones to change into as they get chilly when wet) or nothing in the pool. Your partner will be expected to wear a swimsuit if he intends to enter the water. A small sieve is useful for retrieving debris and a rubber ring or plastic-covered foam pillow (inflatable pillows float away or flip out of reach) can be useful for support in the water; an inflatable gymnastic ball (about 26 inches (65 cms) in diameter) is ideal for sitting on outside the pool.

Checklist for labour
- ❑ Cotton nighties/loose T-shirts . . . .
- ❑ Lip salve and massage oil . . . .
- ❑ Ice cubes in a plastic flask . . . .
- ❑ Mineral water to drink, tiny natural sponge to suck . . . .
- ❑ Battery fan/mineral water spray/water-filled plant spray . . . . .
- ❑ Hot water bottle for a hot or cold compress . . . .
- ❑ Personal stereo, music or story tapes . . . .
- ❑ Camera and film . . . .
- ❑ V-shaped back pillow . . . .
- ❑ Beanbag/bucket to sit on (pad the rim with a towel) . . . .

Other items . . . .

Children at the birth

Talk to your midwife if you plan to have children or young people around during labour. If the birth is to take place in hospital you may need permission. You do not need it to have children present at a home birth, but you will want them to feel welcome. Some women prefer to ask a friend or relative to have small children, but many play it by ear as labour often takes place when children are asleep. There should be somebody there other than your birth partner to look after them if they wake up, however, or if labour takes place in the day.

Toddlers tend to take birth in their stride provided you are calm, but they do not understand that you cannot talk during contractions; they may get upset if you fail to answer them. Young children often have practical worries, such as who is going to make their tea! If they are old enough to understand about birth they need careful preparation so that their first experience is positive. Teenagers can feel especially protective towards you, so they need to be told that you are not depending on them for support and there is no pressure for them to be there.

Make life easy around the birth
- ❑ Fill your freezer or store cupboard with the basics for simple meals; buy biscuits for visitors and extra food and basics like soap if relatives are staying.
- ❑ Cut down on shopping by bulk buying things like detergent or pet food.
- ❑ Buy batteries for a cassette recorder, film for a camera, thank you notes to acknowledge gifts, stamps and birth announcement cards.
- ❑ If you have a toddler pack a bag for her if she is going to stay with somebody; write a diary of her day to help whoever looks after her.
- ❑ Arrange for someone to feed any pets while you are in labour.

Birth planner

☐ Find out about the various approaches to birth. Certain things, such as drips and monitors, or epidurals and assisted deliveries, tend to 'go together'.

☐ Discuss the options with your partner and midwife and decide on the basic approach with which you feel comfortable.

☐ Choose where to give birth – it depends on the approach you prefer.

☐ Book early if you and your partner want to attend antenatal classes, especially small classes.

☐ Think about the details that would make birth easier for you and tell your midwife or write a birth plan.

☐ Hire a pool for a water birth.

☐ In the last two months of pregnancy help your baby adopt an anterior position to make labour easier; massage your perineum to help prevent a tear (see page 186) and practise breathing and relaxation skills until you feel confident.

☐ Pack your labour bag and make domestic arrangements in good time.

Older mothers' experiences

Elizabeth (42): 'I want to feel in control and do everything my way as far as possible. My midwife did not volunteer alternatives but when I asked for information she willingly provided it. I've decided to have as natural a birth as possible in hospital, with the security of knowing technology is there if needed. I'm not afraid to challenge assumptions and get what I want from the system. Four weeks before the birth I felt that the midwives at the hospital where I was booked really wanted me to agree to go along with whatever they thought best. I visited another hospital and the staff there seemed much more open so I asked to be transferred.'

Q: I need live-in help for the month after my baby is born as Michael will be away. How do I find a maternity nurse, and what should I look for?

A: Ask friends for a recommendation as names are often passed from family to family, or approach an agency via Yellow Pages so that candidates are screened for you. Alternatively, place an advertisement (or reply to one) in a magazine such as *The Lady*. Interview candidates and take up references.

A maternity nurse often has a background in nursing or midwifery and is likely to have more training or experience with new babies than a college-leaver. She looks after you and your baby but does not do general domestic chores. If you are keen to breastfeed find out what support she could offer if you ran into a problem. Some maternity nurses have firm ideas and will make sure you are well organised by the time they leave; others are more willing to follow your wishes.

Valerie (44): 'Although I've had to make allowances for my back problem, diabetes and emotional traumas I've enjoyed my pregnancy. Barry and my daughters make me feel that having a baby is rather special. Emma and Claire would like to be at the birth, but they are at an age where I want to be sure that they can handle anything they see or hear.

'I expected everyone to be younger than me at antenatal classes but most of the class were in their thirties and two of us were over forty. I feel well prepared this time round. The main thing I worry about is needing stitches, as it spoiled the first few days when Claire was born. Apart from that I'm looking forward to the birth.'

Q: What can I do to avoid an episiotomy or tear this time round?
A: Massage can help avoid damage your perineum (the tissue between your vagina and anus) when it is stretched thinly by your baby's head during delivery. Every night from about 34 weeks, work vitamin E or wheatgerm oil (or any pure vegetable oil) well into the tissue for a few minutes, then stretch it gently until you feel a burning sensation. You may need help if you cannot reach around your bump, but you will soon notice your perineum becoming more supple.

Write on your birth plan or tell your midwife that you hope to manage without needing stitches, and ask her to help. She may suggest lying on your side for the delivery to reduce the effects of gravity when the tissue is very thin, and she will probably ask you to stop pushing and pant as your baby's head is born.

Anne: (47): 'I'm having a water birth at home. My doctor was rather dismissive and put me off at first, but I kept reading, talking to people who had had them and thinking about it. You can easily be frightened off doing something that feels right for you by someone who has little experience of it and is afraid for you.

'I always wanted to have a baby at home. The thought of being in my own surroundings and free to labour in my own way is very appealing. Life has taught me that there is no point setting my heart on something. I accept that at my age I might need to go to hospital during labour, but I feel completely comfortable with the choice I have made.

'My partner has been behaving very strangely and he does not want to be at the birth, so my daughter Sonia will be my birth partner.'

Q: How can a birth partner help?
A: A birth partner should be a willing slave who sees to your every need with patience and good humour. If your baby's father

prefers not to be there your daughter (or a sister or girlfriend) is a good choice. Sharing the birth of your baby is a privilege that neither of you will ever forget.

In the early stages your daughter could keep you company and cheer you up if labour is slow. She could gently massage your face, hair, shoulders, feet or the sore bit under your bump; or fetch you something to eat or drink. Later on she could help you change position or get in and out of the birth pool. She could keep you cool with a fan or a damp flannel, give you sips of water, remind you to relax and breathe gently, help you to focus on something calming, massage your lower back, and offer encouragement if you temporarily lose confidence.

Ask her simply to be there for you, to smile and look confident even if she does not feel it. Tenderness and a consistent, calm presence are much more important than technique.

9 *Labour and Birth*

LABOUR IS CONTROLLED BY YOUR HYPOTHALAMUS, THE PART OF the brain that is thought to handle emotion and instinct, and stress hormones can affect progress as much as the shape of your pelvis or the position of your baby. Like making love, giving birth is possible more or less anywhere, but easier in some situations than others. Oxytocin, which is partly responsible for orgasm as well as the contractions of labour, and endorphins, the body's natural pain killers, are released more readily when you are relaxed and they can be inhibited by disturbance or tension.

Age is irrelevant to giving birth for most women, but a first labour is often slower than later ones and delivery may take slightly longer when you are older. Before labour starts irregular contractions prepare your uterus and thin your cervix, sporadically over a week or continuously for a day or more. The first stage of labour takes place when contractions strengthen to dilate your cervix progressively, taking a few hours or more than a day. The second stage begins when your baby moves down the birth canal and ends with the birth, typically after an hour or two of pushing. The third stage of labour, the arrival of the placenta, completes the birth.

In a normal labour, contractions become regular and your cervix dilates at a consistent rate. Your baby's head fits into your pelvis and her heartbeat is strong and steady. Your blood pressure, temperature and pulse are within standard range and you do not suffer excessive pain.

Research shows that older women have more interventions, such as drips to speed up labour, even in the absence of any complication. Extra attention can be reassuring, but intervention carries risks as well as benefits. You might want to discuss the issues (see Chapter 10) with your consultant, to find out when it would be considered necessary and what the alternatives are.

Going overdue

Arrange some outings and treats for after your due date to make the days special in some way so that you have something to look forward to. Put a message on your answer phone to deal with 'Are you still here?' enquiries.

The duration of pregnancy is influenced by genetic factors such as the length of your menstrual cycle and your race. For example, your baby is more likely to be born a few days late if you have a long cycle, or early if you are black. There is some evidence that the placenta may age slightly faster in older women, so you are more likely to be offered induction (see page 211) if you go overdue. A failing placenta will not nourish a baby as well as a healthy one, but if your cervix is not ready to dilate induction can lead to a more difficult or painful labour, requiring further interventions. Many women are glad to be offered induction and it is justified in some circumstances; in others you get more than you bargained for. Induction was mentioned frequently in the 'I wish I had known' section in a recent survey of about 10,000 readers of *Practical Parenting* magazine.

If your baby is healthy and you prefer to go into labour spontaneously you could ask to be monitored daily. A baby who has a strong heartbeat and is moving as usual is probably doing fine. If you are a couple of weeks overdue or have been given a date to be induced, try breast stimulation or intercourse to encourage the release of contracting hormones. Alternatively, acupuncture may help, or you could try putting about four drops of clary-sage in your bath. This is an essential oil that has oestrogen-like effects and is sometimes used to help to strengthen contractions.

How labour may start

A 'show':
The mucus plug that seals the cervix during pregnancy often comes away when the cervix begins to thin and soften. It is about as big as an almond and may be streaked with old blood. Contractions may not start for a few hours or days. Contact your midwife if there is fresh bleeding; otherwise wait.

The waters break:
It happens to about 15 per cent of women, but rarely in public because when you are standing the baby's head tends to act as a cork, preventing fluid from escaping. Cover your mattress with plastic and wear a sanitary towel if you are concerned. Contact your midwife or hospital as they like to check you.

Contractions:
This is the most common way for labour to start. For a few hours or days, irregular contractions soften and thin your cervix. They may last 20–30 seconds and feel like mild period pains or dull backache. At some point they'll lengthen, strengthen and become more regular. Contact your midwife or the hospital when you feel you need advice or help (see page 192).

What happens in labour

Labour may involve a short burst of intense contractions that are painful but dilate your cervix faster and shorten labour; or a long period of gentle ones that are easier to handle.

Preparatory phase: In the weeks before labour starts you may feel Braxton Hicks contractions: irregular, painless tightenings that make your uterus feel as hard as a football. They help to tone the muscles and may encourage your baby to adopt a favourable position (see page 177). If it is your first baby they may come and go for many hours, only gradually becoming stronger and more regular. With subsequent babies they may come quite strongly night after night, in waves that last a few hours but fade away just as you start to take them seriously.
What to do: Finish tasks you want to complete before the birth but try not to take them too seriously. Get plenty of rest.

Early labour: Contractions become regular and strong. They may feel like period-type cramps, pains in your back or legs, or a tight feeling across your abdomen that restricts your breathing. You may be excited or nervous or not sure what is going on (see page 192).
What to do: You will notice contractions less if you keep occupied, but it may be hard to concentrate on anything for long. Have plenty of activities to help you pass the time: a new tapestry kit, a jigsaw, cooking, videos, a list of friends to phone, cards to address. Listen to music, have a bath by candle light, walk with your partner under the stars. Ask your midwife to visit you at home for reassurance; phone the labour ward if you need advice about when to go to hospital.

Is this labour?

It can be hard to know whether your cervix is still thinning or has started to dilate. Here are some ways to help you decide:

❑ Change your activity – lie down if you were pottering about, go for a walk or have a bath if you were resting. If the contractions continue, this may be labour.

❑ Can you still drink a cup of tea, chat on the phone, laugh at your partner's jokes? If the answers are 'No, no, and I stopped long ago!', this may be labour.

❑ Are your contractions more purposeful than they were half an hour ago? Look for a build-up in their length and strength.

❑ The interval between contractions is less significant: they may come every five minutes all day when your cervix is only thinning out. Labour contractions tend to be regular, last at least 45 seconds and put you under some pressure.

Strong labour: The fiercer the contractions the faster you will dilate. Early labour is like sailing a yacht in a gentle breeze; strong labour is tackling a storm – tough but exhilarating. Your contractions will be noticeably longer and more purposeful and it will take all your concentration to stay calm and relaxed. You may feel powerful and confident, or disheartened and fragile; or so deeply calm that you doze through this phase.

What to do: Darkness or low lighting may help you to relax and act instinctively, or you could use the techniques you have practised (see pages 178–80) to help you cope. They may be sufficient to manage the pain; if not ask for extra pain relief (see pages 198–203). Think about your baby and deal with one contraction at a time; forget about those in the past or still to come.

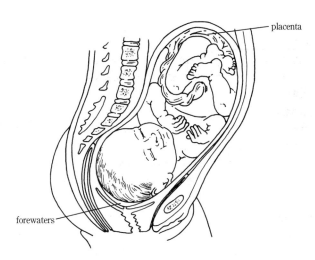

placenta

forewaters

Pre-labour phase. *Before labour begins your contractions draw up your cervix so it becomes shorter and eventually thinner.*

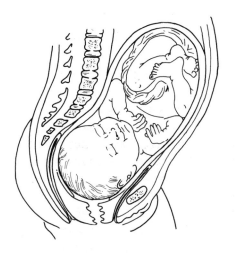

First stage of labour. *Your uterus tips forwards with each contraction as your cervix opens to let your baby into the birth canal.*

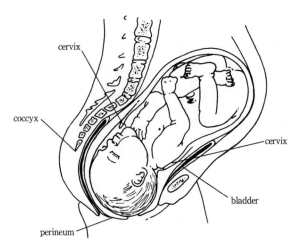

Your baby's head follows the curve of your pelvis, moving your coccyx
(tailbone) aside.

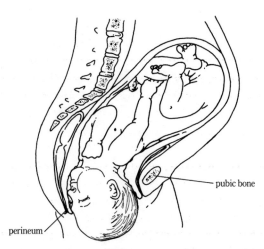

Your baby's head flexes up underneath your pubic arch and emerges,
releasing pressure on your coccyx and perineum. At this point the back
of your baby's head is towards your front and you may be able to
feel her hair.

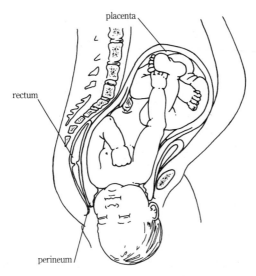

placenta

rectum

perineum

Your baby turns to face your thigh, so that her shoulders fit more easily through your pubic arch and pelvic floor. When her shoulders are born her body tumbles out.

Transition: This short phase, taking a few minutes to over an hour, bridges the first and second stages of labour. You may barely notice it until you feel a strange sensation low down, or your knees buckle under your weight. As the contractions lose their rhythm it can be the last straw, and you may get angry or distressed.

What to do: Tell your midwife who will examine you to check if you are ready to push. If there is a rim of cervix still to dilate, kneel with your bottom in the air to take pressure away and ask for gas and air to help stop you pushing. If you are fully dilated but feel no urge to push get in an upright position and wait for gravity to help your baby move further down the birth canal. Shout if it helps.

The birth: The baby's head feels like an orange moving down your birth canal and the pushing reflex is triggered when it stretches the muscles of your pelvic floor. You may get a burning sensation as the head is about to be delivered.

What to do: Many women instinctively give several small pushes during each contraction and breathe out as they bear down. You may need to try various positions before the urge to push becomes overwhelming. Arch your back and release your pelvic floor so that you 'give' birth. Be patient; it is rarely necessary to hold your breath and strain. Push towards the burning sensation as it will go numb as your baby's head is born. Pant lightly when your midwife tells you to.

The delivery of the placenta: If you have an injection the placenta will arrive within about ten minutes (see page 209). It may take half to one hour to arrive naturally. Compared with the baby's head it feels as soft as a blancmange.

What to do: Enjoy cuddling or breastfeeding your baby. When the placenta has separated from the wall of your uterus your midwife will ask you to push it out.

Giving birth in hospital

Typically, when you go into hospital you and your partner are given a single room and introduced to your midwife, who tests your urine, takes your temperature and blood pressure, feels your baby's position and examines you to check how far dilated you are. Your baby's normal heartbeat may be recorded using a fetal heart monitor for 20 minutes. The delicate hormones that control labour can be disturbed by moving to hospital in early labour, but when you feel at ease they will flow again.

If you are not yet dilating you could ask to go home or stay fully dressed and walk around or visit the hospital café to pass the time. Otherwise, change into something comfortable for labour; there will be a trolley for your clothes and bags. Your midwife will examine you and listen to your baby's heartbeat every so often and you can call her if you need anything. Routines and protocols about things like fetal monitoring, when you may enter a birth pool or when to speed up labour with a drip vary considerably. You may be left to your own devices most of the time, but if you feel uncomfortable with the midwife assigned to you, your partner could ask the sister in charge if someone else may care for you.

When you are ready to push your midwife will stay with you in the labour room or move you to a delivery room and a second midwife will usually help deliver your baby. You can have a cup of tea, cuddle or breastfeed your new baby and be washed or have a bath, before being transferred to a postnatal ward.

Giving birth at home

Home births tend to be relaxed and easy-going; there are fewer routines as your midwife uses her experience to monitor you individually. When you think labour has begun she will come to your home to check you. She may make other calls, leaving you with a number on which to contact her. Once you are in labour she will stay with you, or in another room if you prefer. You can do whatever you like to help you cope, but TENS, gas and air or pethidine are available should you need them.

When you are nearly ready to push, your GP or another midwife will usually come to help. Some midwives prefer to give an injection to bring the placenta away quickly, but others are happy to deliver it naturally. Afterwards you might have a bath with your baby while your midwife clears up. She will leave a number for you to contact her (or a colleague) on for advice at any time, day or night. After a few hours, or next day, she will check you and your baby and then visit as often as necessary.

Labour pain

Labour pain is caused by many things, including pressure on the sensitive membranes that coat your pelvic bones and stretching of resistant muscle fibres. Your expectations and frame of mind influence how you perceive it, however. The brain responds to pain by releasing morphine-like substances (endorphins and enkephalins) to dull sensation and block the nerve fibres, so that they transmit fewer impulses. If you are tense you release stress hormones, which stop your labour to allow you time to relax.

Older women often have experience of coping with pain and manage a normal labour with self-help or alternative therapies, using drugs only if there is complication or a combination of adverse factors. Breathing, relaxation, massage, comfortable positions, visualisation and focusing (see page 179) can be effective ways of handling moderate labour pain. Changes of temperature can block pain messages: fill a hot water bottle with hot or cold water for a compress, wrap a packet of peas or a frozen gel pack in kitchen foil for travelling or ask your hospital to supply ice; trickle cold water over your back or tummy in a birth pool or bath (block the overflow with Blu-tack to make the water deeper). Alternate changes of temperature with massage to sustain the pain relief.

You may prefer to try simple remedies first, keeping stronger options in reserve; or you may feel that there is no point in suffering pain when powerful drugs are available to relieve it, although they may have side-effects for you or your baby.

Alternative therapies for labour pain

Here is a brief guide to some alternative therapies to make labour easier or help you to cope with pain. Some therapies are powerful or have individual effects; the Health Information Service (see *Directory*) can help you find a qualified practitioner.

Acupuncture or acupressure: Special points are stimulated by fine needles or pressure, to free the flow of energy along invisible channels under your skin. During labour, points in your ear, leg or foot are stimulated with needles attached to a device like a TENS machine; or electrodes are attached with sticky pads to points on your leg. After about 20 minutes you may feel relaxed and sleepy.

Aromatherapy: Essential plant oils are massaged into your skin and absorbed into your bloodstream, affecting your nervous and hormone systems. Oils can also be added to a bath, inhaled (try five drops in a room burner) or used in a water spray or compress. For example, geranium or lavender oils help to calm and relax you; neroli can reduce anxiety. Use five drops in two tablespoons of a carrier such as almond oil for massage, or stir four to six drops into a warm bath. Some oils are not suitable for labour, so check first.

Homeopathy: A tiny amount of a substance that causes a symptom can also cure it. For example, caulophyllum tones your uterus; arnica heals bruising; gelsemium, pulsatilla and arsenicum album help fear and anxiety. The stronger the potency the higher the number (6th potency is taken hourly and 30th three hourly, repeating the dose up to six times – healing is triggered when you feel a change). Strong scents or flavours, such as massage oils, peppermint or coffee, may inactivate the remedies.

Hypnosis: You relax deeply until you enter a state of trance where your mind accepts positive suggestions. For instance, you imagine your hand is dipped in ice-cold water until it's numb, and that you can transfer the numbness to any part of your body by touch (glove anaesthesia). In labour your therapist puts you into a trance, or you do this yourself, perhaps using a tape made specially for you.

Medical herbalism uses all the bark or leaves of a plant because the 'active ingredient' is modified by the other substances it contains. For example, raspberry leaf tea can help to soften ligaments: buy tea bags from a health shop and infuse them for 10–15 minutes.

Other forms of pain relief

If self-help or alternative remedies are not sufficient to help you cope with pain you could try one of these.

Gas and air (Entonox): The mixture of nitrous oxide and oxygen, inhaled through a mask or mouthpiece, makes you feel suddenly 'lightheaded'. It can be used in a bath or birth pool and may help you resist pushing urges before you're fully dilated. It has little effect on your baby as it is exhaled almost immediately, and you can stop using it if you dislike the feeling. It may cause nausea or a dry mouth, however, and it does not help everyone. If used in the second stage of labour it can prevent you pushing effectively.

Getting the best out of it: Timing is important: it takes 30 seconds to act so start *to inhale slowly and deeply as soon as you feel a contraction coming.* You will automatically relax so that you do not take too much.

TENS (transcutaneous electrical nerve stimulation):
This sends mild pins and needles through four pads taped to your back. You can vary the pulse frequency, or make it continuous. It does not affect your baby and you can remove it if you find the sensation irritating. It cannot be used in a bath or birth pool.
Getting the best out of it: Follow the instructions carefully so that you position the pads correctly and put it on in early labour as it helps release endorphins, or use it later on as it blocks pain messages at higher frequencies.

Pethidine: This injection relaxes you and distances you from pain for two to four hours, and labour may progress faster, or occasionally slow down. You may feel sick or drowsy and cannot change your mind if you dislike its effect. It can affect the baby's breathing and sucking reflex (a few need an antidote or are sleepy and difficult to feed for several days) so you should be examined just before having it, *especially if it is not your first baby*, as you may have dilated quicker than expected.
Getting the best out of it: A standard dose has more effect if you are petite, vegetarian or generally respond strongly to drugs. It tends to sustain your mood so it may be better to have a small dose when you need it rather than to wait until you are struggling.

Epidural: An anaesthetist has to be available throughout, and local anaesthetic is injected into the space around your spinal cord to numb your abdomen. A fine tube is left in your back for topping up and you have a catheter if bladder sensation is lost and a drip in case fluids are needed. A combination of drugs, or an epidural and a spinal block (placed lower down your back) may be used to give you greater mobility to change your position, but you may not be able to move away from the bed and mobile epidurals have the same side-effects as conventional epidurals.

Epidurals help severe pain; they work better than pethidine for backache, let you rest if labour is long and stop the urge to push too soon if your baby is breech (see pages 217–19). Pain relief is sometimes incomplete, however, and they may lower your blood pressure too much or raise your temperature so that you need to be sponged down. Just under 1 per cent of women get a bad headache afterwards (most get better within ten days). Labour may be accelerated and an episiotomy, assisted delivery or caesarean section (see Chapter 10) are more likely. Some women complain of long-term backache, possibly because they gave birth on their back, and there are occasional reports of complications such as nerve damage.

Getting the best out of it: While it's administered, curl up on your side or sitting, and remain very still. Tell the staff if pain relief is uneven. Forget any reservations about an epidural if you suffer severe pain – circumstances alter cases.

Choosing pain relief

Your choice will depend on local availability and your preference. Self-help, alternative therapies, gas and air and TENS help relieve pain that is moderate, or severe for a short time, such as when you are too close to giving birth for pethidine. Self-help techniques often need practice or preparation and they do not eliminate pain, but they can be used in sequence or combination, have few side-effects, reduce your need for drugs and can be abandoned at any time.

Pethidine or an epidural help severe pain, or moderate pain that continues for a long time. Just as you know if you need paracetamol for a headache, you will know if the pain you feel requires their help. Pethidine may not eliminate pain, but a small dose is likely to have little effect on your baby and is preferable to repeated large doses. An epidural is excellent for severe pain.

Both methods carry small risks and side-effects, but if labour is difficult the benefits generally outweigh these.

Different patterns of labour

In 1963 prolonged labour was defined as lasting over 36 hours. By 1968 this had been reduced to 24 hours and by 1972 to only 12 hours. Nature probably does not intend all women to give birth quickly and those who labour slowly do not always have a problem. Labour patterns differ, just as some athletes can sprint and others run marathons. Here are some ways to cope:

Fast labour: This feels like being caught in a current and swept downstream. You cannot control it and resisting makes it harder. If you let it happen the ride can be almost exhilarating. Focus on relaxing your shoulders and jaw.

Slow labour: Easy at first but tough towards the end when you are getting tired, this requires stamina. It is more comfortable if you are well prepared and you pace yourself. Movement can shift your baby's head slightly and improve progress: try rocking or rotating your pelvis, lifting each leg as though walking in long grass, climbing stairs sideways or raising one hip and then the other by placing your foot on a stool. A slow labour can be especially disheartening in hospital when there is little to take your mind off it and pressure to agree to acceleration (see pages 211–13).

Stop–Go labour: You need patience as this sort of labour can be frustrating and disappointing. Sleep or at least rest if you can. Movement or changes of position may help, but if labour slows down after it is established there is some evidence that a drip to speed it up (and an epidural if necessary) can be beneficial.

Back labour: Some women feel all their contractions in their back. Try a cold compress, a hot water bottle (you will tolerate extremes of temperature so protect your skin), or pressure such as firm massage, or pressing your back against a wall with something hard such as an aerosol can wrapped in a towel against the spot that aches. An epidural may help severe backache.

Avoiding an episiotomy or tear

Many women prefer a small tear which tends to heal easily and may not even need stitches, to an episiotomy (a cut made in the outlet to the birth canal), although this is preferable to a large tear that damages the muscles around the anus. If your baby is distressed or arrives rapidly it may not be possible to avoid damage to your perineum (tissue between the vagina and the anus), but older mothers tend to have more elastic skin and you can improve your chances of avoiding damage still further by massage (see page 186).

Injury to such a delicate area sounds alarming, but you feel nothing at the time as the tissue is stretched. For an episiotomy, local anaesthetic may be injected or it may be performed at the height of a contraction when the tissue is numb. Pain relief given for an assisted delivery (see page 213) is also adequate. Ideally, any stitches necessary should be inserted immediately after delivery while the tissue is still numb. A few could be done without anaesthetic if you dislike the sensation of it wearing off, but if time has elapsed or a longer repair is needed local anaesthetic is given. It may sting, but if stitching hurts ask for more or for gas and air.

Coping with discomfort if you have stitches

❑ Any infection will delay healing so be scrupulous about hygiene.

❑ Bathe your stitches with cold water, or use an ice pack wrapped in a clean towel or the homeopathic remedy arnica to help reduce swelling. Gentle pelvic floor exercises (see page 92) soon after the birth help disperse swelling.

❑ Hold a clean sanitary pad over your stitches to support them when using the toilet. Some women stand in the shower to pass urine so that the flow stings less. Wash afterwards and dab your perineum dry with soft tissue.

❑ Stuff one leg of a pair of old tights with something soft and tie it into a ring to make a pad to sit on.

After the birth

Some newborn babies look grey or blue or bruised from negotiating the pelvis, but their appearance usually improves rapidly over a few hours or days. Your midwife will assess your baby's condition using the Apgar score, awarding points for measures such as breathing and muscle tone. A score of seven to ten is normal; the assessment is repeated five minutes later and lower scores often improve, but if it is still under seven your baby will be watched carefully for a while. A few babies need special care but most recover well.

Bonding is the process of falling in love that enables you to put the needs of your baby before your own. You and your partner may be euphoric after the birth and love your baby straight away, but equally you may be relieved that the birth is over and proud of your achievement but curiously disinterested in your baby.

Babies have a period of alertness and a strong sucking reflex shortly after birth, so holding and feeding your baby makes bonding easier, but it is not something to worry about unduly.

Like falling in love, it may happen instantly or over a period of time. Most parents get there in the end.

A day or so after giving birth you may feel sore and bruised or have a sense of anticlimax. Afterpains, the contractions that shrink your uterus to its normal size, can be painfully strong, especially when you breastfeed or if it is not your first baby. They help release the lochia, a discharge like a heavy period with small clots that lasts from two to six weeks (and sometimes longer), tailing off progressively until it becomes pink or brownish.

Spend some time lying on your tummy with a pillow under your hips each day, however. This will encourage your uterus to tip forward as it settles in your pelvis, so that it is supported by your pubic bone. If you have your baby in hospital and everything is normal you usually go home 6–48 hours after the birth.

Early breast feeds

Your midwife will help you to breastfeed shortly after the birth but if your baby is not interested there is plenty of time. Here are some tips to get you started:

❑ After the birth lie back with your baby resting flat on your tummy, slightly below your breast. Let her wriggle up towards your nipple and nuzzle it; she may open her mouth wide and latch on perfectly.

❑ When you sit up in bed, put a pillow over your knees. Rest your baby with her legs along the pillow and one cheek on your wrist, so that she faces your chest.

❑ Be patient and let her nuzzle your nipple. When she opens her mouth really wide (the 'gape') cup your other hand round the back of her head and guide it quickly towards you, so that she grasps a good mouthful of breast tissue.

❑ To check she is latched on, watch her ear wiggle or her jawbone move. If necessary, break her suction with the corner of your little finger and try again.

Older mothers' experiences

Elizabeth (42): 'Labour was better than I expected. The contractions started like mild period pain in the cervix area and got stronger until it felt like being put in a clamp with a vice-like grip. Breathing helped at first as it gave me something to focus on. At about five centimetres dilated I got disheartened and had a small shot of pethidine which made me feel as though I was floating above the contractions. It didn't take the edge off the pain but made me relax and doze between them, giving me strength for the next one as they came thick and fast. When I was ready to push I suddenly lost confidence again and felt afraid.

'I saw my life change before me and wasn't sure I really wanted a baby! Apart from that moment I always felt in control and the pain wasn't unbearable at any stage. When I held Jessica she was brand new and I felt like a queen.'

Q: How can I recover from the birth as fast as possible?
A: As you were fit and healthy before the birth and had a straightforward delivery you are likely to recover fairly quickly, but it would be unrealistic to expect too much of yourself too soon. In the first month get as much rest as possible, so that you can cope with the progressive effects of disturbed sleep.

Gentle postnatal exercises will help you to get your figure back and your pelvic floor to return to normal. You may have been shown some at the hospital, or you could get a book or a video. When you are older you tend to listen to your body more, and although you may get tired you may also be content to live at a slower pace and learn about Jessica's needs without pushing yourself. Give yourself up to a year to get fit again.

Sue (39): 'When Jack was born my labour started slowly so it was easier to cope. The contractions came and went and I felt perfectly normal between them. I thought of labour as a job to be accomplished and tried to be positive, reminding myself that my uterus was working powerfully as it should. I made myself breathe calmly and relax with each contraction, which is easier when you're more mature and realistic. I felt my mind was free to handle labour in whatever way seemed right. I knew my midwife would make sure the baby was safe.

'Most women underestimate the amount of pain involved in labour, but my body took over and got on with giving birth. Afterwards I was surprised that I never thought about pain relief. This time I know what to expect and I know I can cope with the pain. I'm more worried about not getting to hospital in time.'

Q: What should my husband do if he has to deliver our baby?
A: If you think there is no time to get to hospital phone for help rather than end up delivering on the back seat of the car. Assume that the birth will be normal and that only common sense is required. Kenneth should stay and reassure you when the baby is coming, but if there is time he could put something soft on the floor, and get a duvet to put around you and the baby to keep you warm. A newborn baby is wet and slippery and needs to be held firmly.

Some babies are shocked or collect mucus from the birth canal as they arrive, but most recover quickly and breathe without problems. Kenneth could wipe mucus from the baby's mouth but he should leave the cord as it will pulsate for several minutes to provide a dual breathing system. As soon as the baby is breathing he can phone for help if there was no time before the birth. A doctor or midwife will come immediately to see to the cord and placenta.

Anne (47): 'Everything is ready for the birth and Sonia can come at any time. I've hired a birth pool and put a line of candles on the sideboard. Each evening I light them and swish around in warm water for an hour or so. On land I'm awkward and heavy, but in the water I feel light and free. I chose a water birth at home because it is as 'low tech' as you can get and I worry about intervention, but I know my midwife will suggest transfer to hospital if she thinks intervention may become necessary.

'Sonia was born three weeks early but I'm ten days overdue this time. It's hard to handle well-meaning enquiries when I'm pretty fed up with waiting myself. I feel like a conjurer who can't do her tricks! My midwife comes every day to monitor me and my cervix is soft and slightly dilated, so we'll try to start labour off tomorrow using a recipe that's said to be effective: 50 ml of castor oil mixed with six squeezed oranges and a tablespoon of sugar. I can't wait!'

Q: What are the advantages of letting the placenta come away naturally instead of having an injection to bring it away quickly?
A: An injection will usually bring the placenta away within five to ten minutes and may reduce the risk of serious bleeding after the birth. The cord has to be clamped and cut immediately, however, because as the uterus contracts strongly in response to the drug it could pump too much blood into the baby. The placenta is usually delivered by controlled cord traction: the midwife puts a hand on your abdomen and carefully delivers the placenta before the cervix closes, using the cord.

If labour has been normal and your midwife is experienced and confident about delivering the placenta naturally you may prefer this. The cord is left to pulsate and the baby gets a useful amount of extra blood, but not too much as the jelly-like substance within the cord swells up and the blood supply is gradually cut off. The placenta usually arrives within 15–30 minutes but occasionally takes longer. If you appear to be bleeding more than expected you can be given an injection to make your uterus contract at any time after your baby has arrived. Do discuss the pros and cons of each approach with your midwife.

10   *Interventions and Special Births*

LABOUR IS NOT ESPECIALLY RISKY FOR WOMEN OVER 35 BUT THEY have more interventions, partly because they are more likely to have breech or multiple births and pre-existing illness that leads to complications. Research also shows that they have interventions that would not be considered necessary for someone younger. Perhaps this reflects unwarranted anxiety associated with age.

Technology is not something either to fear or to welcome uncritically. It often benefits small and premature babies; it may assist an individual but it does not improve overall outcomes for healthy women with normal labours. Most hospitals say they only intervene when essential, but what is essential is a matter of opinion.

If you and your baby are healthy and your baby is ready to be born intervention should not be routine as it is rarely the only option. In some cases it helps to ensure safety but in others the benefits are less certain: setting up a drip can shorten labour but could also cause a baby to become distressed, for instance. Both you and your doctor have to live with the consequences of any decisions made.

Unless you are very confident and assertive, you will only exercise choice within the limits 'allowed' by the staff in hospital. People choose to do many things in life that are not essential and that carry risks. Some doctors, midwives and mothers feel safer using technology during labour 'just in case'; others prefer to avoid it except in serious circumstances, as it may solve one problem only to cause a different one. Harmful repercussions from the overuse of technology do occur, but like unforeseen complications in an otherwise straightforward labour, they are rare.

If you have thought about the issues surrounding intervention you are less likely to get any unpleasant surprises. You do not have to be an expert; all you need is an overview and enough confidence to ask questions; older mothers tend to have this. Except in an emergency when there might not be time, intervention should always be discussed and your feelings taken into account.

Help during labour

When intervention seems necessary it alters your view of it. Nobody knows in advance how their labour will progress and you might change your mind at the time or be glad of it because a complication arises. You can always query why it has been suggested, or ask 'will my baby be safe if I do not have this?'

Induction: Between 10 and 30 per cent of women have labour started off artificially. Labour is not always longer or more painful, although it may be if you have to be induced before your uterus and cervix are ready because you or your baby are at risk; for example, if your baby is not growing well.

Other factors being equal, induction is more likely to be suggested when you are over 35 but it may not be essential for your sake or your baby's. Some hospitals have a routine policy, regardless of individual need. Some doctors induce all older mothers around their due date; others allow a couple of weeks while monitoring the baby frequently. Induction may also be offered if you have had a difficult labour previously, your baby is lying in an awkward position or you are overdue, but it is usually open to discussion.

Hospitals differ, but typically you are admitted the day before induction is planned. The midwife checks to see if your cervix is soft and if not she inserts a prostaglandin pessary or some gel to ripen it. One dose may be enough if you are overdue, but more than one may be necessary if your cervix is not ready for labour. A hormone drip may be set up to stimulate contractions (this remains until after the birth) and your waters may be broken using an instrument rather like a plastic crochet hook. This is painless, but the internal examination may be uncomfortable.

Most babies cope well with induction, but you will be monitored by electrodes attached to soft elastic belts around your abdomen or by a scalp electrode attached to your baby's head by a clip or tiny suction cup.

Active management: Length of labour is not linked to age but some women are encouraged to have labour speeded up because that is hospital policy. Labour starts naturally, and then the

---

Coping with induction or active management

❑ Prostaglandin pessaries or gel can produce colicky 'hormone' pains, but these should pass when the true contractions begin. Ask for pain relief if necessary.

❑ If a drip makes your contractions so strong that they are hard to cope with, ask whether it can be turned down a little.

❑ A belt monitor is less invasive than a scalp electrode although it restricts your freedom to move. You could overcome this if you change position every half hour or so; ask the midwife to reposition the monitor.

process is similar to induction: your progress is checked every two to four hours and the drip is increased until your cervix dilates at a prescribed rate. It is important that your midwife is sure you really are in labour, as some women dilate slowly to three or four centimetres, when the contractions strengthen naturally and progress increases rapidly.

If progress remains slow once you are in strong labour, or your waters have broken, active management can avoid a prolonged labour with its increased risk of infection and caesarean section. On average, however, it reduces the length of labour by less than an hour and if the drip fails to dilate your cervix effectively or the baby becomes distressed a caesarean section is needed.

Assisted delivery: Forceps and ventouse are used to turn the baby's head so that it fits under your pubic arch, or to prevent it sliding back after a contraction so that the baby makes progress with each push. When a baby is breech or premature they can control the speed of the delivery so that it is neither too fast nor too slow.

Forceps are shaped like salad servers to fit around a baby's head and a ventouse, which is becoming increasingly popular, is a small suction cap. The choice depends on the circumstances and what the doctor feels confident using.

You may have an epidural, a spinal block (placed lower down your back) or possibly a pudendal block (local anaesthetic injected into the vagina) for pain relief. Usually an episiotomy is performed to give extra room. Your baby may be born with marks from forceps or a swelling where a ventouse cup was applied, but these usually fade rapidly. If it is thought the baby might be at any risk, caesarean section is performed instead of an assisted delivery.

Bleeding after the birth: Your midwife may give you an injection or tablet to bring the placenta away within about ten minutes

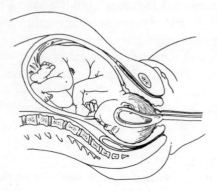

Forceps. *Without causing damage, forceps hold the baby's head securely so that the doctor can turn it slightly or stop it from slipping back in the birth canal.*

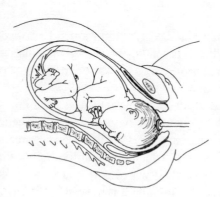

Ventouse. *A ventouse or vacuum extractor looks like a shallow cup. It fits onto the crown of the baby's head and is held securely in place by suction. A forceps or ventouse delivery can make a difficult birth easier.*

(see page 209). In about 3 per cent of births the placenta fails to come away, partially or completely. A retained placenta stops your uterus from shrinking and can lead to excessive bleeding. It is more common if it has happened at a preceding birth, or if you have had a previous caesarean section, as your uterus has scar tissue. The placenta is gently removed under general anaesthetic.

Heavy bleeding that is difficult to stop is rare and unlikely to be life-threatening if treated promptly. Although it is associated with conditions that are more common when you are older, such as multiple births or fibroids, the cause is more likely to be a long labour or difficult delivery. Abdominal massage or drugs usually help your uterus to contract. If further measures are needed a drip for fluids can be set up or a blood transfusion arranged. Occasionally the uterus has to be packed with gauze, and very rarely, if all else fails, a hysterectomy is necessary.

Pre-term labour

Overall 7 to 10 per cent of births occur before the 37th week of pregnancy. About half have a known risk for premature labour, such as drink or drug abuse, poor nutrition, housing or financial problems, stressful travel or work, physical trauma, multiple birth, placental problems, vaginal infection, fibroids, illnesses such as diabetes or pre-eclampsia, or a maternal family history of prematurity. When obstetric history, smoking and pre-pregnancy health are taken into account, older mothers are at no greater risk of pre-term labour.

The first problem a premature baby faces is breathing. Immature lungs lack surfactant, a chemical that helps keep them inflated, but new drugs and technology mean that even babies who arrive four months early have a chance of survival. With good care about 70 per cent who are born at 28 weeks grow up with no problems.

If you think you might be going into labour early lie down for an hour; call your midwife if you get four or more contractions. In hospital it may be possible to stop your contractions with drugs to give your baby (or babies) extra time to grow and mature, or you may be given steroids to help mature your baby's lungs if pre-term birth seems inevitable. It has been suggested that dehydration may contribute to falling blood volume and pre-term labour for a few women, so drinking a glass or two of water is a simple remedy worth trying, but do not delay seeking medical help if you have any of these symptoms:

❑   low, cramp-like pains with or without nausea, diarrhoea or indigestion.

❑   low backache that is persistent or rhythmical, or a change in backache.

❑   a vaginal discharge that is pinkish or streaked with blood.

❑   a trickle of fluid so that your pants are repeatedly damp and your waters may be leaking, or a gush suggesting that they have broken.

❑   an intuitive feeling that something is wrong.

Multiple birth

Maturity at birth is the single most important factor influencing a baby's health, and pre-term labour is ten times more common when you are expecting more than one baby. The uterus is so stretched that some women do not feel the contractions that may signal it, but for some reason extra support from your midwife if you are expecting more than one baby appears to help avoid premature birth.

About half of all twins and three-quarters of triplets are born before the 37th week of pregnancy. The same proportions (but only about 10 per cent of single babies) weigh less than 2,500 g, the international definition of low birth weight.

You are more likely to carry your babies to term if you are well nourished and have no risk factors for prematurity. Increasing the amount of food you eat may give you more energy, and plenty of rest benefits all mothers towards the end of pregnancy. It can ease the discomfort when you are carrying more than one baby and make extra calories available to help growth.

Aim to lie down or at least put your feet up for an hour, two or three times a day. There is no evidence that bed rest makes any difference if you are expecting twins, but if you are carrying triplets or more, or your cervix has started to dilate early, it may help avoid pre-term labour.

Labour tends to be slightly shorter with twins, and many deliveries are straightforward. Each baby is likely to be monitored and extra staff will be present when the babies are born, including one or more paediatricians. The second twin usually arrives within about 20 minutes of the first. More than two babies may be delivered by caesarean section, but some doctors feel vaginal delivery is easier as they tend to be smaller.

When there is more than one baby, however, there is more than one set of circumstances. Depending on how the babies are lying, and how they cope with labour, there could be a mixture of normal and assisted deliveries, or even a vaginal delivery and a caesarean section.

Breech birth

Most babies settle head down before birth but 3–4 per cent are in a breech or bottom down position. Women with large families (who tend to be older) are more likely to have a breech baby, and one study suggests that, compared with younger women, more than twice as many first babies born to women over 35 are breech.

YOUR BABY'S POSITION

Vertex (head down) presentations

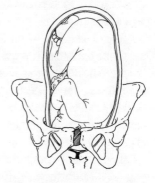

Posterior *where the baby faces the mother's abdominal wall*

Anterior *where the baby faces the mother's spine. This is the commonest presentation*

Breech (bottom down) presentations

Full breech *presentation where the thighs are flexed against the body and the knees are bent.*

Frank breech *where the thighs are flexed but the legs are pointed upwards.*

Some doctors attempt to turn the baby (external version) just before birth, using drugs to relax your uterus. This is successful in about 80 per cent of cases and reduces the caesarean section rate by half.

If you have delivered a previous baby easily the size and position of this baby could be checked at 38 to 40 weeks by scan, although the margin allowed for error can mean that a baby judged to be large is actually quite small. Generally, a well curled up baby can be safely delivered bottom first if the mother's pelvis is adequate and the doctor is experienced and confident. Older women are often encouraged to have an elective caesarean section at about 38 weeks, however. If there is a problem with your pelvis or your baby is lying awkwardly as well as bottom down this option might be safest.

For a vaginal breech delivery, blood is taken for cross matching and a drip is inserted in your arm, to save precious moments in an emergency. You may have more internal examinations, to check that your cervix is fully open before you push, so that the baby's head passes through it easily. Some doctors suggest an epidural for a breech birth, to help reduce the urge to push too soon; taking gas and air or kneeling with your hips in the air can also be effective. Pressure (not distress) may cause your baby to pass meconium, the tarry substance from his intestines.

A breech delivery is usually conducted by a registrar, a doctor specialising in obstetrics. Some are confident enough to deliver you in any position, but most like you to lie on your back with your legs in stirrups. You may have an episiotomy, and your baby's head may be delivered with forceps or the doctor may use his or her hands to keep the head well flexed.

Caesarean section

In Britain about one baby in six is born by caesarean section. You may want to ask the hospitals in your area for their latest figures. The rate is higher for women over 35, as you might expect, because they have more factors like illness or twins. When there are no complications older women are still twice as likely to have a caesarean birth. This reflects the judgment of individual obstetricians and some are ultra-cautious. A caesarean birth is not an easy option for a mother, however; if there are no complications vaginal delivery is both safer and easier to recover from.

An elective caesarean is planned in advance to avoid a complication during labour. For example, you might have pre-eclampsia, diabetes, low-lying fibroids, heart or kidney disease, placenta or cord problems or previous surgery to repair your vagina. The pelvis and the baby tend to adapt well to each other during labour so it is not possible to say there will be disproportion between the two in advance, but an elective caesarean can avoid the uncertainty of normal labour if a baby is premature or very small; or if you have lost a baby previously or had extensive fertility treatment.

Even when pregnancy has been normal a baby might show signs of stress, or contractions might be long and strong without dilating the cervix. If there is an unexpected problem, an emergency (not pre-planned) caesarean section can ensure that you and your baby come through safely. Dire emergencies are rare, however; there is usually plenty of warning and no cause for panic, although it is good practice to carry out a caesarean section within about half an hour of deciding that it is necessary.

An elective caesarean can be performed under local anaesthetic and, except in a crisis, so can an emergency caesarean. You feel sensation but no pain and are awake to welcome your baby; your partner can be there, and you avoid the small risks associated with general anaesthetic. An epidural is deeper than it would be for labour and it can be topped up. A spinal block is sometimes used instead; this is inserted further down your spine than an epidural and can be set up more rapidly but it cannot be topped up. General anaesthetic is given in a crisis where speed is essential, if an operation under spinal block takes longer than expected, if you prefer it or if you simply change your mind about being awake.

The operation: For an elective caesarean you may go into hospital the previous day to meet the surgeon, anaesthetist and paediatrician and for the staff to make routine health checks.

Before the operation you remove jewellery (tape can be put round your wedding ring) contact lenses, make-up and nail polish (so that your colour is visible during the operation) and put on a cotton gown. You may be given something to neutralise stomach acid, the top part of your pubic hair is shaved and a catheter may be inserted to keep your bladder empty. A drip is set up for intravenous fluids, a blood pressure cuff is put on to your arm and electrodes are taped to your chest to monitor your heart and pulse. A diathermy plate (part of the equipment used to control bleeding) may be strapped to your leg.

For an epidural you may have elastic stockings to help maintain your blood pressure, and a frame with sterile drapes is placed across your chest to block your view. The anaesthetist makes sure you are numb before the operation starts. For a general anaesthetic you breathe oxygen from a mask and have an injection of a light anaesthetic to cover the few minutes it takes to deliver your baby, and a deeper one for stitching the wound, which takes about 45 minutes. As you drift off to sleep a narrow tube is passed into your windpipe and the midwife presses gently on your throat to stop anything going down the wrong way.

Afterwards: Most babies are fine, but some need help to breathe or special care for the same reason that the operation was required. Women vary, but pain can be severe at first. It may be controlled by injection or epidural top-up, by PCA (patient controlled analgesia) where you give yourself pain relief via a machine that stops overdoses or by TENS and self-help such as breathing techniques. You may have injections to help prevent deep vein thrombosis (DVT or blood clots in the leg) and suppositories or tablets to help reduce inflammation. After a few days paracetamol may be sufficient.

Breastfeeding may take patience as you will have a sore scar. Ask for help to find a good position: lie your baby on a soft pillow over the scar, or tuck her legs under your arm; or lie on your side with the baby beside you, for example. Bonding is likely to be the same as after a normal birth.

Physically most women feel wobbly at first and need help to lift, feed and care for their baby. If you are healthy, recovery after caesarean section is likely to be rapid, although you may run out of energy quickly. You usually leave hospital in less than a week but will be advised to avoid lifting, tasks that pull

Caesarean birth – tips for coping

In Hospital: Slip on shoes and slippers to avoid bending; wire coat hanger to retrieve things from the floor; footstool to get on and off a high bed; waist-high or G-string pants to avoid the scar; fennel or peppermint tea for wind; high fibre food to avoid constipation; cushion to protect the scar from the seat-belt on the way home.

At Home: Soothe an itchy scar with baby lotion kept in the fridge; wear loose clothing with pockets to carry things; keep sleeping and nappy changing equipment upstairs and downstairs to save journeys; change nappies on a waist-high table or chest of drawers; use a Thermos flask and have a drink and snack beside you before starting to breastfeed, to keep up your energy.

General: Delegate as much as possible; never refuse any help; an extra pair of hands for a few weeks could be well worth the cost, especially if you have other children to look after.

on the scar, and driving (as you may not be up to coping in an emergency) for four to six weeks.

Special care baby unit

A baby who needs extra attention after the birth, perhaps because of low birth weight, prematurity, a disability or a difficult delivery, usually spends time in SCBU (special care baby unit). Depending on the problem a baby may receive special or intensive care for a few hours or days, or for several weeks. If more specialised care is needed a transfer to another centre may be arranged, and you may be able to go with your baby. If this is not possible (perhaps because you have other children) ask for a photo to help you feel closer at such a difficult time.

It can be a distressing experience for a mother recovering from giving birth, and perhaps from the anxiety preceding it. Your baby will look fragile among all the winking lights and complex machinery, but you will be able to visit frequently or stay. The staff will encourage you to look after your baby as much as possible, with help where necessary, and you will be fully involved in any decisions that need to be made.

Even when you know in advance that there might be a problem the reality comes as a shock; fears for your baby can make you feel frighteningly vulnerable. You may have to make far-reaching decisions with too little time and information available, and to trust doctors with whom you have not been able to build up a relationship, but most medical professionals genuinely care and try to do their job well. Ultimately, technical brilliance may be more important than bedside manner.

If your baby is desperately ill put all your energy into coping day to day and expect nothing else of yourself. Enlist all the help you can if you have other children and make it up to them when the immediate crisis is over.

Coming to terms with your birth experience

However carefully you plan there is no guarantee that labour will go the way you hope. Preparation may make it easier, but a baby who stays the wrong way round or a labour that grinds on long after you have lost interest cannot always be foreseen. You are not responsible for such situations and although intervention does not benefit every labour it certainly makes some easier.

If your labour is a disappointment ('failure' is not really an appropriate term), you lose something important: your hopes and expectations and with them some confidence and self-esteem. You may feel depressed, self-critical or angry that the staff who cared for you are largely to blame for your experience. Some women are so glad that the birth is over and their baby is healthy, however, that they suppress negative feelings until later, perhaps when a friend has a lovely birth.

Labour cannot be changed in retrospect but it can help if you understand what happened and why. Contact the hospital and ask to see a midwife who can explain. A copy of your notes should be available, although you might have to pay for them. What happened may have been unavoidable or there may be lessons to be learned, by you or the staff concerned. Anyone can make a mistake or wish with hindsight that they had made a different decision; if this can be acknowledged they can learn from the experience.

Understandably, some doctors and midwives are nervous about being sued and may be defensive, or try to soothe you without really listening to what you are saying. In the long run, fear of litigation will lead to doctors practising defensive medicine. Many women simply want to understand what happened; and if it could have been avoided, for this to be taken on board so that it does not happen again.

Feelings cannot be right or wrong; they simply exist, and often there is no answer to the question 'Why did this happen to me?' The pain of disappointment has to be worked through until you can accept your experience and move forward. Here are some tips that may help:

❑   Talk to your partner or someone who will listen and accept how you feel without brushing you aside. You may need to go over it again and again.

❑   Talk to the staff who cared for you (make an appointment, even if it was months ago) to find out the reason for the problem and if it is likely to occur again or could be avoided another time. If somebody's attitude upset you, it can help you to feel your experience is acknowledged – and them to learn from a mistake.

❑   Try not to blame yourself if you feel you were ignorant or unrealistic about labour – everybody learns some things the hard way.

❑   Find a good antenatal teacher to help and support you if you decide to have another baby, or contact the Birth Crisis Network (see *Directory*).

Losing a baby

The loss of a baby is hard to talk about. It is relatively rare, but sadly it could happen to anyone. Statistically, the risk is higher for mothers who are ill, have a complication during pregnancy, are socially deprived or who smoke.

The death of a baby in late pregnancy or around the birth is unexpected. You may be recovering from a caesarean section, or from the stress of watching your beloved child fight for life. If only you and your partner knew or looked after your baby there are no memories to share with family and friends, and this can make you feel very lonely. Most parents are glad they saw a baby who died before or at birth, even if they did not want to at first;

as time passes they treasure both the memory and keepsakes such as a footprint or photograph.

Unless your baby was very premature you will have made preparations so there will be reminders everywhere. Cruelly, your hormones will fluctuate, you will have a period-like discharge (lochia) and you will produce milk as though your baby were alive. Your midwife may suggest wearing a tight bra and taking paracetamol for a day or two until your breasts settle down. Some women have 'empty arms' and desperately long to cuddle someone else's baby.

Friends who are pregnant or have young children may be afraid to visit for fear of upsetting you, and 'breaking the ice' becomes harder as time goes on. You may want friends to visit unannounced so that you do not feel you should have tidied up, or you may prefer a phone call first. Try to tell your partner or a close friend how you feel, so that he or she can explain to other people.

Some friends may avoid you completely or say 'perhaps it was for the best', or 'be grateful for the others' if you have other children or lost a twin or triplet. Such comments are inappropriate as you will long only for the baby you have lost, but people do not mean to be hurtful or dismissive; they simply have no experience of something so traumatic and do not know what to do or say.

Bereavement changes everyone, but losing a child is especially hard as it denies you both the reality of what your baby meant to you and all your dreams for the future. Dreams can be especially hard to let go, and when you are older there is the added stress of feeling that time may have run out.

You will never forget and nor will you want to. At first, nothing will ease the desolation, but if you can grieve you will gradually accept your loss, restructure your life and begin to take an interest in other relationships or projects.

Grieving

There are recognisable phases on the way towards accepting any sort of loss, although you may not pass through stages in a special order and there are no rules about how long it takes. The initial shock brings thoughts like, 'This can't be happening', or 'I'll do anything if only it is all right'. Then, as reality sinks in and life's certainties temporarily disappear, you may become disorganised. You will depend on others for help at first, although you may feel uncomfortable doing so.

Grieving involves tremendous emotional energy; it is exhausting. Tears are part of the process and can bring great relief, but you may feel that you ought to be positive, or be embarrassed if they spill out. You may blame yourself or someone else, or even think that you are going mad. You may talk about your loss all the time; or withdraw, longing to be with your child and feeling that life is no longer worth living. You and your partner may be drawn together or split apart by the intensity of the experience.

You cannot look forward until shock and despair have passed, but the process of recovery will begin eventually. Although time heals the wounds, grief does not disappear after a few weeks. A scent, a tune or an anniversary will bring painful memories and you may still need support when everybody else appears to have forgotten your loss. Months later you may want to share the experience with someone who has been through it and really understands (see *Directory*).

Older mothers' experiences

Valerie (44): 'I was induced at 38 weeks because of my diabetes. It's not routine, but the doctor said it was advisable in my case. I felt sad because I'd been looking forward to the excitement of labour starting naturally. I was continuously monitored and as

I didn't want Barry to see me in pain I had an epidural.

'Mark was delivered by forceps and his blood glucose level was tested straight away. He did not feed well and had to go to SCBU to have a drip until his pancreas adapted and he produced the right amount of insulin for the amount of milk he was taking. I knew a stay in SCBU was possible but I didn't really expect it and I went to pieces, needing constant reassurance that Mark would be all right. The staff had much sicker babies to look after, but they were very patient. One nurse sat with me every time I expressed my milk and was so positive that I began to relax.'

Q: What are the main points for someone who has diabetes to keep in mind around the birth and afterwards?
A: As the understanding and management of diabetes in pregnancy improves more women are able to have a normal birth. If labour starts spontaneously special instructions (depending on the circumstances) may be given about whether to inject insulin and eat before going to hospital. Once in hospital some women check their own blood glucose levels and keep a record on a chart. Others have a drip connected to an insulin infusion pump and a bag of dextrose solution, which controls their diabetes during labour. Pain relief does not affect glucose levels.

After the birth insulin requirements often drop dramatically, especially if you are breastfeeding. With a new baby taking your attention it is easy to forget what dose you need and when, so some women make a chart to remind them.

Motherhood can be overwhelming and disorientating at first, even without diabetes to manage, so it is also a good idea to make sure you have adequate supplies of insulin to tide you over the first few weeks.

Lesley (36): 'I was expecting a normal delivery but my waters broke early and one twin was lying across my uterus so I had a caesarean section. It wasn't a real emergency and it happened within hours rather than minutes. I was wheeled to the operating theatre on a trolley, which was a new experience: the staff waiting there looked like a row of masked sentries.

'I was given a spinal block and felt pressure followed by warmth travelling down my legs, then a rummaging sensation as though someone was looking for keys at the bottom of a shopping bag. There was a wonderful sense of release as Sam was born. He cried immediately and was laid on my chest. Then Thomas was delivered and whisked away for a whiff of oxygen. Within minutes he was back and my arms were full of babies. Phil sat beside me in a gown and cap, with tears in his eyes. Nothing could have been more perfect.'

Q: Am I likely to need another caesarean section or could I have a normal delivery next time?

A: If everything is straightforward you should be able to have a normal delivery, but talk to your obstetrician early in your next pregnancy. The possibility of scar rupture is sometimes put forward as a reason for a repeat caesarean, but research shows that only about one in 200 lower segment or bikini scars begin to separate, and it is very rare for there to be any danger to the mother or baby. You should be watched closely by an experienced midwife if a hormone drip is needed to strengthen contractions, as this can put extra stress on the scar. If labour does not make progress within about two hours of setting up a drip the staff would probably want to stop and work out why.

Another complication could arise during pregnancy or birth, or there might be something about your uterus that makes it more comfortable for your baby to lie sideways, for example, but 50–80 per cent of women achieve a vaginal birth after a caesarean (VBAC).

Anne (47): 'After a day labouring at home, in and out of the birth pool, my contractions died away. When my midwife suggested going to hospital I felt tired and disappointed, but it was the right decision. I had a drip and an epidural and Chloe was delivered by ventouse, without an episiotomy. It was far less daunting than I imagined and I'll never be so against intervention again.

'Choice is important to me because I'm used to making my own decisions. It makes me feel in control, and feeling in control makes all the difference. The birth was a very good experience despite my reservations about intervention.'

Q: Can a woman insist on having a caesarean section in the name of choice?
A: Some doctors are reluctant to agree to this because the disadvantages of caesarean birth can outweigh the benefits. For example, it carries the risks associated with any major surgery and recovery may be less straightforward than for normal birth. It is linked with more infections, depression, ill health and problems with breastfeeding and resuming a normal sex life. When a uterus has scar tissue there is an increased risk of ectopic pregnancy, placental problems and postpartum haemorrhage.

Some women ask for a caesarean because they are afraid of labour, but a caesarean can only sidestep this fear. On the other hand, good midwifery care around the birth, including extra support to handle threatening situations, can help women find an inner strength that comes from conquering a fear; this lasts well beyond birth.

11 *New Baby*

BEFORE YOUR BABY ARRIVES THERE ARE ENJOYABLE CHOICES TO be made about baby clothes and equipment, and after the birth there are the practical tasks of looking after a baby which can also be a source of great delight.

There is plenty of research to show that breastfeeding is the best way of feeding a baby; this is acknowledged by the World Health Organisation, the medical profession and even by baby milk manufacturers. Many older mothers are keen to breastfeed, but it works best when you and your baby are relaxed. It is not always easy right from the start; the technique generally has to be learned, so patience is essential and pressure from any source can be counter-productive.

Breastfeeding is a partnership. Most babies can be persuaded to co-operate, but a few will not despite all efforts to encourage them. Some women have to give up sooner than they want because the right information or support is not available; or the stress of overcoming a problem is just too great, or family or work commitments cannot be reconciled with breastfeeding. You may be disappointed if breastfeeding does not work out, but there is little point in feeling guilty when something is not your fault. A happy feeding relationship may be more important than how you feed your baby; both breastmilk and formula are nourishing.

Some women choose to bottle feed for their own good reasons and there should be no blame attached to this decision. If bottle feeding is the best choice for your circumstances there are compensations: your baby is less dependent on you for all her needs, other people can share the pleasure of feeding her, and some women find it more acceptable to bottle feed in a public place.

Why breastfeed?

❑   The more breastmilk is analysed the more complex it appears to be; no formula can match it exactly. For example, the balance of nutrients like calcium, phosphorus and magnesium (important for growth and healthy bones) differ in breastmilk and formula; breastmilk contains more lactose (milk sugar) than cow's milk so sucrose or glucose may be added to formula.

❑   Standards set for formula take account of nutrients considered important at the time. Zinc and certain fatty acids are now added to some formula milk, but many enzymes and hormones identified in breastmilk are not added as their purpose is not understood. This may or may not affect a baby's health in the long-term.

❑   Your body naturally adjusts the composition of your milk whenever necessary. If your baby is born prematurely your milk will compensate, and it will change as your baby grows to fulfil her different needs. If she is feverish or the weather is hot it will adjust to satisfy her thirst. The fat composition of breastmilk changes during the feed, triggering an appetite control mechanism that tells your baby when she has had enough.

❑ Your baby stimulates your breasts to produce the amount of milk she requires. If she is hungry she sucks more strongly or more often, gradually increasing your supply until it matches her needs. This delicate mechanism is designed to handle variety, both in individual babies and in their day to day appetites.

❑ Breastmilk is naturally free of bacteria. It contains substances to fight common childhood illnesses, and antibodies to combat infections caused by bacteria and viruses. Bottle-fed babies are twice as likely to be admitted to hospital with a respiratory infection, and five times more likely to be admitted with diarrhoea.

❑ Colostrum also contains antibodies. This is produced in the first few days after birth and is thought to coat the intestines and prevent anything that could set up an infection or allergic reaction from reaching the bloodstream. It also helps a baby handle smaller amounts of liquid as her kidneys adjust to independent life.

❑ After the birth, breastfeeding helps to shrink your uterus and your body returns to normal faster. You always have food and comfort available for your baby, and your chances of conceiving are naturally reduced (see page 263).

Baby kit

The bewildering array of equipment on the market and the many companies competing for your business may both confuse you and tempt you to spend lavishly, especially if it is your first baby. If you can afford to equip a nursery without worrying about the cost, enjoy yourself! Buying for a baby is fun and you will not want your head to rule your heart entirely.

Nevertheless, practical considerations are important as most parents have some sort of a budget to stick to. Some items seem like a good idea but actually spend more time sitting on top of the wardrobe; others are so versatile that they fail to do any job well. Ask what friends or relatives have found useful, bearing in mind that one parent's godsend clutters up another parent's wardrobe. Think about how long something will be used, the amount of wear and tear it will get and whether it will really make your life easier. Consumer magazines such as *Which?* in Britain publish independent tests of major baby items, and baby magazines such

---

Checklist of clothing and equipment

One on, one in the wash and one spare is a minimum guide for how many of each garment to buy, but a few extra will make life easier.

To help you plan, here is a checklist of basic items:

❑ Vests ....
❑ Stretch suits or nightgowns ....
❑ Jackets or jerseys ....
❑ Shawls or blankets ....
❑ Snowsuit, hat, mittens (for a winter baby) ....
❑ Nappies ....
❑ Changing mat or table, cotton wool, cream ....
❑ Car safety seat ....
❑ Carrycot or Moses basket ....
❑ Pram or buggy ....
❑ Baby carrier or sling ....
❑ Cot and pram sheets and blankets ....
❑ Bathing equipment (bath or bowl, towels, soap
   or similar) ....
❑ Bottles, sterilising equipment and formula
   (if bottle feeding) ....
❑ Breast pads and a bottle (if breast feeding) ....
   Other ....

as *Practical Parenting* provide helpful reports every month to guide you.

Friends, relatives or colleagues at work are likely to give you presents such as first-size clothes and nursery items. Bear this in mind when buying, and make a note of a few things in case you are asked what you would like.

Caring for a baby

On balance maturity makes life much easier when you have a new baby. You are more likely to listen to your body, rest when tired and let your baby take the lead. You may be better organised than you were when younger and experience may make you more tolerant of disruption, knowing that nothing lasts for ever.

When you have achieved a senior position in your career, however, it can be hard to remember what it was like to be a beginner, thrown in at the deep end not knowing quite what was expected of you. Caring for a baby can feel like this, and some older women secretly fear at first that it has all been a big mistake. It is distressing to feel that you do not know what to do with a tiny baby when you have reached the stage in life of being able to handle most situations.

If you feel this way you may suffer the added burden of pretending to be thrilled with your baby because everyone else expects it. It will relieve the pressure and help resolve your feelings if you find somebody sympathetic – your partner, a friend or your midwife, perhaps – to talk to about how you really feel. You are not an unnatural or unsuitable mother; you will grow to enjoy many aspects of parenthood and love your baby fiercely given time. The initial reality can simply be a shock.

Having more than one baby, or a baby with a disability, means extra work and more adjustment than usual. Twins or triplets have novelty value and you may get more attention and offers of help. Friends and relatives who are prepared to shop, cook or look after other children can free you to concentrate on your baby, give a toddler some much needed attention or simply rest and renew your energy.

If tests suggest your baby has a named disability you can obtain information and support beforehand. Sometimes the news comes as a shock or the outcome is uknown, however, and the early days are darkened by fears and uncertainties.

Seek all the information you need and accept all offers of help. The medical team will advise you about caring for your baby and help you to decide the best method of feeding. You could express milk (see page 245–6) for your baby, and although breastfeeding may be difficult in some cases you may still succeed with skilled support. A breastfeeding group or the relevant voluntary organisation (see *Directory*) may be able to put you in touch with the right expert.

The first three months

Life for you: You need to rest, recover and reorientate after the birth and your baby needs to adjust to a new environment. Gradually you will get to know what your baby wants and how to supply it as easily as possible, forming a relationship that works for both of you. Many older mothers feel deeply fulfilled and enjoy this period enormously.

After the birth you may feel bruised and uncomfortable for several days, or longer if you have stitches or a caesarean scar. Many women feel weepy or overwhelmed when their milk comes in a few days later, partly because of the sudden hormone changes that take place when the placenta is delivered. If you can give yourself space and rest as much as possible (especially if you have other small children) you will have a good chance of recovering well. Your health visitor will call from time to time, to make sure that both you and your baby are well and to answer any queries you may have.

By the second month the aches and pains that follow a normal delivery are usually over. If you had a caesarean birth you will be feeling stronger, although you may still run out of energy quickly. The lochia diminishes to a pinkish discharge, often with bright red bleeding for a day or two if you do too much.

About six weeks after the birth your GP or the hospital will offer you a postnatal check-up. This is an opportunity to ask any questions relating to the birth and discuss your own health. If you feel low, say so without smiling brightly or your body language will communicate that you are fine and your doctor may not realise you are asking for help. Postnatal depression is an illness, not an inadequacy, and it can be treated in various ways (see page 255).

It generally takes six weeks for the uterus to return to its pre-pregnant state, but complete recovery after a birth takes longer. Your pelvic floor may not be back to normal, and you may not have felt ready to attempt intercourse, for instance. If you have been doing pelvic floor exercises (50–100 a day for three months – see page 92) and are making no progress, or you have any other problems, you can make an appointment to see your GP for help at any time.

By the third month life is generally more predictable and some sort of routine may gradually evolve. A flexible routine works well for many mothers and babies. It may take you six months to a year to fully recover emotionally and physically even after a normal birth, however, so continue to be kind to yourself!

Life for your baby: Some babies adapt more easily to their new environment than others. As you get to know your baby's ways you will discover what works for both of you. Friends, relatives, books and baby magazines can offer helpful advice, or you could contact your health visitor or one of the organisations in the

Directory. There is no shortage of advice, and older women often feel more confident to ask for it; and to ignore any that does not work for them.

Breastfeeding is established for many women by the second month, and for most women by the third month after the birth. Some babies need feeding every two to three hours at first, but many bottle-fed and some breastfed babies go for longer between feeds. During the night your baby may wake every couple of hours or sleep for about six hours at a stretch. Some babies have their clocks reversed, sleeping well in daylight and waking up at night. If you are breastfeeding you could try to gently encourage your baby to feed more often during the day, so that your milk supply does not adjust to larger or more frequent feeds at night.

Many babies have a growth spurt at about six to eight weeks, and another at about three months. They are fretful and feed frequently to build up your milk supply, producing a definite increase after a couple of days. Some babies get into the habit of continual snack feeding, however. If this happens you may want to encourage your baby to wait two to three hours between feeds, using a dummy or walking around to distract her, instead of putting her to your breast as soon as she cries. After a few days she may happily space out her feeds, sucking longer each time to compensate.

After the first month or so babies often need entertaining as they are less likely to sleep. Some are happy to lie and watch the world go by, but others prefer to be held close to you, and many are fretful every evening for the first few weeks, wanting to be cuddled constantly and screaming if put down. At this age you will not 'make a rod for your own back' by giving in! By the end of the third month most babies are more settled and predictable.

Practical babycare

There are no rules about bringing up a baby: different eras and cultures have different ideas. For example, babies used to be fed every four hours and this is still normal in some European countries; in Britain they have more individual schedules. If a mature mother feels out of tune with whatever is the norm, or her baby does not fit easily into the prevailing routine, she is less likely to worry about doing her own thing. Here are some options – the decisions are yours!

Sleeping: You could
❑ sleep with your baby beside your bed to make night feeds easier.
❑ put the cot in another room if your baby is so snuffly that you cannot sleep.
❑ have your baby in bed with you, unless you take anything that could make you sleep deeply, or like so many covers that your baby could overheat.
❑ bring your baby into bed for part of the night, for example after a feed.

Bathing: You could
❑ wash your baby in a wash-basin, sink or washing up bowl for a few weeks.
❑ put her in the bath with you, your partner or your other children.
❑ use a baby bath in the big bath, where it may be easier to fill and empty.
❑ bath her every other day, or twice a week. 'Top and tail' her by washing her face and nappy area on the other days.
❑ bath her at a time that suits you both, be it morning, afternoon or evening.

Crying: You could
❑ respond immediately with food or comfort if your baby cries in the first month.
❑ distinguish between fretting (she can wait a little), persistent crying (respond soon) and screaming (respond now).
❑ leave her for ten minutes if she is grizzling or crying persistently to see if she stops (some babies cry persistently before they drop off to sleep).

❑   give her a dummy if she has colic (abdominal pain), or cries
excessively for no apparent reason. You can get rid of it when
she is more settled (by three to five months).

Bottle feeding

Baby formula is usually made from cow's milk or soya, modified
so that the balance of fats and minerals resembles breast milk
more closely. Your choice of formula will be guided by what suits
your baby's digestion, but before you choose ask the manufacturers for nutritional information and compare brands – the
product you buy may be your baby's sole or main source of nutrition for several months.

The instructions for making up bottles vary slightly with the
product. Usually you boil tap water, cool it and fill each bottle to
the right level using the measuring scale on the side; measure the
formula using the scoop provided, level it off with the back of a
knife, add it to the water, screw the bottle caps on and shake to
dissolve the powder. If you bottle feed twins or triplets it saves
time to weigh the formula instead of using scoops; measure the
amount of water in a plastic jug, mix in the powder, pour it into
the bottles and store them in the fridge for up to 24 hours.

When feeding your baby, keep the bottle teat full so that she
does not gulp air with the feed. You may want to cuddle her close
to your breast, so that she has skin to skin contact (this can be
comforting for both of you if you have reluctantly changed from
breast to bottle). If your baby takes in wind during a feed, sit her
up halfway through and again at the end, and rub her back to help
her bring it up.

Breastfeeding

Breastfeeding may be enjoyable right from the start or there may be problems to overcome, but older mothers tend to be patient, less inclined to rush at life and more likely to succeed if they encounter difficulties. You can breastfeed more than one baby – it can take dedication but your supply adjusts to the demand.

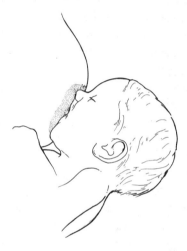

Good positioning at breast

A newborn baby's reflexes last for a few days, long enough for her to learn to breastfeed. If her feet touch a surface she moves each leg as if she is crawling, and when something touches her palm, her hand grips it firmly enough to support her weight; so she can reach her mother's breast without help if necessary.

The pigmentation of the areola (skin around the nipple) and the smell of colostrum (the forerunner of milk) guide her like homing devices. Her rooting reflex encourages her to open her mouth wide and explore the breast. Eventually she grasps the right bit; the nipple touches her palate and triggers her sucking reflex.

Good positioning

1. Sit upright, comfortably supported, and lay your baby on her side on a pillow across your knee with her chest against yours and her nose near your nipple; or lie on your side with your lower arm extended and line your baby up facing you.

2. If sitting, support her head on your wrist or forearm (not the crook of your elbow), and cup your other palm around her head, ready to guide it.

3. When she opens her mouth wide (like a yawn) guide her head towards you so that she takes a good mouthful of breast, her chin close to your breast. Bring her onto your breast rather than putting your breast into her mouth.

4. If she is well latched on you will see her jawbone move or her ears wiggle as she sucks. If not, break her suction by sliding your little finger into the corner of her mouth and patiently try again.

Thinking about how her reflexes assist a baby will help you to position her successfully. Her chest is flat against yours and the curve of your breast tips her head back (like opening the airway when giving mouth to mouth resuscitation), and her nose passes your nipple first. She roots or searches and her mouth opens wide, enabling her to take a good mouthful of breast tissue with her chin close in to your breast and her nose free for breathing.

A baby in a good position will take a better feed and help you avoid problems such as sore nipples, blocked ducts and mastitis. A little knowledge can get you off to a good start and extra help is available if you need it (see *Directory*).

Establishing breastfeeding: It generally takes two to six weeks for breastfeeding to be fully established, and the fewer the rules the easier it is. All you really need is patience, and skilled individual help if you encounter a problem. Some babies are difficult to feed even if you have breastfed a previous baby successfully; a baby with a very small mouth may be unable to take in enough breast tissue to stimulate your milk supply, or may make your nipples sore, for example.

You will know when breastfeeding is established as you will feel relaxed and confident, and will let your milk down easily. The let-down reflex is under the influence of the hormone oxytocin, which tends to be easily switched off by anxiety or disturbance. It becomes less affected by your emotional state and more reliable every day because it is conditioned by your baby's sucking; and as you get used to breastfeeding the delicate mechanism fine-tunes to suit you and your baby.

Many breastfed babies dislike bottles and refuse to take them. If you want to bottle feed when you return to work offer a little boiled water (some babies prefer expressed milk) in a bottle, perhaps to help delay a feed if your baby wakes early. A baby who is easily bottle fed in the early weeks may forget how to do it by the time she is three or four months old, so start in the first month and keep it up once or twice a week until you are ready to introduce more bottles.

Common breastfeeding problems

Most breastfeeding problems can be solved with perseverance, but there are as many solutions as there are individual women and babies. The golden rule is to seek help early. Try these remedies or ask a friend or relative, your midwife, health visitor or a breastfeeding counsellor (see *Directory*) for help before you are so desperate that you are about to give up completely.

PROBLEM	WHAT TO DO
Sore nipples: A sharp pain at the start of a feed is usually caused by a rush of milk from the let-down reflex forcing the ducts open. It disappears as breastfeeding becomes established. Pain that lasts throughout a feed may be caused by damage to the nipple tissue, often from poor positioning.	Handle let-down pain by relaxing your shoulders and focusing on the breathing you learned for labour. If your nipple tissue is sore, check that your baby is latched on properly (see page 242). Some women expose their nipples to dry them off naturally, as breastmilk seems to help healing; others dry them with tissues after a feed and use a suitable ointment (ask your midwife to suggest one).
Engorgement: Swollen, hard breasts with nipples that are almost flat may be caused by extra fluid during the transition from colostrum to milk on the third or fourth day after the birth, or by a long gap between feeds.	Putting your baby to the breast frequently for practice in the early days can help avoid engorgement as you both learn what to do by the time the milk comes in. If she cannot grasp the nipple try a warm bath or a hot compress to soften it. A cold compress, such as a packet of frozen peas wrapped in a tea towel, can ease swelling caused by extra fluid. A cold compress followed by a hot one may help and some women swear by cabbage leaves tucked inside their bra.
Too much milk: Some women produce a gush of milk so splendid that their baby chokes and their bra gets soaked between feeds.	Your milk supply will usually adjust to your baby's needs in a week or two. Try feeding while lying on your back so that your baby sucks against gravity; or catch the first flow in a sterile container (store it for later use or discard it). Some women offer one breast at each feed to provide less frequent stimulation.
Too little milk: Your baby fails to put on weight and constantly cries and stuffs her fingers in her mouth. Some women produce milk more easily than others, but as supply adjusts to the demand most can provide enough for their own baby.	Check to make sure your baby is well positioned as this affects the strength of suck. Feed more frequently for two days to help your supply increase but it could take two weeks before the supply becomes balanced, so be patient. It may help to rest, eat more or drink some water each time you feed; occasionally, taking more exercise or vigorous arm-swinging helps. Well-fed babies can be fretful by nature, however, or enjoy sucking their fists when not hungry.

PROBLEM	WHAT TO DO
Blocked ducts: These may occur when the milk does not flow well. Pressure from clothing or a natural narrowing of the ducts in one area of the breast may cause a small clot of milk – you can often feel a lump.	Gently massage the lump while your baby feeds. Strong sucking by a hungry baby will help to keep ducts clear, so start each feed on the affected side for a few days; tuck your baby's legs under your arm or feed lying down for a change.
Mastitis: Part of your breast becomes hot and inflamed, or you feel as though you have 'flu. It may happen if you neglect blocked ducts, or if your baby is poorly positioned or has fed less well because of a change in your routine.	It is vital to catch it early so that it does not get worse. Feed frequently on the affected breast to keep it empty, making sure your baby is well positioned. Rest, take care of yourself and if there is no improvement in six–eight hours, or you start to feel feverish, contact your GP immediately as you may need antibiotics.

Expressing and storing milk: When breastfeeding is fully established you may want to express and store milk to supply bottles when someone else is caring for your baby. Hand expressing needs no special equipment but takes practice. Cup your hand under your breast and press it towards your rib-cage; rhythmically squeeze the milk sacs under the areola with your thumb and forefinger. Catch the droplets, spurt or spray of milk in a clean container. If you find it hard to get the knack it may help to use warm compresses or massage your breasts gently first, or to practise when your baby is feeding from the other breast.

Many women find it easier to use a hand or battery operated breast pump but some models are likely to be more successful than others, depending on the shape of your breasts. It is difficult to test them before buying, but you may be able to borrow different models from friends to try out.

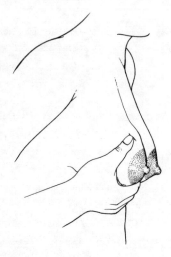

When using hand expression, catch the milk in a cup or any other clean container

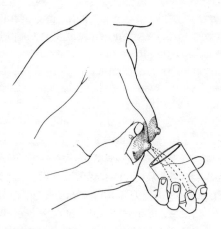

Electric pumps require little effort and are generally the most efficient. A fully automatic one can empty both breasts at once, a great time-saver. They have come down in price, and if you are pumping regularly because your baby needs special care or you are working full time they may be worth the cost. You may want to hire one for a short period, to see how you get on with it (see *Directory*).

Store milk in plastic fridge containers or special sterile poly-thene bags, topping up with more milk collected the same day. It will keep for 24–48 hours in a fridge and for about three months in a freezer. If you express regularly label the milk with the date and rotate your stock (the composition of the milk will be ideal for your baby on the day it was expressed). You may want to freeze the milk in small quantities as any surplus should be used within 24 hours or discarded; it cannot be refrozen. Thaw milk in the fridge, or in hot water just before the feed (a microwave may heat it unevenly) and shake the container if the milk has separated.

Use a cool bag with frozen ice-packs if you are taking expressed breast milk to your childminder. You may want to provide written guidelines for her about how you would like the milk stored, thawed and used.

Older mothers' experiences

Valerie (44): 'I felt really sorry for myself a few days after the birth. My body ached all over, I was totally exhausted, breast-feeding was a nightmare and my stitches hurt so much that I could hardly walk. Barry, Emma and Claire were clearly thrilled with the baby and I didn't want to spoil it by moaning that I felt awful. I'd like to say that I bounced back, but it was a long, slow haul.

'There is great pressure on women to feel perfectly fulfilled by motherhood, and I didn't at first, even though I had longed to have

a baby. It was not easy for me to admit to feeling depressed.
Nurses expect to give support to other people, not need it themselves. We are over the worst and I feel a lot better now. I'm
starting to relax and enjoy Mark and it's a great comfort to
know that I can get through difficulties and that the rest of the
family pulls together to help me.'

Q: At times I still feel distant from Mark, as though I'm caring
for somebody else's child while they are on holiday. Is this normal
and when will it change?
A: It is not unusual for women who have waited some time, or
suffered a loss during pregnancy, to be disorientated when a baby
finally arrives. Longing for a baby can distort your feelings; some
are suppressed while others are idealised and reality can be an
anti-climax. These feelings can also follow a stressful pregnancy,
a disappointing birth, or even a birth you have been dreading but
that turns out well. Perhaps it is hard to replace one strong
emotion with another, and when a change for the better occurs
your emotions switch off for a rest.

If this phase has not passed by the time Mark is a few months
old talk to your doctor. Some women find it hard to relax and
enjoy their baby; they feel they do not deserve or cannot allow
themselves great happiness. Feelings are not right or wrong,
they simply exist; but if they prevent you from enjoying your
life and your family get help to change them.

Lesley (36): 'I was over the moon from the moment the babies
were born and I'm still on cloud nine. I have a routine to save the
energy of thinking what to do all the time, but twins are not as
tiring as I'd expected, even after a caesarean section. My local
Twins Club (see *Directory*) is proving invaluable for support –
talking to a mother who has been through the same experience is
a great encouragement.

'Sam was born first and he is much stronger than Thomas; but one baby feeding well establishes the milk supply, making it easier for the other. I used to feed them separately as they liked different schedules, but now they are a few weeks old I breast-feed them together, using the "football" hold with their legs tucked under each of my arms. If they cry a lot I know I will be able to cope more easily by looking after myself, so I eat and drink more to boost my milk supply and take resting seriously for a few days.'

Q: Any tips for making life with twins as easy as possible for the next few months?
A: Make sandwiches at breakfast time and put them in the fridge to avoid missing lunch; keep a bottle of juice, disposable cups and fruit bars out on a table so that it is easy to keep your strength up. Buy cheap, plastic storage boxes to throw dirty washing or other clutter into for instant tidying. Later, they can be used to store toys.

Bath each twin every other day and 'top and tail' them in between. Change their clothes completely only once a day, using bibs to deal with dribbles. Change and dress them together on a playpen mat or square of PVC cloth.

Ask your family for help, too, suggesting specific tasks to encourage them to share the chores as well as the delights of looking after the twins. It will make all the difference in the months to come.

Sue (39): 'The birth was brilliant and I recovered much faster than last time as I made the huge adjustment to being on call twenty-four hours a day, seven days a week after Jack was born. That's what tires you out!

'Now I'm just astonished at the strength of the love that I feel for both children. Every other achievement pales into insignificance beside motherhood, something I could never have dreamt of before I had them. When I held Amy and Jack stroked her face and kissed her I was overwhelmed by the feeling that I might have missed all this joy because my career and freedom were more important.'

Q: Jack hates sharing my attention and chooses the times when I'm occupied with Amy to be naughty which is extremely wearing. How can I cope?

A: It takes most small children about three months to adjust their map of the world to include a new baby. If Jack watches to see your reaction when he is being naughty, giving him attention may reinforce his behaviour. Try casually saying something like 'I wonder if we have enough bread for tea – I must go and look' and sweeping out of the room with Amy. This will deprive him of an audience and give you time to think of something positive to occupy him.

Every few months bright children need more of a challenge to absorb their attention; the same old jigsaw no longer holds any attraction, but they become co-operative again when they learn something new. Kenneth could help by finding a skill to pass on, such as simple woodwork or cooking.

Videos, story tapes and children's TV all have their place in keeping the peace when you have a new baby. A treasure bag containing dressing up clothes, special art materials or anything that you know will really absorb his attention may also help, if you only bring it out at times when you are desperate for peace, so that it keeps its novelty value.

12 *The Early Months*

THERE IS SOMETHING WARM AND INTIMATE ABOUT MOTHERHOOD, a sleepy head on your shoulder, a sparkling smile in the morning. But let us not get too sentimental. The early months with a baby take you from antenatal optimism to postnatal realism. Pain goes with giving birth, exhaustion goes with parenthood and one small baby can seem like a descent from control into chaos, especially for anyone whose life is normally orderly. This does not detract from the rewards, summed up in a single word: fulfilment; but an impossibly romanticised view of motherhood can make every woman feel guilty when she fails to live up to the soft-focus images.

Voluntary simplicity, the slower and more quality conscious lifestyle brought about by choosing to swap a certain level of income for more pleasure, is an attractive idea; but if you have got into a ritual of having breakfast in bed with the Sunday papers and touching up chipped paintwork straight away so that your house stays immaculate, it takes time to change.

Older parents have had longer to form habits and simply because of this they can find it hard to adapt to a tiny tyrant whose every cry tugs at their heartstrings. When you feel low or tired all the time, especially if you have had doubts beforehand, you can see your baby as an enemy who disrupts your life and drives a wedge between you and your partner. A child's demands can be as much of an irritation as a guest who has rather over-stayed his welcome.

In spite of this, the majority of older women enjoy motherhood enormously. One reason may be that they have established a career, done their travelling and are content to settle down. Another may be because they know themselves better and take their health and other needs seriously. It is always easier to cope with the ups and downs of parenthood if you feel well, so looking after yourself when you have a baby is a necessity rather than a luxury.

Your health

First time older mothers take 11 months on average to recover physically after a birth, and those who already have a child take about seven months. You will recover faster if you are fit but if you had difficult labour, a caesarean section or any infection it may take longer. Your six week check-up will allow you to discuss contraception and any immediate postnatal problems with your GP, but problems can occur after this and can be debilitating at a time when you need all your energy. Make an appointment to see your GP again if necessary.

Postnatal exercises

Your hormones will be settling down for several months after the birth and it may be hard to find time for anything other than your baby, so allow about a year to get fully fit again. An unrealistic tar-get may put unnecessary pressure on you.

These exercises gently tone your abdominal muscles, which in turn help support your internal organs. Repeat each one slowly six times, working up to twelve repetitions. Be guided by your body and stop if you feel tired. If you had a caesarean section omit any that pull on your scar, and try again after a week or two.

1.   *Stretch and Curl:* Kneel or sit cross-legged on the floor. Stretch your back, raising one arm in the air; lower your arm and curl your back slowly into a slump. Stretch and curl using each arm alternately.

2.   *Leg Sliding:* Lie on your back with your knees bent. Keeping the small of your back firmly pressed to the floor, slide your feet slowly away from you. When your back begins to arch, draw your legs up and try again. If you can straighten your legs completely without arching your back, start in the same position but lift your head and shoulders, stretching your hands towards your knees.

3.   *Hip Hitch:* Lie on your back with your left knee bent. Place your right hand on your abdomen, between your hip and pubic bones. Keeping your right leg straight, draw your hip up towards your shoulder so that you feel your abdominal muscles working under your hand. Repeat on the other side.

4.   *Sitting Twist:* Sit with your knees bent and feet together, supporting yourself with your arms behind you. Keeping your feet together, bend your knees down to the floor one side, then the other.

5.   *Diagonal Stretch:* Sit with your knees bent, leaning back onto your elbows. Stretch your left hand diagonally so that it passes your right knee and you feel your abdominal muscles working. Repeat on the other side.

Backache: Lying on your back when giving birth, perhaps for an assisted delivery, can contribute to backache because the base of your spine is unable to move in response to pressure from your baby's head. Sometimes there is pain where an epidural was inserted, or the coccyx (the bones at the end of the spine) becomes bruised. This can be more comfortable if you sit on a soft cushion, or a piece of foam rubber in the bath, but it may take several months to heal completely.

Some women injure their back by moving awkwardly or straining while their ligaments are still soft. To protect your back try to sit straight when breastfeeding and avoid lifting and twisting at the same time, for example. The Alexander technique, often taught at local authority evening classes, could help you to be more aware of how you use your back. If back pain is severe, or does not subside after taking care about how you use your body for a week or two, consult your GP or a registered osteopath or chiropractor.

Headaches: Older mothers report fewer headaches than younger mothers, but if you suffer regularly it is worth keeping a notebook to record what you eat, what the weather is like, how the day went and so on. Over a period of time you may be able to detect a pattern that narrows down the likely cause, so that you can eliminate it at least some of the time instead of taking painkillers.

Pelvic floor: Many women are dismayed to find that for several weeks after the birth their pelvic floor muscles are so weak that they leak urine if they attempt anything strenuous. Pelvic floor exercises (see page 92) can tone and strengthen the muscles, but both quality and quantity are important. They should feel as if you are pulling your vagina towards your heart, an internal movement not involving your abdominal or buttock muscles.

Lie on the floor with your hips on a pillow and legs raised on the bed, so that gravity helps. Breathing naturally, tighten your pelvic floor as much, and hold it for as long, as is comfortable. If the muscles tremble you are over-straining them. You may feel little sensation at first, even after a caesarean section, but you should make noticeable progress in less than three months if you do about 50 repetitions a day in groups of 6 to 10, stopping as soon as the muscles tire. If you need help after this your GP may refer you to a physiotherapist or suggest other treatment.

Prolapse: Age, gravity and having children can put the best of pelvic floors under strain. The ligaments holding the uterus in place may stretch so that it descends into the vagina (uterine prolapse), but more commonly after childbirth the front or rear wall of the vagina sags (cystocele or rectocele, respectively) and can be felt as a slight bulge at the entrance to the vagina. A cystocele may cause leakage or an urge to pass water frequently; a rectocele can cause difficulty opening your bowels.

For a mild vaginal prolapse, pelvic floor exercises in the position described above may help; progress them by putting your hands on your inner thighs to give resistance (or your partner could help) while you press your knees together, tighten your abdomen and buttock muscles and draw up your pelvic floor. Some women find it helps to increase their intake of vitamins B, C and E, or to tone the muscles gently by spraying them with cold water in the shower. Your GP can refer you to an obstetric physiotherapist for electrotherapy treatment to tighten the vagina, but in some cases a prolapse that causes problems needs surgery.

Postnatal depression: This is not associated with age but it is linked to isolation, lack of support, physical stress and a history of depression. It is more common after having a first baby or a caesarean section, and there is some evidence that up to 40 per cent of depression is already present during late pregnancy. Older women are more likely to have support from a partner or family and to feel in control of their lives, however, factors that reduce the chances of suffering from it.

If you think you may be depressed (see *Symptoms of depression*), tackle it before it becomes so entrenched that you have neither the will nor the energy to do so. Try simple remedies first:

talk to your partner or a friend about how you feel, take a few hours' break from babycare or ask your partner to organise an outing. If this fails to do the trick or does not seem worth the effort, or if your partner, family or health visitor are worried (you may not be the best judge after a birth), talk to your doctor. Two weeks is long enough to suffer before seeking help.

Drug treatments include tranquillisers and antidepressants. At least 70 per cent of women respond to antidepressants, but it may be several weeks before you feel a noticeable difference; newer drugs act faster but may cause breastfeeding problems.

Symptoms of depression

If you have four or more of these symptoms for two weeks, talk to your GP:

- ❑ loss of interest and enjoyment in your baby.
- ❑ feeling overwhelmed by the everyday tasks of caring for a baby, or feeling useless, inadequate, hopeless, irritable, a bad mother.
- ❑ utter fatigue, even after a reasonable night's sleep.
- ❑ disturbed sleep, or waking early in the morning, even if your baby sleeps well.
- ❑ constant butterflies in your tummy so that you dread your baby waking up.
- ❑ a need to stick rigidly to a routine, for security.
- ❑ feeling uneasy or agitated, so that you cannot rest when your baby sleeps.
- ❑ feeling worse at a certain time of day, usually in the morning.
- ❑ avoiding people, for example by making excuses to decline invitations.
- ❑ weight loss or gain and disinterest in food; forgetting to eat or constant eating.
- ❑ feeling the world is bleak and grey.
- ❑ repeated thoughts of harming yourself or your baby; these are common and a sure sign that you need help.

Psychological treatments include counselling, psychotherapy and cognitive therapy (see page 258). A combination of pills for symptoms and psychological help for problems often works best.

If you feel utterly alone, isolated inside a bubble where you cannot help yourself or imagine being helped, you may benefit from a short spell of treatment in hospital. It is well worth pressing to be referred to a specialist unit where you can take your baby, even if it means travelling some distance. In a mother and baby unit you will meet many women in your situation; you will see them get better – which is a reassurance in itself. The experience of the staff and the treatments available will be geared to the special needs of mothers in a way that is not possible in a general unit treating all patients with depression.

Phobia, obsession and panic attacks: A phobia is an irrational fear: the fear is real but the danger is not. An obsessive-compulsive reaction involves intrusive thoughts (often about harming your baby) or repetitive actions that you feel powerless to suppress; a panic attack is an extreme fear reaction to a harmless event. These conditions tend to be worse if you are anxious or stressed, and having a baby can trigger or cause a relapse in any of them. They affect your quality of life and, if they become serious, the way you bring up your child.

Women often feel embarrassed or powerless to change so they heroically struggle on alone, but medication or cognitive-behavioural therapy (to change your thought patterns and behaviour) can be dramatically successful. There may be a waiting list for psychological treatments; the sooner you ask for help the better.

A brief guide to some talking therapies

Psychotherapy: This offers support, insight and the possibility of change. It can range from short-term support for problems such as divorce or illness (sometimes described as counselling) through to weekly sessions for two to five years that aim to encourage deep insights into a problem by relating it to difficulties in early relationships. Long-term psychotherapy is usually only available privately.

Cognitive Therapy: This deliberately aims to change illogical ways of thinking, or break damaging thought patterns by challenging how you see the world. You have weekly sessions over a few months and practise in between. Can help problems such as depression or obsessive-compulsive disorder.

Counselling: This term is imprecise and can describe anything from telephone help to solve a breastfeeding problem (advice) to sessions over several weeks to talk through a relationship difficulty (supportive psychotherapy). Some counsellors have minimal training, or work from a particular moral or religious perspective. Get a recommendation if possible; if you use Yellow Pages talk to several about their training and what they can offer before committing yourself.

Talking to your GP:

Recovering from having a baby is complex, but it is often assumed that once your uterus is back to normal so are you. This makes women reluctant to complain; if they do and their doctor cannot diagnose anything, they think they are making a fuss. Anxiety can mimic symptoms of other illnesses, but a problem is not neurosis or hypochondria just because it is hard to diagnose.

A symptom may be vague or embarrassing to explain; you may not mention it when you first visit your GP because something else seemed more important. The problem may be hard to pin down, because aches and pains or tiredness form part of everyday experience to some degree and cannot be accurately measured.

If you feel something is wrong, persevere; write things down so that you do not forget them, or try to explain to your GP in a different way.

Getting back to normal

Life will never be the same as it was before you had a child. A different sort of normality will evolve, with the usual high and low points. Babies are delightful, but changing nappies and wiping up sick are not the most thrilling of activities. Although more rewarding than many domestic tasks, the repetitiveness of babycare can come as a shock to an older mother who has had an interesting career.

For the past few years the ideal of good mothering has been to respond to your baby's needs: to feed on demand, provide a good deal of stimulation and never leave your baby to cry. Like all ideals, this works better for some mothers and babies than for others. There are babies who would happily feed all day given half a chance, and there are babies who like attention so much that they soak up all that is on offer and then scream from over-stimulation and sheer exhaustion.

A balance has to be struck, for everyone's sake, and flexible routines make life a great deal easier. They give you time for other activities such as getting out and about and meeting people, so that you do not feel you are constantly on duty.

Most babies like a rhythm to their day, so that they know to expect a sleep after lunch, a walk later on, a bath and nursery rhymes before bed or whatever. To establish a routine, watch your baby's natural rhythms and once a pattern emerges that works for you both, reinforce it. For example, if he tends to be sleepy around mid-day, put him in his room with the curtains drawn, so that he learns that this signifies time to nap. Eventually the routine itself will help him to feel sleepy.

It may take time and effort to find activities that you can do with your baby, and at the same time forge friendships with like-minded people, but it is well worth it. Other mothers understand how you feel, are interested when your baby achieves a milestone, provide ideas when you are at your wits' end over some problem and find your toddler lovable when you secretly fear that he is turning into a thug. There are a number of addresses in the Directory to help you contact other mothers.

You and your partner

Some men believe that women are so wonderful that they bounce back from birth in a matter of days and carry on as though nothing had happened. Some women give the appearance of doing so, but many more push themselves to live up to pretty unrealistic expectations.

One advantage of being older, that maturity and experience

Entertaining a baby in the first three months
Active, alert babies quickly get bored before they can hold and explore objects. Here are some ideas for entertaining them for short periods:

❑ Tie three sprung clothes pegs or bulldog clips to short lengths of ribbon (or string) and tie the ribbons to a wire coat hanger. Hang it from a hook in the ceiling, a clothes airer, a camera tripod or a broom handle tied to a chair back, so that it is at the right height for your baby to watch (use string if necessary). Near it keep a box of bright objects (socks, coloured ribbons, scarf or flower, postcards, pictures torn from magazines, rubber glove or part-inflated balloon, kitchen foil, paper plates, packaging). Clip them on, change them frequently.

❑ Buy a brightly coloured helium balloon (from a greetings card shop) and tie it to your baby's ankle so that he can make it move as he kicks.

❑ Tie one end of a ribbon to your baby's wrist or ankle and the other end to a mobile. In a day or two your baby will learn how to make the mobile dance; tie the ribbon to a different limb so he can work out what to do again.

give you the edge in the parenting game, can also be something of a banana skin. You may feel the need to prove yourself, have more invested in the idea of 'getting it right' because you waited to have a baby, or you have other children. You may have high expectations of yourself, believing you can handle change and keep a strong relationship with your partner.

After birth, a mother often becomes preoccupied with the baby while a father provides financial and emotional support for her. Each may find the role of willing slave more difficult than they expected. You cannot foresee or control the sort of birth you have, your child's nature, the way your hormones will behave or how your partner will react, but all these can make a mockery of your expectations. One way to resolve difficulties is to talk about what you thought would happen, and what actually happened.

Women of all ages complain that their menfolk lack energy or do not help as much as they should. The issue often lies in perceptions of what needs doing. It can be quite difficult to work out an equitable division of parental labour, because of different commitments and because it is easier to let things slide than to have meaningful discussions (also known as rows). If one person feels put upon, however, discussion is essential, as secret resentment can poison a relationship.

Two working parents may be so tired and stressed that they constantly try to dump everything on each other. If you are under too much pressure, unbelievably petty arguments can be hurtful. It can be easier to say yes to your boss than to your partner; to give attention to your job with its defined tasks, projects and deadlines than to your relationship, which you assume will always be there tomorrow.

If your partner agreed to become a father largely because you were desperate to have a baby he may resent fatherhood although he loves his child; but equally he may rise to the challenge and find he enjoys it. Many older men take to family life with enthusiasm, relishing the chance to be close to their child; or to be the hands-on father they never were with their first family because work commitments when they were in their twenties would not allow it or because they thought it was women's work in those days.

Sex after birth

Your sex life is constantly shifting and what worked well at one point will not be right at another. On average it takes around twelve months to readjust sexually after a birth and older mothers take slightly longer than younger ones. Fuelled by adrenalin and euphoria, things may go wonderfully well at first, only to hit a bad patch several months later. Sex or the lack of it can cause major tensions in any relationship, so if you are not making space in your life for it, ask yourself why.

Apart from the sheer physical exhaustion of looking after a baby, your postnatal figure may make you feel undesirable and breastfeeding hormones may have depressed your libido. Your partner may have continued to do what he wants when he wants, leaving you feeling resentful instead of emotionally and practically supported. You may be so afraid that intimacy will lead to painful sex or to another pregnancy that you withdraw affection, finding it easier to cuddle the baby.

Some mothers put their baby first, second and third; father trails in last, surplus to requirements. Some men feel disturbed by the birth, ambivalent now you are a mother; others are under intense pressure at work.

For a man who feels unsettled or displaced from a central role in the family, sex may become more important than ever as a demonstration that he is loved, a major reassurance of his importance. Feelings of rejection, loneliness, inadequacy or guilt can grow and affect performance. If he has not had sex for several months he may climax very quickly, leaving him with a sense of failure and you wondering if it was worth the effort.

Modern partnerships are based on give and take and most women want to receive as well as give emotional support. If the sexual side of your relationship is not going well you or your partner will probably feel angry or resentful. Delicate feelings can be hard to put into words, but older couples often find it easier to show tenderness and laugh together. Better communication comes with maturity and once you can discuss the problem you are closer to finding a solution.

Love can be kept alive in a thousand tiny ways. You could lower your expectations for a while and find other ways of giving and receiving attention. You could be inventive over when and how you have sex, perfect the art of the quickie (with practice you can pick up sex where you left off as easily as a conversation), flirt over breakfast (small babies have no idea what you are up to). If penetration is painful you could be referred to a gynaecologist, or have ultrasound treatment, even months after the birth, and if your sex drive is low because of a hormonal imbalance it could be treated with low levels of the hormone testosterone.

If you definitely do not want another baby, the most reliable contraception includes hormone methods such as injections and the pill (combined or progestogen-only), the sympto-thermal method, barriers such as the diaphragm or condom used with a spermicide, and intrauterine devices. If you are concerned about side-effects or health risks or are breastfeeding you may prefer to avoid hormone methods. Older women who just want to reduce the chances of another pregnancy often use a slightly less reliable method, such as a barrier method or spermicide alone, or withdrawal.

Research suggests that breastfeeding (the lactational amenorrhoea method or LAM) is as reliable as some hormone or barrier methods for six months after the birth, if you are breastfeeding fully (offering no supplements) and have no periods. There are addresses in the Directory for information about all these methods.

Adjusting in special situations

You get together with your partner in a specific set of circumstances, and although you have no knowledge of how life will turn out you expect them to stay more or less the same. The pressures that result from something like lengthy IVF treatment or deciding to adopt are much greater than normal. There is an implicit expectation that if you get your heart's desire – a precious baby that cost you dearly – you live happily ever after; but you are still the same person.

Any traumatic event, such as losing a baby, produces needs that it may be unrealistic to expect your partner to fully meet. You cannot say how you or your partner will respond. Some couples pull together; others cannot, or they part once the crisis is over. A couple who are unable to help each other may sink into a cycle of guilt and blame. Finding their needs are not fulfilled by their partner they begin to draw on their own resources: the 'weaker' partner becomes strong and the dynamics of the relationship change. One partner feels angry that the relationship is different and blames the other, who caused the change or who has changed.

Putting all your energy into whatever it takes to have a baby can distract you from problems in your relationship with your partner, which are still there afterwards. A hormone imbalance that made conceiving difficult may need extra time to settle down after the birth. Longing and hoping for a child can leave you, after the initial euphoria, with an almighty sense of anti-climax.

If you feel negative towards your partner, your baby or motherhood generally you may feel guilty and reluctant to admit it, at least until you feel better. Yet this is the experience of many women in stressful situations. It may help if you accept the way you feel for the moment and allow time to recover. Then you can tackle any problem that needs attention without blaming yourself or your partner for it.

Older mothers' experiences

Valerie (44): 'Barry's firm has been taken over and if he is made redundant I shall have to look for a job, just when I'm starting to enjoy Mark. I wouldn't have missed the last few months for the world, but some of it has been hard. I came through postnatal depression with a combination of pills and counselling – accepting that motherhood is a mixture of roses and rotten eggs took some effort.

'Age does influence my actions because I want to get the most out of each day while I can. Nothing lasts for long, good or bad. Younger mothers worry about the phases children go through, but I know Mark will feed himself, get out of nappies, stop screaming, and sleep through the night – one day!'

Q: I'm aware that I'm vulnerable to depression. How can I help to avoid it?
A: The key may be to become your own best friend. Depression rarely hits like a thunderbolt, so learn to notice the early signs and use avoidance strategies. When you are depressed you will not be able to summon up the energy to do the things that would help, so set your strategies in place beforehand.

You need companionship, to avoid isolation and to feel comfortable asking for help when necessary. Depression is so common that many people are understanding and some friends will offer support – nurture these friendships.

Find activities to turn to when you begin to feel low. A creative project could lift your mood and there is increasing evidence that moderate physical exercise, such as taking a brisk walk for half an hour (or even scrubbing a floor) can combat depression by releasing mood-lifting endorphins in the brain. Smile when you feel negative, as lifting your face muscles can help to lift your mood.

Some women write down everything they feel grateful for:

home, children, partner's support, friends and family, having survived traumas in their past, to look at when they feel low, but others find this makes them feel guilty! Do whatever works for you.

Lesley (36): 'There have been a few occasions when I've said I wished I'd never had the twins, but I wouldn't really change anything. Phil and I both get tired, but what parent doesn't? Phil notices it about halfway through the evening after a long day at work, especially if one of the boys has been unsettled during the night which happens quite often. Sometimes we wonder how we'll keep going, but we're in it together and sharing makes life smoother.

'As Sam and Thomas are six months old now we feel we're through the worst and we want to bring our large family together to share our pleasure and celebrate their birth. I can honestly say we have never enjoyed life so much.'

Q: Any suggestions for a meaningful celebration for families who do not want a religious naming ceremony?
A: You and Phil could write a simple testimony of what the twins mean to you and your hopes for their futures. If you have alternative 'godparents' or special friends, they could affirm their commitment to support the boys, to help them to grow to independence and develop their own beliefs and values, for example.

All the other adults with a special relationship to the twins could light a candle (night lights floating in water or placed in a circle look pretty), and each child could bring a flower or a small shiny object to give to the babies. With a poem or a reading (for example, the famous lines from Kahlil Gibran's *The Prophet,* 'Your children are not your children. They are the sons and daughters of Life's longing for itself . . .' or a passage from Laurie Lee's essay *The Firstborn,* or something from Beatrix Potter) and music at the beginning and end, you have the makings of a short eloquent ceremony. The Humanist Association (see *Directory*) has a self-help guide to naming ceremonies, including suggestions for readings and music, but many families devise their own.

Sue (39): 'Tiredness is something I expected with two children to look after, and in the early weeks I put it down to hormonal changes, stress because Jack was being difficult or even mild anxiety. I tried having an afternoon nap so that I wasn't overtired and I stopped drinking strong coffee. I'm sensitive to noise at night, and I had Amy in a cot beside our bed so I sometimes slept badly and woke at every little snuffle. I knew something wasn't right, as I felt exhausted even when I had a good night's sleep.

'Then my hair started to come out. My pillow was covered with hair every morning, and handfuls came out when I used a brush or comb. My doctor thought I was anaemic at first, but eventually diagnosed a thyroid problem. I have to take tablets regularly, but now I feel fine.'

Q: Is it common to lose hair after giving birth?
A: About one woman in ten suffers a degree of hair loss in the year after having a baby. Sometimes it is a temporary response to disruption of the normal hair growth cycle in pregnancy, but it can also be caused by an auto immune disease (alopecia) which causes hair follicles to 'switch off' and fail to produce new hair. There may be no obvious reason for this, although it can be triggered by stress, trauma, certain drugs, and in your case a thyroid problem.

Most women who suffer hair loss have 'diffuse alopecia', a marked thinning of the hair that causes great distress and can be a serious blow to their confidence. Various treatments can be tried, however, and there is a growing number of specialists interested in the condition (see *Directory*).

At-a-glance chart

There is a network of experts, experienced carers, supporters and other parents who can help you to make the most of parenting. There are addresses in the Directory, but this chart may help you locate sources of help more quickly.

Help with Babycare		
GENERAL	HEALTH	DISABILITY/SPECIAL NEEDS
Midwife, health visitor Your family Voluntary groups Childminder/nanny Books, magazines	Midwife, health visitor Your GP Voluntary groups Telephone helplines Alternative therapists	The Maternity Alliance ParentAbility Specialist voluntary groups Disabled Living Foundation

Help for Mothers		
GENERAL	BEREAVEMENT	RELATIONSHIPS
Midwife, health visitor Voluntary groups Your doctor Your family Friends, other mothers	Your family Another mother Bereavement counsellor Your GP, vicar, church elder Voluntary groups	Voluntary groups (eg Relate) Your family Relationship counsellor Your GP, vicar or spiritual adviser

General Help (To find the addresses of many national charities and smaller local groups)		
DIRECTORIES, ETC	PUBLIC LIBRARY	CITIZENS' ADVICE BUREAU
Phone Book Yellow Pages Thompson's Directory Local bookshop Local paper	Reference sections of large libraries keep the Directory of British Associations, listing 1000s of organisations by subject. Look at it yourself or ask the librarian to track down information for you.	Trained volunteers give confidential advice on many topics including debt, consumer rights and benefit regulations. If they cannot help they pass you on to someone who can. Local branch is in the Phone Book.

13   *Work and Motherhood*

ALL MOTHERS ARE WORKING MOTHERS, PAID OR UNPAID. WOMEN with small children often work for financial reasons but for older women, especially with a partner in full-time work, research shows that personal reasons are more important in deciding whether to work full-time or part-time or to stay at home when they have a baby.

Many older women look forward to full-time motherhood, which can provide freedom and autonomy, especially for women who have not had a fulfilling career. It can be more rewarding, however, when separated from general domestic duties. Work in the home is never-ending; its status is low and the pay is non-existent.

Paid work gives you independence, a break from childcare, a separate identity and the feeling of participating in society, and in some professions a career break would mean losing touch. Women in higher-status occupations, including many who delay motherhood, are more likely to return to work. By the time you reach your mid-thirties or forties your career may have reached a stage where it cannot be put on hold, or your lifestyle may demand that you continue to work.

What is right for one woman or one family will not be right for another, and this variety should be something to celebrate. It can be equally rewarding to be a full-time mother or return full-time to your career; if neither of these options is right for you there may be a part-time alternative. You can only choose one life and it will have advantages and disadvantages, but on the whole, older women are remarkably positive about their choices.

Working during pregnancy

There are few occupations that cannot be continued during pregnancy although jobs that involve long shifts, constant travel or heavy lifting, or where you are not able to sit down when you need to, may be more tiring. If you are not sure whether to continue work during your pregnancy talk to your GP. Some types of antenatal care (see page 128) may be easier to combine with work commitments.

Travelling to and from work and handling a demanding job while coping with sickness or heartburn (see page 147–8 for some remedies) is stressful, but working can also provide company, help your finances, keep you fit and distract from minor discomforts. A sedentary job could be more restful than staying at home if you might be tempted to spring clean or redecorate the house.

Many women take their time before announcing a pregnancy to work mates or their employer, because of the risk of a miscarriage or an adverse test result. Freelance or contract workers such as entertainers sometimes drop out for a few months instead of announcing a pregnancy, as some employers appear reluctant to engage a woman with a child unless she has proved that she can cope.

Some women are able to ignore the physiological changes of

pregnancy and carry on as usual, but in general the more you listen to your body and take care of it, the better it operates. You may have to ask for a chair, a glass of water or whatever, if colleagues are unaware of your needs, and carry a mineral spray or a battery fan to keep cool. Taking a taxi instead of struggling on public transport can help you to keep up a near-normal work schedule.

There is a reasonable choice of maternity wear suitable for business use and your basics will probably get heavy wear for several months. Loose waistbands, a well-fitting bra and layers that you can shed are more comfortable, with support tights and shoes with low heels if you have to stand a lot.

Women vary considerably in how energetic they feel when pregnant. You do not have to leave work on the date you become entitled to maternity leave but can work for as long as you wish, provided your employer agrees and you feel well. You cannot carry forward all the extra weeks to increase your time off after the birth, however. Slowing down in the later weeks of pregnancy can help you to adjust to the rhythm of life with a small baby, and many women find working can be increasingly tiring. If you have a complication or are expecting twins you may need to take sick leave before you are eligible for maternity leave.

Should you work if you have a child?

About half of all women with children under 5 go out to work, but only 1 in 16 works full-time. Many mothers return to work after the birth of a first child but give up when more children arrive because of the cost of childcare.

Children need to be nurtured as they grow up, but despite the strong feelings and research findings that are regularly aired on the subject, it is difficult to prove that mothers, rather than fathers

Your rights during pregnancy

Four basic rights apply to pregnant women. Your local social security office can give you details of the complex regulations and the Maternity Alliance or the Citizens' Advice Bureau (see page 268) can help with work-related problems. The first right is universal and the others depend on qualifying conditions.

1. Paid time off for antenatal check-ups, and antenatal classes if your GP or midwife considers them essential to your care.
2. Protection against unfair dismissal during pregnancy. If your job is unsuitable your employer must offer an alternative if one is available.
3. Statutory maternity pay or allowance. Your employer may provide additional arrangements under a special agreement.
4. Statutory maternity leave and the right to return to your job afterwards, if you give notice that you intend to do so.

or other significant adults, are vital to their welfare. The sort of care that builds self-esteem is often provided by mothers but could be shared by other people. Working is unlikely to harm a child, although always putting work first or never being around might.

As long as caring is seen as the primary responsibility of women there is no real incentive to introduce flexible working practices that would benefit everyone with family responsibilities. Fathers miss out on a close relationship with their children and many would like to share childcare more equally.

Despite the stresses of combining full-time work with motherhood it can be satisfying. So can working part-time, or full-time motherhood. Each has pros and cons; in the end it boils down to choice and personal circumstances. All parents face pressures: men and women, full-time carers, full and part-time workers. Most women occasionally worry or feel guilty that their child might be missing out, so the best you can do is to make the choice that is right for you and your circumstances.

Working after the birth

The revolution that took women into the work force has not been matched by a similar change in the lives of men, or in the attitudes of employers. There may be good intentions, but the shape and nature of life in the workplace does not make it easy for working mothers, who often take on the main responsibility of running the family as well. Consequently they often choose not to use their qualifications.

In some professions there is an assumption that a man who has a child can carry on as if nothing had changed, but an equally well-qualified woman should stop work and look after the family. Choice has almost come to mean not whether to be a working mother, but whether to be a mother at all.

Few women with children are able to work excessive and unpredictable hours or always be available, so it is easier to combine a career with motherhood in occupations where there is an understanding of family needs. When being seen to be committed means working long hours and socialising after work is part of the job, there may be little understanding or respect for someone who has to get home on time to take over from the nanny. Not wanting anyone to think that they are less than dedicated now they have a baby, many women overcompensate at work.

There may be a long way to go before most employers are family-friendly, but things are changing. Women are not victims; they shape their lives, balancing family and work according to their priorities and acquiring the sort of flexible attitude that stands them in good stead in a rapidly changing job market.

Full-time work

It takes skill and determination to combine the drive required for a career with the floating, inner world of motherhood, but it can be stimulating and worthwhile. Apart from the wage or salary, full-time work provides independence, a challenge and the confidence that comes from using your skills or training.

Full-time workers are less likely than part-timers to be marginalised or passed over for promotion, but there is some evidence that career development slows down and mothers are given less demanding roles. This suits many women as some of the energy they gave to their career is now directed elsewhere, although they often try to keep domestic problems away from the office in case they score badly when reliability and total commitment are counted up.

There is tension between a family and a full-time career for most parents, although it is generally easier if you have only one child. You may miss out on your child's milestones, and on time for yourself with nobody making claims on you. You may not fulfil either your work or your mothering role as well as you would wish, and feel you are constantly over-stretched.

In the morning, when you have already been on the go for an hour and a half, some of your colleagues have had nothing more taxing to do than run a shower. After work whoever looks after your child may go off duty, plunging you straight into your domestic role without time to wind down and adjust. A little voice in your head may say 'Why am I doing this?'

Working hard and being a workaholic are not the same thing, however, and women tend to be better than men at drawing the line between the two. You are unlikely to need your job to give you a sense of self-worth, as some men do. You have other things in your life and, aware of the need for balance, you may be well organised and confident enough to do what the job requires and then walk away.

Part-time work

Women who work part-time report less stress than their full-time colleagues and in many ways are happy with their working lives. They do not have to leave their child for so long and it is often easier to find childcare, although it may be more expensive when paid for by the hour. Part-timers may sacrifice employment status, pay and perhaps job satisfaction, however, and they have less access to training and development and less progression in their careers, so they feel less positive about their career prospects.

Many part-time jobs are unskilled and low paid, with no employment rights. The better jobs tend to go to women who did them before they had a child, and whose employer does not want to lose them. If you would like to return to your job part-time, you could present a proposal to your manager or personnel officer explaining how it would benefit not you but the company; you may be surprised at what you can achieve, even if a similar request has been refused in the past.

Job sharing: This can work especially well at senior levels or between partners. Two people can divide the hours, pay, holidays and benefits of the job between them in whatever way suits them, sometimes solving the need for childcare at the same time. You could apply together for an advertised position, approach an employment agency or apply to share a job already held full-time by one of you. If your employer is used to job sharing arrangements (see *Directory* if not) approach them direct and see if they can match you up.

Freelance or occasional work: Short-term contracts or engagements lasting a few weeks or months can be difficult if you are the main breadwinner as you have to look for the next contract as soon as you start work on the current one; but some women like them as they can hold their place in their professional field while enjoying blocks of time with their children between jobs. Temporary work obtained through an employment agency also gives some women the flexibility they want, although it is often low paid, with little continuity and no employment rights.

Self-employment: Running your own business can be satisfying if you are self-motivated and like a challenge; you can balance your life and take time off when you need it. You may have to find work, complete it, deal with your own tax and insurance and set boundaries, but motherhood teaches you to prioritise, to juggle several different jobs and complete them on time, managerial skills that can be vital for success. Many women say the quality of their home life improves when they take on a new venture, although if the business is successful, stopping work can be harder than starting!

The flood of women into the work force has created the need for traditional service jobs, such as cleaning, ironing, childcare and ready-made food. Caring for your own or somebody else's elderly relative could also fit in well with bringing up your child. These growth areas offer obvious opportunities; but some large high street chains were also started on the kitchen table. The library or Citizens' Advice Bureau can give you advice about starting a business.

Working from home

An increasing number of jobs can be done partially or completely from home. This can be ideal when you have a baby as you can organise the hours to suit yourself, but it is usually difficult to look after a child at the same time.

Most work needs space and no interruptions. If you use a computer your child (or even the family cat) can discover functions you never knew existed or wipe out hours of effort at the touch of a button. Pins posted into your sewing machine can bring the production line to a halt, and a baby crying in the background or a toddler who grabs the phone before you reach it can give the impression of chaos to clients who do not have children.

You may be able to work in the evenings (although this cuts into time spent with your partner), or ask friends to help out when you have a busy week, reciprocating in quieter times. Alternatively, childcare may be the answer.

Full-time motherhood

As a baby develops, motherhood can be increasingly rewarding. Full-time mothers have a gentler pace and often a better quality of life. They have the time to take up new interests and seek out new friendships, the satisfaction of doing what they feel is best for their family. For many older women retirement is a relief after years of working, and things that were necessities when they were single and child-free are reassessed as luxuries and never missed.

Domestic life can be as stressful as any job, however. Sometimes you will sit back, look at your family and feel completely fulfilled; most of the time you will be caught up in the battle against chaos. Much routine child care lacks stimulation and some women are shocked to find they are bored, have lost confidence, or cannot accomplish tasks that were simple before they had a child; some miss having their own money, or feel they are not supporting their partner or being useful.

You need time off – nobody can perform a job well twenty-four hours a day, seven days a week with no breaks – and friendships with other mothers who have small children. Friends with older children may airily dismiss your concerns about your baby's sleeping habits or diet as they are preoccupied with different challenges, such as teenagers or choosing secondary schools.

If you have previously put all your energy into your career it can take a year or so to adjust to the different rhythm of full-time motherhood.

Career break: Staying at home with a baby gives you the chance to reassess your life and decide whether you want to go back to the same career at a later date or change tracks. As more women seek to continue their career or start a new one after a break, retraining opportunities abound and employers are increasingly receptive to women returners. You are not obliged to record your date of birth or age on a CV or job application form, even when there is a space for it; having a young child should speak for itself.

There are similarities between running a home and family and managing a workplace. Women returning to work after a career break are often equal in managerial skills to anyone in the world of business. At home you set and work to a budget, balance books, manage support services and ensure adequate supplies of food and clean clothes to keep the household running smoothly. You sort out disputes, persuade a reluctant toddler to put her coat on, organise corporate meetings (or dinner parties) for your partner's colleagues who are essential to the family budget. All these skills should make you more desirable as an employee.

Childcare

A child develops self-esteem when people listen to her, remember things that are important to her such as birthdays, spend time with her, set appropriate boundaries and take an interest in things that interest her. However many toys or treats a child gets, nothing can substitute for knowing that somebody thinks she is the best thing since sliced bread, that she (as distinct from her education, her clothing or her social life) is a priority to you. If she always comes after your work she will assume she is less important. Children thrive when cared for by someone who likes children in general, and someone who likes this one in particular.

Ideally, whoever you trust to look after your child should like children and the things they enjoy and not be doing it solely for the money. Caring for and parenting children are two distinct roles, however. A carer gives your child attention, stimulates her and keeps her safe while you work; she picks up and comforts your child when you are not there, but at the end of the day she goes home to her own life. You do not want your child to be distraught when her carer inevitably moves on.

Mothering is a different quality of attention. Your child *is* your life and the privilege of being fully accepted, which means being at the receiving end of both her deepest love and her worst behaviour, should be yours.

If your job is time consuming or demanding you may feel torn between it and your child no matter how good your childcare is. Getting the best is not always easy, especially if money is short or the childcare available is less than ideal. If your arrangement breaks down it can be a disaster and you may feel ready to accept any alternative, even if you do not know the person.

Constant change is unsettling for most children, but an arrangement that does not work out can usually be altered, and most parents succeed in arranging suitable care among the many possible options.

Childminders: A childminder has to be checked by and registered with the local authority. There are rules about the number and ages of the children (including her own) she may take and you usually have a contract setting out commitments on both sides, including back-up arrangements for illness or holidays (see *Directory*).

Childminders are usually experienced mothers who stay at

home to bring up their own children, and the relationship can be delicate. Women who have chosen to work sometimes feel they are being judged, or find it difficult to ask what their child has been up to all day. A childminder may be more flexible about irregular hours than a nursery or nanny, however.

Your local social services department can send you a list of registered childminders, or you may find one by recommendation. Alternatively you could ask a friend who has chosen full-time motherhood to look after your baby; she will need to register but this is not daunting. A relative can childmind without registering, and many women feel happiest with this arrangement. It can be awkward if a difference of opinion arises, however, and if payment is refused you may feel you are taking unfair advantage of goodwill.

Role sharing or reversal: In areas that have lost traditional industries, such as mining, at least half of the main carers of children are men. It can be a practical solution if you earn more or have greater job security than your partner, or if he is self-employed, his career is winding down or he can take an early retirement or a redundancy package. After the initial adjustment, a father who is at home all day generally experiences the same joys and frustrations as a mother and has a similar need for company in the evening, joint decision-making, appreciation for the job he is doing and regular time off to do what he wants.

If you change the name on your family allowance book the time your partner spends looking after your child will earn him credits towards his pension. You could tell the tax office if you wish to receive the married couples' allowance and make use of your partner's personal allowance by transferring investments into his name.

Au pairs: An *au pair* works for up to five hours a day, with two free days a week, in exchange for living expenses plus an allowance. Hours are flexible and she can help with chores, care for children and babysit. She is not qualified in childcare and would not expect to take sole charge of a baby.

Find an *au pair* through an agency (try Yellow Pages, or *The Lady*). You are unlikely to meet her until she comes to your home (although you can speak on the phone beforehand). Her English may be imperfect and a teenager away from home for the first time can be homesick. Some *au pairs* are very capable, however, and it may be a cost-effective solution if you work from home.

Nannies: A nanny has a recognised childcare qualification, or extensive experience of looking after children. She takes sole charge, but does not do general domestic tasks: she washes your child's clothes but not the family's, for instance. Nannies can live in or out, and they tend to move on after a year or so.

Although not a cheap option – in addition to her salary and insurance there may be higher household bills and the expense of a car to ferry children around – your child will get individual attention in familiar surroundings and there will be someone to look after her if she is ill, a distinct advantage if you have a demanding job.

Some mothers share a nanny on a daily basis if they work part-time; or to look after both children if they work full-time. Find a family to share with first and then look for someone suitable. These arrangements need mutual tolerance at first but they help with the cost and provide companionship for your child.

Nurseries: Social services departments register and inspect nurseries. The Children Act (1989) recommends a ratio of three babies per carer for the under 2s, four children per carer for 2 and 3 year olds, and eight per carer for 4–5 year olds. Nurseries are usually provided by companies or private individuals and some do not take babies because they need extra staff. Local authority nursery places are generally allocated on a 'needs' basis, for example to lone parents.

Nurseries are usually open from 8 am to 6 pm, to cover the working day. Your child has several carers rather than one 'mother figure' and there should be a variety of play equipment available and sufficient staff so that she gets some individual

---

Choosing childcare

Choice of childcare is usually limited by the cost, what is available and your circumstances. If you have several options you can take into account convenience, your child's age and temperament and how you and your partner feel about the options. Here are some considerations:

- ❑ How many hours' care do you want and do you want it in one place?
- ❑ Do you want a family environment, a well-equipped nursery or care in your own home?
- ❑ Is it important to you that your child gets one-to-one attention, or do you want her to have the companionship of other children?
- ❑ Which is more convenient – childcare in or near your own home, close to your work or near where your partner works? A long journey to a superb nursery may prove less workable than a childminder just round the corner.
- ❑ Do you want a carer who is young and enthusiastic, or somebody more mature and experienced?
- ❑ Are you likely to need flexibility, for example over arrangements for picking your child up or looking after her if she is unwell?
- ❑ Do you want your carer to supply your child's food, or to provide it yourself?
- ❑ Do you have strong feelings about things like the lifestyle, values, religious beliefs or attitude to discipline of whoever cares for your child?

attention, not just comfort when she is upset.

There is often considerable demand for nursery places but you may want to put your name down even if you are told there is little likelihood of a place; families move and places become available unexpectedly.

Returning to work

Returning to work a few weeks after the birth is physically and emotionally stressful, and most older women prefer to take several months off if they can. Even then it can be a wrench, although a well-planned and phased return is easier.

Settling your baby: Whatever sort of care you choose, you will worry about leaving your baby as the time to return to work draws near. A few dry runs, leaving your child for a morning or afternoon, may make the day you return to work less stressful. Dry runs can streamline your routine, make getting away in the morning easier and reassure you that your baby can settle – you will probably miss her more than she misses you at first.

Back-up care: If your child falls ill you will need back-up care. Most women feel torn if they have to leave a child who is unwell, but if you or your partner cannot leave work at short notice a friend or relative might take over from a nursery or childminder, or you might make a reciprocal arrangement with a friend's or colleague's nanny. Other working mothers understand the problem only too well and you may have a ready-made support network that you can call on. As a last resort, some working women are forced to call in sick when their child is ill.

Breastfeeding and work: Depending on your circumstances you may be able to continue to breastfeed while working full or part-time. Many women find their supply adjusts to breast-feeding mornings and evening, and they leave bottles of formula or expressed milk for the day. Some need to express milk at work to avoid getting engorged (see page 245–7); they either discard this or keep it in a fridge with the container in a plastic box marked with their name to avoid confusion.

If it is impractical or too stressful to combine breastfeeding and work you will be more comfortable and avoid engorgement if you drop one breastfeed per week, starting with the smallest a month or so before you return to work. If you have not intro-duced bottles before your baby may resist (see page 287), but keep trying as she may suddenly change her mind. A breast-feeding support group (see *Directory*) can give individual advice.

Combining full-time work and motherhood

❑ You do not have to carry on as if you did not have a baby. Pace yourself at work or get extra help; make allowances and expect other people to accept this.

❑ Put your feet up in your lunch break and for half an hour when you get home.

❑ Accept all help offered and turn a blind eye if things are not done your way.

❑ Eat as healthily as possible.

❑ List what needs doing and ask yourself what would happen if each item was not done or if you asked someone else to do it.

❑ Look for short cuts if something is essential.

❑ The best time-saver is saying 'no'! Decide if a request is unrea-sonable, you lack the necessary expertise, it takes lower priority than what you are doing or someone else could do it just as easily.

Older mothers' experiences

Elizabeth (42): 'Compared with men, women's pay drops steeply during the years of motherhood and never recovers, and although this is unfair I can see why. Mothers could put as much into their careers as many fathers do but they realise what they would be missing. They know how quickly a child grows and that real relationships can't be built in a spare five minutes.

'I no longer socialise or spend time at the gym like I used to because Jessica draws me home. I think about her at odd moments in the day and wonder what she's up to and I treasure my time with her. I'm committed to my career but I also wish I could put it 'on hold' and enjoy her early years to the full. Back on the career ladder, yes, but I seem to have lost my head for heights.'

Q: I've decided to take Jessica out of nursery care and have a full-time nanny. Where can I get advice about insurance, pay and contracts?
A: You could find a nanny through an agency, when the initial selection and other details will be done for you. Alternatively you could contact a local college or advertise locally or nationally. The organisations in the Directory can provide sample contracts to use for a nanny or a childminder, plus information on rates of pay and national insurance and guidance on interviewing candidates.

Follow up references, ask to speak directly to a previous employer; check qualifications, registration certificates and so on. College leavers have been vetted at the start of their course, but other carers may not. While not wishing to be overly suspicious of everyone, trust your instinct if something does not feel right.

Valerie (44): 'Barry was made redundant and as it is easy for me to get work as a nurse we have role reversed. We both found it difficult to adjust at first. I missed Mark and envied Barry who could watch him develop, while I came home exhausted every night from a job where I'm under pressure.

'I noticed things like dust on the sideboard and pizza served up too frequently for tea. Barry found it hard because he had held a responsible supervisory job and felt he couldn't even organise one baby and get the chores done now. He was lonely and walked for miles with Mark in a backpack.

'Eventually we found a compromise that suits us. Barry has a part-time job and Mark goes to a childminder two days a week. Although I'm not at my best in the morning and end up screaming on the days we all have to get out of the house on time, to my surprise I have started to enjoy the challenge of a career again.'

Q: How can I make the start to the day more relaxed?
A: Do your thinking and preparation the night before so that you can get ready like a robot. A kitchen timer could limit the time everyone spends in the bathroom if this causes conflict. Breakfast could be laid the night before, or everyone could be responsible for making their own and washing the plates up. You and Barry can share feeding Mark and getting him ready for the child-minder. Allow half an hour more than you need at first, so that if something happens you have time in hand.

It will save nagging or panic if your daughters are responsible for their own PE kit, sandwiches, homework and so on. Remind them to get everything ready the night before, then trust them. This will be hard at first if you are used to thinking for them, but a routine where everyone knows what is expected and you do not feel 'in charge' will help.

Sue (39): 'I had a mixed reception when I returned to work. Many colleagues welcomed me, but the woman who took over during my maternity leave was unhappy at being demoted and tried to sideline me. It was not pleasant. My brain is scrambled from exhaustion so I may be hypersensitive to criticism, but I feel some disapproval of working mothers and I never mention babies unless someone asks.

'Sometimes I work from home, although only in the evening. It's difficult if the children are around as I cannot concentrate if I hear crying and when they are giggling I always want to go and join in the fun.

'Motherhood is so different from the world of work but I love leading a double life. I love coming across story books fighting for space with lipstick and spare bibs in my bag. It's hard if I've had a bad night with one of the children, but I still feel that combining motherhood and work gives me the best of both worlds.'

Q: Jack took a bottle happily but Amy screams with rage. How can I persuade her?
A: Ideally, you offer boiled water or expressed breast milk once or twice a week from birth to keep a baby used to the different action required when sucking from a teat (see page 243), but having had no problems with Jack it is understandable that you did not anticipate any with Amy.

If she is hungry your husband or someone else is likely to have more success in persuading her to take a bottle as she will associate you with breastfeeding and get very cross when denied what she wants. You could try introducing a bottle halfway through a feed, or when she is sleepy. She might prefer a different teat shape, one with fewer holes so that the milk does not choke her, or more holes so that it flows faster (heat a darning needle on the cooker to make them). It may not be worth spending a fortune on a range of teats in the hope that one will suit her, however, as it often makes little difference.

She may suddenly change her mind when she gets used to having a bottle popped in her mouth, or she may continue to resist with spirited determination. If so you could try her on a small cup or a feeding beaker with a spout. Some babies take to these more happily than to a bottle, and she will get plenty of chance to suck if you are still breastfeeding part of the time.

14   *Motherhood Alone*

ABOUT ONE FAMILY IN FIVE IS HEADED BY A LONE PARENT. NINE out of ten lone parents are women and about half have a child under the age of 4. Relatively few chose to have a child without a partner; some are alone through bereavement or, more often, the breakdown of a relationship.

When something breaks down, life is temporarily thrown into disarray. If it is a washing machine, we blame the manufacturer and demand greater reliability or better servicing, although sometimes it is better to change the model. When a partnership breaks down and children are involved there are calls for stronger measures to keep couples together – more encouragement to marry or stricter divorce laws; or for better services to mend relationships – more counselling, more mediation. Working at the relationship is considered responsible; getting out before you go under is not generally seen as an acceptable option.

Lone parents struggling to be both mother and father to their child often feel that other people are looking over their shoulder. They are a handy target for politicians searching for sound bites and simple solutions, blamed if they leave their children to go out to work, but equally blamed if they stay at home and exist on welfare benefits, attitudes that make it harder to be a good mother.

Anyone bringing up a child on their own will face some difficulties that are not faced by those within a partnership. Lack of money is probably the single biggest problem for a lone mother, because society is generally geared to men as earners and women as carers. What is often viewed as the 'problem' of lone mothers may be partly the result of inequality in earning ability between the sexes.

You can be a happy family with or without a father, however. Bringing up a child alone and turning what you first thought of as a bleak future into something positive can be an achievement to be proud of.

Going solo: Setting out to have a baby without creating a two-parent family takes thought and commitment, but women who decide to go solo have usually considered carefully how their lives will change and really want a child. They tend to be older and more financially stable, with good employment prospects. A lone mother who does not need welfare benefits may face less disapproval. Women who go solo often have a mature outlook on life and generally feel more positive than someone who got pregnant by accident or whose partner let her down.

Some women separate the roles of lover and father, to avoid judging every boyfriend according to his suitability as a father until the 'right' man turns up. You may prefer the anonymity of donor insemination to achieve a pregnancy; or you may feel that a child needs to know his father and shun a quick fling with a test tube or a stranger in favour of a close friend who wants a child without a traditional family relationship.

This needs caution (see page 110), but if you go into it with your eyes open it may be preferable to entering a partnership because you are desperate to have a baby, and then watching your child lose the father he loves because you got together for the wrong reasons and your relationship fails.

Mostly alone: A growing number of women have a partner away from home for weeks or months at a time. Men who work in the City or take business trips abroad, sports stars, sailors and sales reps, musicians and heavy goods drivers often dip in and out of family life, leaving their partner with the responsibilities of a lone parent most of the time.

Absence makes the heart grow fonder but the reunion is not always a second honeymoon. You may feel envious of your partner's lifestyle and he of yours. After caring for your child alone you may want to talk when your partner gets home; he may want to make love and then crash out, so that you feel you are providing hotel service with sex thrown in and he feels rejected when you refuse.

When you take full responsibility for running a family, getting the car or the boiler serviced and coping if your child is ill, you become self-reliant. On his return your partner may feel redundant, a stranger to his child, a guest in his own home with no real role to play. You may resent him making decisions when he has not played as big a part in your child's life as you have.

Adjusting can be harder than you anticipate; differences of opinion can lie buried until they explode. Time when you should be enjoying each other's company may be spent bickering about who is hard done by or whether he is going to mend the iron.

Constant separation strains a relationship, and although it works in the short term it can lead to growing apart in the longer term. It helps to keep in touch by fax, phone or e-mail so that your partner knows what is going on in his absence, and to share the load by listening to each other talk through the day. You may need to recognise the need for reassurance that sex can provide, make family time a priority, and spend time together renewing your relationship without your child.

Bereavement: If your partner dies you are left with all the practical problems of lone motherhood and an overwhelming sense of unfairness. You may have had the stress of coping during an illness, or the sudden shock of an accident, the hand of fate that changes your future irrevocably. Married women receive widow's benefit at first, but unless your partner made provisions finance may be a long-term worry, as it is for many lone mothers.

You are likely to receive great sympathy at first. Friends and family generally rally round to offer practical help, but coming to terms with your own, and if he is old enough your child's grief, can take months or even years (see page 227). It may feel worse rather than better as time passes and the process of adapting to a different future begins. Some people may assume that you never had a partner or were deserted, which can be hurtful, but your child is less likely to lose his self-esteem.

Separation or divorce: There is something specific about the break-up of an established family that affects a child more than losing his father through death or being brought up by his mother alone from an early age. Children of separated or divorced parents show more signs of difficult behaviour and do less well at school, findings that have not changed over the past forty years. If a child has to face the fact that his father does not want to support him or even see him, his self-esteem may be damaged; and the feeling of rejection may get sharper as he grows up.

Hurt feelings are involved in the most amicably handled separation and it may be hard to overcome these if you feel that contact with your ex-partner could harm your child. 'Reasonable access' may be one more thing that you cannot agree about. Given the importance to a child of an ongoing relationship with his father, however (even an imperfect one) it is worth struggling to find a solution. Mediation services (see *Directory*) may help, and they can also suggest ways to minimise damage to your child if your partner fails to maintain contact.

To discover that your partner is leaving you when you are pregnant or have a young child can feel like the end of the world. You may lose a major source of financial and practical support, along with self-esteem and your extended family. If your partner found somebody else when you thought you were going through the normal ups and downs of any relationship, you are likely to feel humiliated and unable to trust your own judgment.

If you have left your partner, because of abuse or because you have found somebody else, you may feel responsible for both the separation and any distress or negative behaviour your child exhibits. This is a heavy burden of guilt to carry, even when your decision was the only one possible in the circumstances.

Advantages of being alone

- ❑ You can please yourself about when you eat and where you go.
- ❑ You are never torn between your partner's needs and your baby's needs.
- ❑ The decisions are yours alone; there are no disagreements over what is right or wrong for your child.
- ❑ Everything is down to you. You do not need to persuade a partner to take his share or suffer the frustration of doing nothing because you cannot agree.
- ❑ There is less resentment, and resentment is extremely draining if the reality of a partnership does not come up to expectations.
- ❑ If you work you may receive more support and understanding as a lone mother.
- ❑ Relying on yourself is liberating; you come to realise that if you can do this you can do anything.

Lesbian women who become mothers when married, but separate when they discover their true sexuality, often face even
more disapproval if they come out. Gossip will hurt and there
is no way round this; but it may help to realise that some people
make scapegoats by projecting their own failings on to others.

When you have recently separated you may worry about
people judging you; or be afraid of breaking down when telling
people (although tears can open up communication). Burying
your head in the sand and denying what has happened is a
way of gradually coming to terms with and coping after any
traumatic event. You may lose confidence, feel sad, angry,
lonely and afraid of having nobody to share the responsibility,
but bringing a child up alone is not the catastrophe it may seem
at first.

Pregnancy and birth

If you are facing pregnancy and birth alone by choice you are
likely to feel more in control than if a partnership you expected
to be permanent breaks down when the responsibility of a baby
is on the cards. During pregnancy hormone changes make you
emotionally vulnerable and a relationship in tatters may seem
catastrophic.

Everyone feels panicky sometimes during pregnancy, but
knowing that you are ultimately responsible for your baby can
also give you a great sense of independence. You do not necessarily miss out on sharing the joys of feeling your baby move or
the worry of deciding about tests just because your baby's father
is absent. Family and friends tend to step back when you have a
stable relationship, not wishing to intrude, but if you are alone
they may be thrilled by the chance to share your pregnancy and
support you at a special time.

You could choose a godmother or special friend for your child and include her where possible, for example at your antenatal check up or scan appointments. You may be surprised at how many people offer to support you at the birth, even your baby's father. Think about who you would like as your birth partner (see page 186). If whoever you choose has not attended a birth, lend a pregnancy book or suggest attending antenatal classes together. Anyone you like can attend a home birth and most hospitals allow you a choice of birth partner.

In some ways it is easier to be alone right from the start. At least you know where you stand and do not worry about your child losing a relationship with his father. When a man decides not to be involved during pregnancy you grieve. Then you recover and get on with your life.

Your child's father

A father who is not married to the mother of his child has no legal rights over the child. If he applies to the courts for parental responsibility, however, it will be automatically granted provided he can show an ongoing relationship with the child and is not considered a danger. This gives him similar rights to a married father but does not deal with things like maintenance or access, which have to be negotiated separately. A third to half of divorced men quietly drop out of their child's life, however. Keeping up the relationship may take more time or effort than they feel able to give and other priorities take over.

A child benefits from regular contact with his father, even occasionally, so that he gets to know a real person instead of constructing a fantasy figure. If you are both determined to put your child first you are less likely to use him to work out emotional problems with each other. A mother can make visits difficult, or a father may be unreliable, cancelling visits at the last minute. It does not help to criticise, however angry you feel. Either partner can go back to court to reassess contact arrangements.

An unmarried father is legally obliged to support his child whether he has contact or not, but some men feel they are not responsible when the child's mother appears financially independent. If you cannot agree, an amount of maintenance is set by the Child Support Agency, with power to deduct it from the father's salary. This is almost impossible to enforce, however, as an obstructive man can make endless difficulties.

Morally it may be absolutely right that a father contributes to his child's upkeep, but you cannot make someone care or behave decently against their will. Rules that were intended to make fathers think twice before abandoning their children have simply made some men rebel against payment and demand access rights. Realistically, you could spend a great deal of money and emotional energy with little or no chance of success. It may be better to channel energy into something more positive.

If an unmarried father wants to appear on the birth certificate he has to register the birth himself; or be added at a later date with the mother's consent. A child can be given any surname so some women register both and use the one that seems more convenient; others choose a different surname altogether.

Money matters

Motherhood is no bar to working if you have a marketable skill, and women who are financially secure sometimes prefer to bring a child up alone rather than remain in an unsatisfactory relationship. Working is easier and financially more rewarding if you have a well-paid job and only one child, perhaps because you have delayed having a baby until your career is established.

For most lone mothers, however, childcare needs are greater and money is tighter than if they had a partner. If you live on Income Support, like 70 per cent of lone parents, benefit rules and childcare problems can make it difficult to work, and your weekly income may be less than half that of a two-parent family.

Money gives you equality, choice and self-respect, and it can be a shock to face a reduced income when you have sole responsibility to provide for your child. You may feel humiliated to be in this situation if you are used to having your own money, but maturity and experience of life can also make it easier to cope. The best way to survive is to ask for advice before you need help (see *Directory*).

Some women work part-time to keep up skills or make a little extra money, while others study, train in something like aromatherapy that could provide flexible self-employment, or set up a business that they can expand as their child grows up.

Lone parents who work full-time say it helps to devote half an hour to playing with their child as soon as they get home, before they change their clothes, make a meal, or do anything other than fetching a snack if they are hungry. This can be a winding down process for both of you; your child gets your full attention and you feel you have put your relationship first.

It can also produce a positive atmosphere that makes the next few hours go more smoothly, an easy little routine that shows your child that he is more important to you than anything else. Some things may have to go, but if the only moments you can spare for your child are fitted in after chores are done you will feel less good about yourself as a mother.

Planning a budget

To plan a budget, fill in the chart as accurately as possible, overestimating your expenditure where there is doubt. Phone the enquiry number on your last bill if you are not sure what you spend on gas or electricity. If your income is weekly divide the relevant costs to get a weekly total; if it is monthly multiply the weekly costs by four and divide the annual costs by twelve to get comparable totals.

If the right-hand total exceeds the left, or is too close for comfort you need to cut down your expenses or increase your income to make ends meet. The Citizens' Advice Bureau (see phone book) can offer advice.

INCOME

Wage or Salary ....
Child Benefit ....
Interest on Savings ....
Any other income ....
....
....
....

EXPENDITURE

Mortgage or rent ....
Gas ....
Electricity ....
Telephone ....
Council Tax ....
Insurance (car, household, etc.) .....
Food ....
Car or other travel expenses ....
Your clothes ....
Your child's clothes, nappies, etc. ...
Entertainment ....
TV Licence ....
Childcare ....
Birthday/Christmas presents ......
Holidays ....
Other ....
....
....

TOTAL   **TOTAL**

Your child's needs

Lone mothers often blame themselves for failing to create the traditional family that many people consider ideal, but two-parent families do not have a monopoly on love and security. You have to plan carefully and put your child first, but the joy of motherhood does not depend on having a partner.

A child needs male and female role models and you need companions of both sexes, if you are both to be rounded individuals who enjoy life together and separately. When you are too tired to make an effort it is tempting to transfer your need for love and affection to your baby, who returns it unquestioningly. A child grows up, however, and cannot satisfy adult needs; other adults must fulfil them.

There is no substitute for contact with a wide variety of people. Other women sometimes leave a lone mother out of social occasions, considering her off-limits where their partners are concerned, or assuming she has no money or time (she may actually have more time without a partner to consider), so it can take effort and thought; but no more than ensuring an only child has companions or a country child has access to culture.

Your child needs to know there are people who will look after him if anything happens to you and if you foster close relationships with other adults and children and try to keep in touch with step siblings, cousins and grandparents, you and your child will not become everything to each other.

Having all your eggs in one basket can intensify your relationship. You may become afraid of what might happen to your child and over-compensate by giving in to demands you know are unreasonable. For instance, sleeping in your bed may be hard to discourage, especially if your partner has left, but an older child needs to find his own independence. Your situation is not responsible for behaviour that is part of normal development, however. Most children go through phases of preferring one parent to the other, for example, or playing one person off against another; if you are alone it may be a grandparent or your childminder.

As a lone parent you face up to yourself because there is nobody else to blame. The stakes are higher and it is easy to be over-protective, but you can equally develop a caring, honest relationship with your child.

If you make time to spend together, if you put your energy into enjoying life and ask for help when you need it, you will make a good job of motherhood. Your child will not miss out.

Looking after yourself

When you are bringing up a child under pressure, without the respite and reassurance that a mother who has a partner enjoys, you may compare lives and think yours is harder. It can be a relief

---

Ten small ways to make yourself feel better

- ❑ Read a magazine article or one chapter of a novel.
- ❑ Have a bath by candlelight.
- ❑ Watch the shape of your child's face, the fineness of his skin while he sleeps.
- ❑ Think about something you look forward to – an outing, a friend's visit, springtime.
- ❑ Give yourself a small treat.
- ❑ Get rid of negative feelings by talking into a tape recorder.
- ❑ Tear up magazines or paper, or jump on a cushion to release tension.
- ❑ Cuddle your baby and tell yourself you are as good a mother as any other.
- ❑ Go for a swim at your local leisure centre and put your baby in the creche.
- ❑ . . . . (fill this one in yourself)

to push the baby into somebody else's arms and retire for a good scream, but when you have small children maintaining a harmonious relationship with your partner is also challenging. The grass is rarely greener on the other side of the fence. Most mothers learn to enjoy what they have.

At times you may feel guilty, frustrated and afraid, resentful or angry if you have to cope with a drop in your standard of living or work when you wanted to stay at home with your baby. These can be destructive emotions, however. To make a good life for yourself and your child it may be more positive to conserve energy for mothering, for building relationships with family and friends, for having fun.

When everything depends on you it is important to be in good shape and not to become so stressed out (see pages 319–20) that you cannot shake off minor illnesses. Whatever makes you relaxed and positive should be a top priority. If you become depressed (see page 255) talk to your GP as soon as possible so that you get help.

A good and caring mother, alone or in a partnership, can be swamped by the daily struggle if she always puts her child's needs first. You need to be adequately selfish as a mother, and even more so when you are on your own.

A major source of stress for some women is the fear of having their child taken away if they are seen not to be coping. If the pressure on you is so great that you are afraid you might harm your child, use the voluntary agencies (see *Directory*) as a buffer. They are neutral and can tell you what is likely to happen, so that it is easier to ask for any help you need before it is too late. You owe it to yourself and to your child.

Getting support: Most mothers find the first few months of a baby's life stressful and need practical help and someone to talk to. A father cannot always fulfil the need for companionship, or give you ideas and help you get worries in proportion, in the way another mother can. Voluntary groups (see *Directory*) can help you contact other mothers, who understand your stresses and joys.

Once you trust someone enough to moan occasionally without losing face it is surprising how much it helps to get worries off your chest. It can be easier to develop this sort of relationship when you are alone because you do not hold back out of loyalty to a partner, and you may be able to develop strong mutual support.

A lone mother can manage extremely well if she constructs a pyramid of good women, each willing and able to give a little help. Such a pyramid is virtually indestructible. The bottom layer comprises anyone who offers help, however casually. Next come those you can call on occasionally for support, and then come those you can rely on regularly. There may be several layers to your pyramid or only a few, but the more people you include the less help you need from any one person and the more secure you will be.

Repaying a favour

❑ A small or occasional favour only needs appreciative thanks.

❑ Be on the lookout for doing something in return: pick up a prescription, offer a pair of hands to help put up a shelf, search out information at the library.

❑ Use your talents to bake a cake, make a casserole, give a massage, send a hand-made card saying thank you.

❑ Say it with flowers or a bottle of wine, on a birthday or other occasion so that it is not seen as payment.

❑ Swap creatively: friends who work full time may value help with ironing, gardening, someone to wait in for a service call, in return for babysitting.

❑ Support a working mother: offer back-up childcare, take a child to the dentist or pick him up from school, in return for babysitting or weekend respite.

When you are older your own parents or your baby's other grandparents may be unable to give much assistance, but other relatives or your baby's father (even if you do not live together) may be able to help. If they are already stretched by their own families or jobs the net may have to be cast wider. A baby is often a novelty to neighbours and friends who are childless or have grown-up children and they may be glad to help if you tell them what they can do.

The first step to creating a support pyramid is to get in the habit of accepting every offer of help – even to hold your baby while you open your front door – rather than automatically saying that you can manage. The second is to exclude nobody unless they are clearly unsuitable. Accepting help does not commit you or the person offering it to a long-term relationship. Even brief help is help and you soon learn to judge who is likely to stay the course and join your support pyramid.

A balanced life

A balanced life does not simply evolve. When there are many demands on you and nobody to give you a break or make sure you are all right, you need to plan in order to make time for work, mothering and chores while leaving space to lead a life of your own. Although you may feel that muddling is all you can manage, in the long term you and your child will benefit if you make time every day to recharge your batteries. Some women find it works to designate half an hour a week as planning time, so that it becomes as much of a routine as going to the supermarket.

Look at your daily and weekly schedules to make sure you have time for recreation as well as for work and family (see page 318). Some needs can be combined: for example, lunch with work mates is also adult time, and playing with your child after a bath is recreation as well as good mothering. A tiny baby who fusses

Make the most of motherhood alone

❑ You *can* be a happy family, and you *can* bring up a well-adjusted child on your own. Many of the joys of parenthood do not depend on a father being present.

❑ Try not to see every problem as the result of being a lone mother. There are practical difficulties in any family.

❑ Expect to struggle to carve out some time for yourself – all mothers do.

❑ Try to avoid you and your child becoming everything to each other.

❑ Deliver cuddles but also discipline. Switch to a firm tone that your child can recognise, or a no-nonsense catch phrase such as 'Enough!'

❑ Parenthood is the real test of maturity – not all partnerships are loving and more break up under the stress of having a baby than at any other time.

❑ In a balanced life, expect to get some things wrong and some things right. A perfect mother would be a hard act for a child to follow.

may settle in a baby sling while you get on with chores. An older baby may benefit from learning to amuse himself for short periods. A kitchen timer can help you organise time and a catch phrase such as 'Time for chores' can tell a small child what to expect.

The best thing you can do for your child is to survive as an individual. You may find another partner in time, but a new companion is a friend first so the more you relax and let things happen without making a big deal of it the better. Your child does not have to like your friends; nor is he auditioning another parent. Being open and honest all along the line will stand you in good stead if a friendship develops into something more.

Older mothers' experiences

Elizabeth (42): 'Michael's work schedule means that he's away for weeks at a time so I take on all the responsibility and set my routine in place without him. Then he comes home and wants to go out and about as we did before Jessica arrived, because he's not really tuned in to a baby's needs. I rearrange the household around him and sometimes I resent the extra work.

'Jessica is growing fast and her needs change each time Michael sees her. He doesn't always know how to handle her so he gets her overexcited. She expects attention while he's here, and when he goes again there's a vacant space where Daddy should be. It hasn't been easy, but we've learned to talk more since we had Jessica. If you can do that you can work things out.'

Q: How can I keep contact with other mothers when I work full-time and can't go out in the evenings because I'm on my own?
A: Working and lone mothers often feel that they miss out on the sharing that goes on among groups of mothers, because the timing, location or effort involved make it hard to join in. You may be able to find a regular babysitter so that you can attend a working mothers' group that meets in the evenings, however. Lone parent groups (see *Directory*) often have weekend meetings or joint outings for the children.

As you are shouldering a lot of responsibility you may feel too tired to make an effort at times, but the challenge is to find mothers with a similar outlook to yours so that friendships develop and the pleasure outweighs the effort. You could invite mothers from your antenatal class to come round for coffee and a chat in the evening; your health visitor may provide contacts or you may get to know someone at work, or whose child attends the creche at the local leisure centre with yours, to share weekend outings.

Anne (47): 'My partner left just before Chloe was born and refused to see her. Breaking up is worse when you aren't married because there's no tidy ending as there is with divorce. People assume that the relationship doesn't matter so much. You let your dreams go and suffer for what might have been, not what actually was.

'When your hormones are all over the place things get dreadfully out of perspective. I felt history was repeating itself, and I knew in my heart that I could cope because I'd done it once. After my divorce I thought I'd never go through such pain again and I felt great sadness, for Chloe and for me.

'Many children grow up these days without a father present and it's better than having one who doesn't get on with the household. I look after my own mother as well as Chloe and it's stressful at times, but nobody can influence me or take me over and make me go in a direction I don't want to go in.

'I wouldn't swap my life for anything now, because it's so easy to be in charge of what's happening and to do it my way. Motherhood is a great healer and nothing can take the joy away.'

Q: As I'm unwaged, how can I kit out Chloe on a budget?
A: You can save a great deal by improvising, judging how long something will last and waiting until you are sure you really need something before buying it. Some women use a washing up bowl or wash basin instead of a baby bath, a square of plastic as a changing mat and a wash bag for carrying a nappy and bottom cream around, for example. Cots, prams and clothes, may be so tiny that they will be outgrown in a matter of weeks and a new purchase will be necessary, but friends may pass on tiny clothes that are almost new, or lend you equipment like a Moses basket or small car seat that will be useful only for a short time.

Second-hand equipment obtained through friends, car boot or NCT sales (see *Directory*), specialist shops or your local paper can also cut costs. The library can help you with current safety regulations and you will want to check that equipment like a pushchair, that is likely to get heavy use over a couple of years, has not had too much wear.

15 *Family Life*

MOTHERHOOD IS A STEALTHY PROCESS THAT CHANGES YOU MORE profoundly than you realise and produces some dramatic turnabouts. You become more passionate about some things, more tolerant of others. Boy racers showing off in sports cars suddenly become potential child killers. Paedophiles are no longer people to be understood but to be angry about: it is *your* child at risk. From criticising a mother who gives her child a packet of biscuits in the supermarket to keep him quiet, or sits him in front of a video while she gulps her tea in peace, you decide it is not such a bad idea after all. Things that were moral issues now become simply practical.

Every generation has its images of the good mother: she provides food, smiles, sticking plasters, stimulating activities; she always puts her child's needs first. Each generation discovers new rules for raising children: feed your baby four hourly, feed him on demand, let him sleep in your bed, banish him to his own. Nature is expected to help you transform yourself from an individual into the current ideal of motherhood. Those who never quite manage to stick to the rules are looked down on as spineless by their own generation, only to be called heroines by the next.

Mothers have the ability to give over and over again; this is real enough, and for some women it is a strength that reaffirms their sense of self. For others it produces conflict, and anxiety about not being good enough. You may be astonished at your capacity to love your child, but for most mothers coping and not coping exist side by side. Older mothers often have great expectations of their ability to cope and, if your standards are high, failure to meet them can be all the more devastating to your self-esteem.

Myth and reality

You managed a sales team, ran a hospital ward, made important decisions. You expect to be efficient at whatever you decide to do. You imagine you will have your baby, drop her off at a nursery and go about your business; but whether you intend it or not, she is your business. Her anger or displeasure is yours: if she is happy so are you, if she cries inconsolably you despair.

Another day goes by and the most significant thing you have produced is a stunning finger painting or a shopping list. At work you can usually point to something at the end of the week: a report written, eighty cases of champagne delivered. As a parent the time-span is different: to deliver a happy, responsible human being in eighteen years' time; a goal so far away and with so little feedback along the line that it seems you achieve nothing at all after a week of reading stories, sorting out squabbles or persuading a little person to eat up her greens.

Family life is chaotic. The reality is a child to bath, a washing machine to fill, a meal to purée; no time for a mid-life crisis; no time to pluck your eyebrows or even to cut your toenails! It can be hard to admit the chaos because it feels like failure when you want to be seen as competent. No mother can control her child's reaction to the world, however, so it is not in her power to make sure that things always go well. The nature of small children causes mayhem, not lack of nurturing skills; and learning to live in the here and now makes motherhood rewarding but also hard.

Most women have to live with their own romantic fantasy of motherhood, the ghost on their shoulder that watches and judges all the decisions they make. A working mother may have to sacrifice her carefully constructed images because she is too busy to keep up with them, but the fantasy can crumble just as easily when you are at home all the time. If you have given up a career for motherhood there is not even the respite of feeling in control at work. It is painful to lower your expectations and let the dream go, but feeling guilty is a normal consequence of the way reality cannot live up to the rosy myth of motherhood.

There are many moments of bliss and stretches of ordinary contentment, of course, but equally, there are few mothers, even in stable partnerships, who do not at times dream of walking out and leaving it all behind. It can be terrifying as well as enriching to realise just how emotionally tied you are when you have a child; but what you do not realise beforehand is that, like a dove, you can fly where you wish; you stay because you want to.

If you are generally confident and your baby is alert and responsive, however, you are likely to be doing fine. The more realistic about standards you become the more freedom you will have to enjoy family life for what it is: warm and funny, infuriating and frustrating, and in the long run unbelievably worthwhile.

Special situations

Adoption: Older parents who adopt often take an older child or a child with special needs. Such a placement makes extra demands, yet you may face parenthood without the months of pregnancy to prepare you, with no maternity leave or parenting classes and sometimes with only a hazy knowledge of what to expect.

You may have a long settling-in period and excellent professional support; or short notice and limited back-up. If you adopt abroad there may be a stressful period of travelling, searching, coping with foreign procedures. Your hopes may be raised and dashed repeatedly while you are powerless to complain. You may have to negotiate contact with the birth mother or siblings in an 'open' adoption; cope with hospital appointments, learning programmes or disturbed behaviour.

An older child sometimes has a honeymoon period of exemplary conduct before she relaxes and dares to behave badly. If she has had repeated breakdowns in her relationships she may take many months to trust you, testing you severely as though she knows how to destroy but not how to build relationships. This is profoundly unsettling, even for an experienced parent.

You are bound to wonder if you would have felt so desperate had she been your own child; but the question is irrelevant as the circumstances would be different. Not having carried or given birth does not make you less of a mother, but you may need more support (see *Directory*) and self-care while you rise to the challenges.

Disability or chronic illness: If your child has a disability or a long-term illness you are also likely to be under greater stress than most mothers while you adjust. The first hurdle is telling people; it is hard to say 'It's a girl, but . . .' conscious that they are ready with congratulations and will not know what to say.

Most parents need to mourn the loss of their dream child before they can settle down and see any future, but the outlook is often positive.

There are many sources of help for children with a physical or mental disability, from specially adapted equipment (see *Directory*) to amazing opportunity groups. Depending on the nature of the problem and local resources, information may be given to you or you may have to ferret it out yourself, but maturity and experience generally make it easier to get what you require.

Most mothers do not see themselves as victims and they make an effort to keep family life as normal and balanced as possible. A child with a disability may need extra care over a long period of time and some women look for a job, as a break from childcare and to enable them to buy the best equipment, often only available privately. It may take perseverance to find someone prepared to take on the responsibility of caring for a child with a disability, and employment flexible enough to let you attend hospital appointments frequently (see *Directory*).

If you or your partner have a chronic illness or disability you may be able to get hold of adapted equipment to make caring for a baby easier. Family life will be different but children usually adapt to a parent's disability with remarkable sensitivity. Most parents with a long-term health problem lead a gentler pace of life anyway, and have learned to be patient; both ideal qualities for positive parenting.

Family relationships

The way you or your partner were brought up affects the roles you play and the style of parenting you adopt within your family. Relationships are built on past experiences, seamlessly woven into the personality of each person.

The child of late parents, for example, is the most precious thing in their lives. To be the apple of your parents' eye is fine when you are young but a child who grows up over-indulged or over-protected may spend a lot of time searching for a partner who thinks as highly of him as his parents, until he realises that no-one will ever think of him like that again. Having his own child reminds him what it feels like to be at the centre of the world, only this time he has to do the giving.

For economic reasons some people live at home until their late twenties or early thirties. A prolonged adolescence free from responsibility can make it hard to grow up when they have a child. They may not want to become authority figures and avoid taking tough decisions for their children's welfare because they depend on them for emotional support; a reversal of the normal adult–child roles.

Only children are sometimes exceptionally generous but find sharing difficult when they grow up, especially when it comes to important relationships. They find it easier to give something away, or to withdraw from the race than to compete. A woman who was brought up as an only child may find it hard to share her own child with her partner, or a man may resent sharing his partner with his child.

There are many variations on similar themes, many different motivations that contribute to the richness of behaviour within a family. Take the various roles played: you may have children at different stages of maturity, be caring for elderly parents, pursuing a career, juggling a series of part-time jobs; your partner may have reached an age where he is struggling to hold his position at work and he may live apart from his older children, but be stepfather to yours and father to a new baby. Everyone does not bring up their children on a level playing field.

Step families: A new baby can bridge two families constructively; but the past can also interfere with the present. At a time when you feel vulnerable it may be difficult to share your partner; children may be insecure in a step relationship simply because they have already experienced family breakdown.

If your partner has other children he may fall over backwards to comply with their mother's demands, to ensure that he can see them or because he feels more secure with you than with her. If he does not confront demands that you see as unreasonable, however, you could end up feeling that your objections are petty or that he is not supporting you.

Some women have to live with the ghost of a past partner of exemplary mothering ability. It is daunting to compete with a 'perfect' mother, who cannot be challenged if she is not there or whose added experience may be all too real if she lives nearby. Any comment or gesture can confirm your fear of not being up to scratch when you already feel threatened. Relationships where one person feels constantly undermined have to overcome this if they are to develop.

Other children

When you have more than one child someone is likely to want your attention almost constantly for the first few months. Many older women have learned to be well-organised, however, and are surprised at how much energy they can muster.

Pre-school children: Much depends on your toddler's nature, but most show jealousy when time they regard as theirs is taken up by a crying baby, or twins who need extra attention. Some are easy-going until the baby is old enough to spoil their games or take their toys, when normal sibling struggles arise.

Most mothers agree that life is generally easier with small children if the routine remains as normal as possible at first. Change is often accompanied by anxiety, and clinging or making a fuss about going to bed can be signs of this; they provide comfort when a child is coping with something new. Tantrums are not the result of some parental failing, but a means of expressing strong feelings when you cannot talk very well; a normal sign of healthy growing up and one way that a child learns self-discipline.

Three ideas for small children

❑ *Painting the stones:* If you have a paved patio, give your toddler a bucket of water and a paintbrush (the size used for wallpaper paste works well) and show her how to paint the paving slabs. Water 'paint' looks interesting but dries quickly, and this keeps a small child amused for a surprisingly long time.

❑ *Telling the day:* 'Once upon a time there was a little girl called (your child's name). She got up in the morning and she (fill in the story of her day).' If this becomes a daily ritual you get to spend one-to-one time with your child (brownie points for good mothering) and as she starts to join in you find out what is important to her or what happened at nursery school; you also get a chance to praise or apologise where necessary. Keep it fun, however.

❑ *Fairy box:* In family life, things do not always go as smoothly for small children as we would wish. When a child has been trying hard and failing, or you feel her ego just needs a boost, the fairies could leave a tiny present for her. Put a special box in a special place. Of course it will be empty most of the time.

School-age children: Striking the fine balance between offering support and stifling a child's growing desire to be independent is one of the challenges of parenthood, but when parents are under pressure school children can be pushed into independence before they are ready: as soon as they are able to do something they are left to get on with it. With a baby to care for, keeping up with a child's busy social life, reading with her every day and supporting school fund-raising events are added pressures, but they are also enjoyable and a chance to give individual attention. You may want to make them a priority and ask your partner, other family members or friends for help with shopping or chores to gain enough time.

Teenagers: Young people often help out willingly, although it may be best to let them take a lead as to how much babycare they want to undertake rather than rely on them too much. They resent being used as unpaid babysitters, except occasionally, and they are not always as confident as they seem. It is easy to brush aside their worries about friendships or exams when you are under pressure; but they need to be listened to, even when they choose the moment you were about to go to bed. They will draw their own conclusions if the baby always comes first.

Part-time housewife, juggling

Parenthood is not really a race – it just feels like it. Few women today have one role in life; most juggle family, household, work and relationships, keeping all the plates in the air with considerable ingenuity.

It does not help a rapidly changing society if women shoulder the burden of bringing up the next generation while men heave a sigh of relief and let them get on with it. In the long run it is in the interests of the whole family to share the work, and in your child's interests not to always tend to him at the expense of yourself.

You make lists to give yourself the illusion of control. Before you had a child you would have got to the end of a list eventually; now things stay on it so long that it is too late to do them and you

Running a babysitting circle

Everybody needs time off, and many a partner knows an evening out is on the cards when the kettle is cleaned in honour of the babysitter. If you are short of money or relatives to babysit, join or start a babysitting circle. Most circles use cardboard tokens marked with time spans (half, one or two hours, for example) for payment. Daytime care, ironing or collecting a child from school can be included for members who cannot babysit in the evenings. Successful circles restrict numbers to about twenty maximum and meet regularly to sort out problems and update lists.

❑ Contact friends who might be interested, or advertise locally.

❑ Agree some simple rules such as sitters must be returned home or offered a bed overnight, double tokens after midnight, no more than thirty tokens to be hoarded.

❑ Appoint a secretary each month to keep track of tokens and match families needing a sitter with those needing tokens (saves phone calls but you may not get the sitters your children like). Alternatively, phone sitters directly (you may swap with two or three regularly but you have access to others if necessary).

❑ List members' names, addresses, phone numbers, children's names and ages, plus the rules and any other agreed details. Give each member a copy.

❑ Start everyone off with an agreed number of tokens, say fifteen hours'-worth.

delete them by default. You stop making lists, but forget all the things you have got to do, which worries you even more. The answer is to feel pleased to get one thing done in a day rather than frustrated because you did not manage the other ten. Walking to the park, finding a lost shoe, making a helicopter out of Lego is getting something done.

Beating tiredness

❑ Take up exercise such as swimming (your library may have details of pools with creche facilities) or walking (see page 90). There is evidence that this helps you to sleep for less time but more soundly.

❑ A change of routine and a new activity can be invigorating. Try your local library for details of courses or classes.

❑ Eat fresh or dried fruit, yogurt or a milkshake if you need an energy boost.

❑ Put your feet up for ten minutes and relax totally (see page 109).

❑ Drink fruit juice or water and cut down on tea and coffee as they inhibit the absorption of zinc and iron, minerals essential for energy (see page 87).

❑ Ask for more help, from your partner, family or friends; or pay someone to help.

Make a list of all the things you did yesterday, or any typical day. Jot down roughly how long each item took and work out the time spent with your child and partner, working, commuting, doing household chores, doing something just for you, asleep, or whatever headings you choose. Draw two circles and on one shade in segments in proportion to your headings; on the other shade in segments so that the balance between activities is nearer to what you would ideally like. You will begin to see where you could make changes. For example, if housework looms larger than you like could you cut down, delegate or get help?

Getting enough sleep

Sleep preoccupies all parents. First-time mothers complain of tiredness most, possibly because the emotional adjustment to parenthood takes energy, but anyone who has a child is likely to go short at least some of the time.

A typical eight-hour night consists of about 25 per cent rapid eye movement (REM) or dreaming sleep, 50 per cent light sleep and 25 per cent deep sleep. The discomforts of late pregnancy help your body adjust to less sleep and although deep sleep is the most important for wellbeing, the need for it decreases with age so it may be easier for an older mother to endure repeated broken nights.

Evidence suggests there is a close relationship between adequate sleep and a strong immune system. To catch up after a disturbed night you need a third to a half of the sleep you missed, because your body goes straight into deep sleep, reducing the amount of REM and light sleep for a couple of nights. You may feel deprived if you go short of REM and light sleep, but the amount that you need is partly determined by habit and mood. Mothers who are happy and in love cope more easily than those who are depressed, for example.

You may not feel brilliant when you are short of sleep, but you can stop worrying as your body will take the amount of deep sleep it needs and your long-term health will not suffer. If you have less than five hours' sleep per night you may feel drowsy during the day, but a short catnap can help to balance this. When you get as much sleep as you need, you build up reserves to help in times of stress or short-term sleep deprivation, such as when a child is ill.

A baby over six months who has previously slept well may start to sleep badly after a minor illness such as a cold or cutting a tooth. To avoid a habit developing allow three broken nights, then decide if the reason for waking still applies. If not you may want to be firm; the longer a habit continues the harder it is to break.

Stress: Stress is like an air mattress: too little air and you sink to the ground, too much and you bounce around like a pea; but the right amount feels comfortable.

Having a baby means you face several potentially stressful challenges relatively close together. As long as you feel in control it is invigorating, motivating and exciting. If pressure is too great, however, you feel negative and may become ill.

Stress can come from outside (your baby's crying or other people's demands), or from within (high expectations of yourself or an unrealistic view of motherhood, for example). Everyone interprets it according to their values and previous experiences and it affects women in different ways.

Most people get an early warning in one of four areas: changes in their body, emotions, mental capability or behaviour. You might get aches and pains – headaches, tension around your neck or a flare-up of a stress-related skin problem or asthma. You might burst into tears easily, become irritable or worry even after receiving reassurance. You might put off decisions, stick rigidly to a set routine or find it hard to concentrate; you might isolate yourself by staying indoors, work more frantically the more exhausted you get, or avoid making time to enjoy yourself. If stress continues you are likely to experience symptoms in all four areas.

Older women have usually learned to recognise their own signs because they have had knocks in life. If you can identify the point at which the upward curve of healthy tension, which improves your energy and enjoyment of life, levels out before descending, you can take simple actions to prevent the downward spiral. If you pour juice from a jug that you never refill, sooner or later there is no juice left, so the aim is to achieve a balance between the amount of challenge in your life and your resources for coping with it.

Coping with stress is individual and you may have developed ways that work for you over the years. Several different strategies can be more effective than a single approach. For example, use your support pyramid (see page 302); go to a class, try an alternative therapy such as reflexology or aromatherapy.

When you have faith in a pill or a therapy it may activate nerve pathways in your brain for self-healing (which could explain why relaxation can reduce high blood pressure). If you accept that the mind influences the body it makes sense to take advantage of it to help restore a sense of feeling well. Try vividly recalling a time when you felt most at peace, full of energy, most enthusiastic. Try meditation for 10–20 minutes a day, repeating a word, phrase or prayer; or a repetitive activity – knitting, jogging, swimming. You need to concentrate totally, however; there is no benefit in doing it while worrying about something else.

A way of relaxing can itself become a problem occasionally. For example, if you sit down with a cup of coffee more frequently, extra caffeine may lead to headaches or difficulty sleeping (drinking herbal or fruit teas could solve this). Alcohol or cigarettes may increase stress in the long-term, and working frantically to finish something so that you can relax may be counterproductive: the more you drive yourself when under pressure the less you may achieve!

Extra help: If you are under a great deal of stress you may want to talk to your GP or contact one of the helplines (see *Directory*). Alternatively a counsellor or therapist might help. Therapy can only change a problem indirectly by giving you another way of looking at it, but it may help you to understand why you behave in certain ways and how you could change. It could help you unravel a problem on neutral ground, give you new ways to cope and support you while you try them out.

Before you seek therapy, however, decide whether you want information, insight into what your problem is or why you have it, or to be supported while you deal with it. For information you may be better off turning to a book, a class, an adviser or a voluntary organisation. For insight, explanation or support you could turn to your partner, friend, family, social worker, clergyman or doctor. If you do not turn to the people who know and care for you ask yourself why; there might be benefits in doing so. If you feel they could not help you may want to see a therapist.

Older mothers' experiences

Elizabeth (42): 'When Jessica was tiny going to work or to the cinema to see a new release simply wasn't on my list of priorities. I couldn't understand women who boasted about being back at their desks six weeks after the birth, or who spared their baby half an hour before dashing out for the evening. I wondered why they bothered to have children at all. Time with Jessica was precious and the inevitable comparisons with other children made me feel both proud of her abilities and worried about her slow development!

'Now I'm changing. I worry less, but there is conflict between my desire to work and to be with her. Motherhood is like a dress hanging in my cupboard, kept out of sight when I'm at work because efficient women have that side of their lives under control. I hate separating work and my family life, but it's hard not to be selfish when you've only had yourself to think of all your adult life.'

Q: What is 'quality time' and how much does a child need?
A: Quality time implies that what parents do when they are with their children matters more than the amount of time they actually spend with them. It can help to take away the guilt that most parents feel about being busy all the time, so long as it does not come to mean slotting in a bit of parent duty whenever you happen to find a gap in your diary.

Playing with a child is not the same as mothering, however. If Jessica does not want to use her quality time in the way that you prefer there can be a conflict between your needs and hers. When she is happily watching paint dry on the wall you may want to wave a toy in front of her in the name of stimulation; if she wants you to watch her making dare devil leaps off the sofa again and again it can be hard to sit and admire them, when you would really like her to settle down for a story or do a nice educational jigsaw with you.

You may find you come closer to a mothering relationship and are less inclined to impose your idea of quality time on Jessica if you carry on with tasks that can easily be put aside when she wants your attention. Sit down, perhaps reading a magazine, and she may start to claim your attention on her own terms.

Valerie (44): 'I'm more laid back with Mark than I was with Emma and Claire. I don't worry about developmental stages, or what other people think of the way I bring him up. I'm also more organised. A washing machine and disposable nappies make life easier, although they also make me feel inadequate. With all these benefits I should find parenting easy, but I don't!

'I've learned to live with chaos because something has to go, but when I'm at my lowest ebb an untidy house seems unbearable. Barry and I have a stormy relationship. We argue because he indulges Mark and the girls think that Mark always gets his own way. We also laugh a lot to ease the stresses and strains.

'Most of the other mums I know are much younger than me and they're talking about having another baby, while for me the next step is the menopause. I envy their youth and years of fertility ahead, but I know I'm incredibly privileged to have had another chance at my age.'

Q: Where can parents who want to do a better job get help?
A: There are helplines and services for any parent whose child has a problem or who has reached crisis point, and courses can give you support and ideas for handling ordinary challenges of family life so that they do not become flash points.

Most courses build on normal parenting skills to help you

handle your relationship with your child more constructively. Some are led by parents who have benefited from them and had some additional training; others are run by professional facilitators and include special interests, such as parenting teenagers or facing divorce. There are some addresses in the Directory.

Lesley (36): 'I'm more tolerant, patient and loving than I would have been ten years ago, and I trust my own instincts more. Sometimes I start the day by reading a story or playing with the boys before doing anything else, so that they know they come before the chores. I wouldn't have done that when I was younger.

'In the evening Phil baths the boys and gets them ready for bed, while I prepare supper. Our relationship has changed because the twins take up a lot of the time and energy that we had for each other, but we try to share everything as much as possible and we've gradually got back to a full, loving relationship.

'Nobody can have everything they want, but everyone can make choices. Some have short-term effects while others stretch ahead into the future. Having a baby is one of these. It was the best thing that has ever happened to us.'

Q: How can I explain to the twins that they were conceived after IVF treatment, and what difference will it make as they grow up?
A: A simple explanation such as mummy gave the eggs and daddy gave the seeds and the doctors helped because part of your tummy didn't work would suffice if the boys ask how they got in your tummy.

To go through the stresses of infertility treatment you really have to want a baby and pull together. IVF or donor insemination children tend to have parents who have more emotional involvement compared with natural conception families. You may worry more or tend to be over-cautious at first, because your children are so precious, but the more calculated risks you take the simpler decisions become. Paradoxically, taking risks can lead to peace of mind and greater enjoyment of life; it makes it easier to accept that disaster occasionally happens.

Sue (39): 'You never know what changes life is going to bring. Amy hated being a baby and rarely slept. I was so tired I lost confidence in my ability to be a good mother. I couldn't ask other people what to do because I felt I should know. Books helped most, because they couldn't make me feel guilty. If you don't like what a book says you can throw it away; you don't feel it's watching to see that you've taken its advice. It took me a while to realise that it wasn't just Jack's nature that had made him easy as a baby. The children are just very different.

'Jack hated sharing and took it out on me because Amy demanded so much attention. Now that she is happy and this jealous phase is over they have a touching relationship. He's proud when Amy attempts something new, and she giggles at all his jokes and watches his daring exploits with rapture. They're a mutual admiration society, and his anger towards me has quite melted.'

Q: I still get angry and frustrated at times. How can I let off steam in a way that doesn't involve taking it out on the family?
A: Take a kitchen timer into the bathroom and set it for two minutes. Turn the shower on full and as the water rushes over you think about all the things that are making you angry. Hiss or shout out your anger if you like, or let tears of frustration flow with the water. When the timer goes off turn the shower down and feel the water soothing you gently, making you feel calm, strong and relaxed.

Anne (47): 'My mother is frail and forgetful. She can't be left on her own for long so I do a lot of rushing around just to stand still. Days go by when I can't get to my sculpture and that is frustrating. I know it won't last for ever. I built my reputation up once and I'll do so again, when Chloe and my mother don't need me so much.

'Finding space for me is what I've missed since my partner left. Unless you're firm with yourself your own needs get left until last when you're caring for other people and there is nobody to look out for you.

'Everything in life has ups and downs, but we're a strong family unit. My grown-up children have their own lives to lead and I don't expect them to help out, but they can transform a difficult evening with a few words of admiration for how I cope, when I haven't felt I was coping at all. I never think about my age. I'm the only mother that Chloe will have, and that's enough!'

Q: I often feel pulled in every direction. How can I hold on to my own identity?
A: Women who care often feel guilty if they do not give selflessly all the time. If you want to enjoy positive relationships, however, you need to create spaces around those you love. Parenting is not something you take on on top of everything else; it is an integral part of you, that you carry out in ways that work for you.

A toddler who screams 'No!' is asserting his identity. It is uncomfortable for everyone around him and he risks disapproval, but making up his own mind is an essential step on his road to independence. There are times when you need to assert yourself just as strongly, and face just as much disapproval, perhaps over a decision to leave Chloe to cry instead of going to her straight away, or to put your mother into respite care once a week when she does not want to go.

This is not easy, but it is a part of being in control and retaining your identity. You may not be able to single-mindedly pursue anything that says 'me' at this stage in your life, but without a doubt the decisions you make are an expression of the essential 'you'.

Directory

Umbrella organisations

- ❑ Maternity Alliance, 45 Beech Street, London EC2P 2LX (0171 588 8582). Alliance of maternity groups; information about rights at work, maternity benefits; general health and employment benefit leaflets.
- ❑ Health Information Service. Freephone 0800 665544 (Mon–Fri). Information on all health matters; for example, help to find or change a health professional, or make a complaint; help to give up smoking, deal with a drug or alcohol problem or contact a specialist self-help or voluntary group; advice about alternative therapies and help to find a local practitioner.
- ❑ National Childbirth Trust (NCT), Alexandra House, Oldham Terrace, London W3 6NH (0181 992 8637). The main voluntary organisation for information on pregnancy, birth and early parenthood; antenatal classes; postnatal support;

breastfeeding counsellors and hire of breast pumps; local groups (sales of nearly new baby equipment). ParentAbility offers information and contacts for parents with disabilities.

Pre-conception and early pregnancy

❑ British Pregnancy Advisory Service (BPAS), Austy Manor, Wooton Wawen, Solihull, West Midlands B95 6BX (0345 304030). Information on infertility and contraception, including natural family planning and sterilisation.

❑ Centre for Pregnancy Nutrition, Clinical Sciences Centre, Northern General Hospital, Herries Road, Sheffield S5 7AU (Eating for Pregnancy helpline: 0114 242 4084, Mon–Fri, 10 am–4 pm). Nutritional advice and database of research.

❑ Family Planning Association, 2–12 Pentonville Road, London N1 9FP (0171 837 4044). Information on contraception, including natural methods, sexual health, licensed sperm clinics, techniques of sperm separation, achieving a successful pregnancy.

❑ Foresight, 28 The Paddock, Godalming, Surrey GU7 1XD (01483 427839). Information on pre-conceptual care.

❑ Miscarriage Association, c/o Clayton Hospital, Northgate, Wakefield, West Yorks WF1 3JS (01924 200799). Information on specialist hospitals and clinics, specific problems, tests and treatments; support and befriending. Ectopic pregnancy support network.

❑ QUIT, Victory House, 170 Tottenham Court Road, London W1P 0HA (freephone 0800 002200). Advice on giving up smoking.

❑ Royal College of Obstetricians and Gynaecologists, 27 Sussex Place, Regent's Park, London NW1 4RG (0171 262

5425). List of obstetricians with a special interest in fetal diagnosis.
- ❑ Women's Nutritional Advisory Service (WNAS), PO Box 268, Lewes, East Sussex BN7 2QN (01273 487366). Telephone consultation on pre-conception care and problems relating to withdrawal of contraceptive pill.

Infertility

- ❑ CHILD, Charter House, 43 St Leonards Road, Bexhill-on-Sea, East Sussex TN40 1JA (01424 732361). Self-help, counselling and information on infertility.
- ❑ DI Network, PO Box 265, Sheffield S3 7YX. Self-help for people considering using sperm, egg or embryo donation.
- ❑ Human Fertilisation and Embryology Authority (HFEA), 30 Artillery Lane, London E1 7LS (0171 377 5077). Licenses clinics for IVF, donor insemination, sperm and egg donation, embryo and sperm storage; provides comprehensive information on treatments and choosing a clinic.
- ❑ ISSUE (National Fertility Association), 114 Litchfield Street, Walsall, WS1 1SZ (01922 722888). Support and counselling; information on aspects of infertility; contacts with other patients; second opinions; factsheets.
- ❑ Women's Health, 52 Featherstone Street, London EC1 8RT (0171 251 6580). Promotes informed decisions about health; information on self-insemination groups and clinics that do not discriminate against age or lesbian and single women; Rights of Women (same address: 0171 251 6577) offers legal advice for women; Lesbian Parenting: 0171 251 6576.

Fetal testing

❑ Association for Children with Life Threatening or Terminal Conditions (ACT), 65 St Michael's Hill, Bristol BS2 8DZ (0117 922 1556). Database and information.

❑ Genetic Interest Group (GIG), Farringdon Point, 25–29 Farringdon Road, London EC1M 3JB (0171 430 0090). Information on regional genetic centres for testing.

❑ Rare Unspecified Chromosome Disorder Support Group, 160 Locket Road, Harrow Weald, Middlesex HA3 7NZ (0181 863 3557). Links up and supports families with rare disorders.

❑ Support Around Termination For Abnormality (SATFA), 73–75 Charlotte Street, London W1P 1LB (0171 631 0285). Information and support for parents making decisions about testing, or who discover that their unborn baby is abnormal.

Disability

❑ Contact a Family (CAF), 170 Tottenham Court Road, London W1P 0HA (0171 383 3555). Directory of specific conditions (some rare); brings families together in a network of support groups.

❑ Disabled Living Foundation, 380–384 Harrow Road, London W9 2HU (0171 289 6111). Specialist advisory service on aids and equipment.

❑ Down's Syndrome Association, 155 Mitcham Road, London SW17 9PG (0181 682 4001). Support and information about Down's syndrome.

❑ Remap, Hazledene, Ightham, Sevenoaks, Kent TN15 9AD (01732 883818). Professional engineers who design aids for people with disabilities or modify existing equipment; includes a special crib for disabled mothers.

Adoption, fostering, surrogacy

❑ British Agencies for Adoption and Fostering, Skyline House, 200 Union Street, London SE1 0LX (0171 593 2000). Umbrella organisation for information on adoption and fostering.

❑ Childlessness Overcome Through Surrogacy (COTS), Lairg, Sutherland IV27 4EF (01549 402401). Self-help for people interested in surrogacy.

❑ National Foster Care Association, 517 Marshalsea Road, London SE1 1EP (0171 357 8015, 1–4 pm, except Weds, Sat, Sun). Information, training packs.

❑ Overseas Adoption Support and Information Services (OASIS), Dan-y-Craig Cottage, Balaclava Road, Glais, Swansea SA7 9HJ (01792 844329). Information and support on overseas adoption.

❑ Parent to Parent Information on Adoption Services (PPIAS), Lower Bodington, Daventry, Northants NN11 6YB (01327 260295). Information on adoption.

❑ Post Adoption Centre, 5 Torriano Mews, Torriano Avenue, London NW5 2RZ (0171 284 0555). Information and counselling for all participants in adoption.

Pregnancy and birth

❑ Action on Pre-Eclampsia (APEC), 2nd Floor, 31–33 College Road, Harrow, Middlesex HA1 1EJ (01923 266778). Information for parents and professionals.

❑ Active Birth Centre, 25 Bickerton Road, London N19 5JT (0171 561 9006). Information about natural birth and water birth; teachers (nationwide); videos; hire of birth pools.

❑ Association for Improvements in the Maternity Services (AIMS), 40 Kingswood Avenue, London NW6 6LS (0181 960 5585). Support and information about maternity rights and choices; list of home birth support groups, independent midwives; information about waterbirth.

❑ Association of Radical Midwives, 62 Greetby Hill, Ormskirk, Lancashire L39 2DT (01695 572776). Supports women's choices when giving birth.

❑ British Diastasis Symphysis Pubis Support Group, Mont Hamel House, Office 2, Chapel Place, Ramsgate, Kent CT11 9RY (01843 587356). Information and support for DSP sufferers.

❑ Caesarean Support Network, 55 Cooil Drive, Douglas, Isle of Man IM2 2HF (01624 661269). Support for women before or after caesarean birth.

❑ Independent Midwives Association, 94 Auckland Road, Upper Norwood, London SE19 2DB (0181 406 3172). Register of independent midwives.

❑ Informed Choice Initiative, PO Box 669, Bristol BS99 5FG (0891 210400). Leaflets for parents and professionals about choices for pregnancy and birth.

❑ Spembly Medical Ltd, Newbury Road, Andover, Hants SP10 4DR (freephone 0800 515413). Hire of TENS machines; can also be hired from Boots Chemists.

❑ Twins and Multiple Births Association (TAMBA), PO Box 30 Little Sutton, South Wirral L66 1TH (twinline: 01732 868000, 7 pm–11 pm, Mon–Fri; 10 am–11 pm weekends). Leaflets, local clubs; specialist support for parents; groups for special needs, infertility, bereavement, single parents, adopted twins, triplets.

❑ Vaginal Birth after Caesarean Information and Support Group (VBAC), 8 Wren Way, Farnborough, Hants GU14 8SZ (01252 543250, 4.30–10.30 pm); Information and practical help for women who want to avoid unnecessary surgery as a method of birth. Please send a stamped self-addressed envelope.

After the birth

- ❑ Association of Breastfeeding Mothers (ABM), PO Box 441, St Albans, Herts AL4 0AS (01727 859189). Information; local support groups.
- ❑ Association for Postnatal Illness (APNI), 25 Jerdan Place, Fulham, London SW6 1BE (0171 386 0868). Information and telephone support.
- ❑ Birth Afterthoughts, Royal Hampshire County Hospital, Winchester, Hants SO22 5DG (01962 863535). Counselling for women who have questions or unresolved feelings about their birth.
- ❑ Birth Crisis Network (01865 300266). Telephone helpline for anyone needing to talk about a traumatic birth experience.
- ❑ Baby Life Support Systems (BLISS), 17–21 Emerald Street, London WC1N 3QL (0500 151617). Support and information for parents of sick or premature babies.
- ❑ CRY-SIS Support Group, BM Cry-sis, London WC1N 3XX (helpline: 0171 404 5011). Self-help and support for parents of crying or high need babies.
- ❑ La Leche League (Great Britain); BM 3424, London WC1N 3XX (0171 242 1278). Breastfeeding information and support; local groups.
- ❑ Meet-a-Mum Association (MAMA), 26 Avenue Road, South Norwood, London SE25 4DX (0181 771 5595). Information and groups to support women who are isolated, lonely or suffering from postnatal depression.

Relationships

- ❑ Exploring Parenthood, 4 Ivory Place, 10a Treadgold Street, London W11 4BP (helpline: 0171 221 6681). Information;

professional counselling; courses on all aspects of parenting.
❑ National NEWPIN, Sutherland House, 35 Sutherland Square, Walworth, London SE17 3EE (0171 703 6326). Support and advice to enhance child–parent relationships.
❑ Families Need Fathers, 134 Curtain Road, London EC2A 3AR (0171 613 5060). Advice on maintaining a child's relationship with both parents during and after family breakdown.
❑ National Stepfamily Association, 3rd Floor, Chapel House, 18 Hatton Place, London EC1N 8RU (helpline: 0990 168388, 2–5 pm, 7–10 pm Mon–Fri). Information packs; support and advice; local groups.
❑ Parent Network, Room 2, Winchester House, 11 Cranmer Road, London SW9 6EJ (0171 735 1214). ParentLink – courses on new ways of handling family stress.
❑ PARENTLINE, Endway House, The Endway, Hadleigh, Essex SS7 2AN (helpline: 01702 559900, 9 am–6 pm Mon–Fri, 1–6pm Sat, regional number in phone book). For anyone experiencing parenting difficulties.
❑ Relate, Herbert Grey College, Little Church Street, Rugby, Warcs CV21 3AP (regional number in the phone book). Counselling for relationships, divorce, co-operation over parenting.

Motherhood and work

❑ New Ways to Work, 309 Upper Street, London N1 2TY (0171 226 4026, Mon, Tues, Thurs 12–3 pm). Information for individuals and employers about flexible work patterns, including sabbaticals, job sharing, voluntary reduced work time, working from home.
❑ Parents at Work, 45 Beech Street, Barbican, London EC2Y 8AD (information line: 0171 628 3578). Information for

working parents; books, including guidance on childcare options and a practical guide to managing stress. Special needs helpline: 0171 588 0802.

Lone parents

❑ Gingerbread, 16–17 Clarkenwell Close, London EC1R 0AA (helpline: 0171 336 8184). Practical and emotional support; advice on rights, benefits; local groups.
❑ National Council for One Parent Families, 255 Kentish Town Road, London NW5 2LX (0171 267 1361). Free information booklets.

Bereavement

❑ The Child Bereavement Trust, Harleyford Estate, Henley Road, Marlow, Bucks SL7 2DX (01628 488101). Support for grieving families.
❑ Child Death Helpline, Bereavement Services Department, Great Ormond Street Hospital, London WC1N 3JH (0800 282986, every evening 7–10 pm, Mon, Weds, Fri 10 am –1 pm). Support for anyone affected by the death of a child from any cause.
❑ Foundation for the Study of Infant Deaths (FSID), 14 Halkin Street, London SW1X 7DP (helpline: 0171 235 1721). Information on cot deaths and infant health; research support and individual befriending for parents coping with a sudden infant death.
❑ Stillbirth and Neonatal Death Society (SANDS), 28 Portland Place, London W1N 4DE (helpline: 0171 436 5881). Befriending after pregnancy loss, stillbirth and neonatal

death; self-help groups; booklet: *Saying Goodbye to Your Baby*.
❑ See also: Miscarriage Association; Twins and Multiple Births Association.

Miscellaneous

❑ Action for Victims of Medical Accidents, Bank Chambers, 1 London Road, Forest Hill, London SE23 3TP (0181 291 2793). Advisory service, referral to specialist solicitors.
❑ Alternative Health Information Bureau, Orchard Villa, Porters Park Drive, Shenley, Herts WD7 9DS (01923 856222). Resources and database for holistic health care.
❑ British Humanist Association, 14 Lamb's Conduit Passage, London W1CR 4RH (0171 430 0908). Booklet: *New Arrivals: A Guide to Non-religious Naming Ceremonies*.
❑ Hairline International, Lyons Court, 1668 High Street, Knowle, West Midlands B93 0LY (fax: 01564 782270). Help if you experience hair loss.
❑ Medela, CMS House, Basford Lane Industrial Estate, Leekbrook, Leek, Staffs ST13 7DT (01538 386650). Breastfeeding products including sterile bags for freezing milk, breast pumps for hire or to buy and supplemental nursing system.
❑ National Association of Nappy Services; c/o Cedar Nappy Services; 50 Cedar Road, Northampton NN1 4RW (0121 693 4949). List of cotton nappy laundries.
❑ Triumph Over Phobia (TOP UK), PO Box 1831, Bath BA2 4YW (01225 330353). Self-help for anyone suffering phobias, panic attacks, anxiety disorders.

❑ Women's Environmental Network (WEN), 87 Worship Street London EC2A 2BE (helpline: 0171 247 3327). Campaigning organisation providing environmental and health information on a wide range of products.

Index

NOTES

NOTES

P·R·A·C·T·I·C·A·L
PARENTING

From pregnancy
to pre-school

**Giving your
child the best
chance**

On sale every month at your local Newsagent,
Supermarket or by subscription

For all enquiries call:
01444 445555

or you can write to us at:
Practical Parenting Subscriptions
FREEPOST CY1061
Haywards Heath
West Sussex
RH16 32A
UK